Puerto Rico

Guadeloupe

Dominica

MARTINIQUE

Saint Lucia

Trinidad
& Tobago

VENEZUELA

COLOMBIA

GUYANA

SOUTH AMERICA

FIRE MOUNTAIN

FIRE MOUNTAIN

HOW ONE MAN SURVIVED THE WORLD'S
WORST VOLCANIC DISASTER

PETER MORGAN

BLOOMSBURY

First published in Great Britain 2003

Copyright © 2003 by Peter Morgan

The moral right of the author has been asserted

Bloomsbury Publishing Plc, 38 Soho Square, London W1D 3HB

A CIP catalogue record for this book
is available from the British Library

ISBN 0 7475 5676 8

10 9 8 7 6 5 4 3 2 1

Typeset by Hewer Text Ltd, Edinburgh
Printed by Clays Ltd, St Ives plc

CONTENTS

Harmony Fairy Cures Sick-Stock Group — 47 Persons Table.
C. Mai B. Trof, R. Bacon leader, E. H. Coro Corn, barbed Hyn, Dub. Po. Dwy for Bay.
Under R. Chrisson, Grand, Gourdes, Scissors Foundr, and 40 other Harmony Workers.

PROLOGUE:

THE MOST MARVELLOUS
MAN ON EARTH

I T W A S the finest collection of freaks ever assembled.

The most stupendous congress of curious creatures and human oddballs the world had ever seen; an eye feast of prodigious proportions; a menagerie of Mother Nature at her most whimsical . . .

When it came to towering temples of adjectives, few could rival the alliterative artistry of Barnum and Bailey, curators of The Greatest Show on Earth. And for its first domestic tour in five years, America's finest three-ring circus had excelled itself in every possible way. No dictionary or thesaurus could do justice to a spectacle so full of surprises, so replete with innovation and embarrassed with riches. Nor could it describe an operation of such military rigour and logistic flair: a tented city of twelve hundred people and a thousand animals, whisking through town after town, entertaining fifteen thousand people per day. No longer would the Great American Public have to put up with feeble imitations. For there was only one Barnum and Bailey's Circus:

A MAMMOTH, MOVING MASS OF MULTITUDINOUS,
MULTIFARIOUS, MAGNITUDINOUS AND MAJESTIC
MAGNIFICENCE!

Which is why, on a cold, clear morning in March 1903, this curious congregation of curios has gathered at Madison Square Garden, New York City. They are about to embark on an eight-month tour of the United States, beginning with a five-week residency at New York's most celebrated venue. Above their heads workmen whirr and weld away, preparing acrobatic swings and platforms. In a quiet corner, a sequined bareback rider rehearses her perilous backflip. Yet the figures shuffling across the arena floor are just as remarkable as any daredevil performer. They have been lured into Barnum and Bailey's Side Show from all four corners of the globe: from the wilds of Borneo to the icy wastes of Russia; from the desert sands of Arabia to the bright blue seas of the Caribbean. These fabulous freaks are, as the caption beneath the photograph reminds us, 'Famous people' in their own right.

High above them all, like twin totem poles, perch the figures of George Auger and Leah May. At eight foot three and seven foot eight respectively, they can fairly claim to be the World's Tallest Man and Woman; a boast which, in Captain Auger's case, is boosted by a suspiciously tall top hat. Far away at their feet, in tiny waistcoats and ballgowns, are the Horvath Family: six extraordinary midget brothers and sisters from the Harz mountains of Germany and truly the most diminutive performers ever seen on a circus stage. To their left, that imperious white moustache and oddly truncated trunk belong to Eli Bowen, Legless Acrobat. According to Barnum's *Book of Wonders*, Eli has been making an exhibition of himself for almost fifty years. His firmest friend is the Armless Wonder, Charles Tripp. 'Years ago', it relates, 'it was regarded as a great joke that the armless man always went to the box office to draw the salary of the legless acrobat as well as his own.' Years of experience have taught Bowen to take such slights in his lopsided stride.

There was one point, however, on which every freak and phrase maker could agree. So huge was the investment, so vaunting the ambition behind this comeback show, that it could not afford to fail. Every soul – from the Moss Haired Girl to the great James A. Bailey himself – hoped for favourable reviews. The value of 'good paper' on a circus tour could never be understated; advance notices and word of mouth were the best way to sell every seat in the house.

Whenever a new act was under consideration, Barnum agents had one simple question: *How d'you think they will draw?* And in that year's Freak Department, the sure-fire draw was of a most unusual kind.

You will find him on the left hand side of the group photograph, hidden away in a corner. Follow George Auger's spade-sized hand to the furthest edge of the frame and you will see a smiling, dark-skinned man in a big straw hat, white cotton shirt and braces. A man whose story was so remarkable that the word carpenters of Barnum and Bailey simply called him, without fear of contradiction or exaggeration, *The Most Marvellous Man on Earth.*

After a triumphant opening stand in New York City, the Greatest Show on Earth began its slow, stately trail across America's East Coast. A harmonious roll of names unfurls beside the painted railway wagons: there go Shenandoah, Scranton and Wilkesbarre; Providence, Fall River and Woonsocket are yet to come. In each town, the Barnum routine is slick and unvarying. A morning parade along State and Main, followed by daily performances at two and eight. An hour before every show, the circus grounds are opened to the public with a sharp whistle shriek. It is time for Barnum and Bailey's famous freaks to limp, hobble and skitter into place and to start earning their keep . . .

Lay-Deez an' Jen-ul-men!
As if from nowhere, a stout little man in a bowler hat and

waistcoat has popped up outside the Side Show tent. His lungs are made of leather, his tongue of purest silver:

Lay-Deez an' Jen-ul-men!

Step this way, my friends, for the FINEST collection of Human Curios ever presented to the American Public!

A spectacle, my friends, both STUPENDOUS and SUBLIME. GORGEOUS and GLORIOUS.

Without equal anywhere in this World – Old or New!

A small crowd starts to gather. The townsfolk are reluctant at first; unsure whether they should linger before such a blasphemous spectacle. Richly painted banners dangle in front of them – *ROB ROY, THE ALBINO CONTORTIONIST! KRAO, THE MISSING LINK: HALF WOMAN, HALF APE!* – tempting and tormenting in equal measure.

Ten cents, Ladies and Gentlemen. That is all we ask. To see the Human Salamander and the Leopard Girl, the Albino Bone Bender and the Lion Faced Boy!

As proof of his good intentions, the Bally Man invites one of his protégés to come forward. A grotesquely thin old man steps through the curtain, dressed in a dove-grey morning suit and maroon bow tie. The old fellow bows gently, leaning on his ebony cane.

J.W. Coffee, Ladies and Gentlemen. Undoubtedly the THINNEST man alive – The Champion Featherweight of the World, Requiring TWO to make a shadow . . . The Skeleton Dude!

Laughter and applause. The Bally Man's voice falls to a stage whisper.

And there is yet more within, my friends. Much more.

For one night only, we are proud to exhibit THE MOST MARVEL-LOUS MAN ON EARTH!

He is getting louder now, more insistent.

The sole survivor of the World's Most Horrible Cataclysm!

A man whose name is written in FIRE!

A modern miracle . . .

Alive and here today to tell his own incredible story!

Right on cue, a calamitous crash of cymbal and bass drum comes through the Side Show curtain, as if the entire Farally band has fallen off its podium. The hullabaloo quickly turns into a mazurka played in triple-fast time, a nonsense noise of cornets and slide trombone. *Hurry Up – Ladies and Gentlemen, Boys and Girls! Hurry Up!* It is enough to draw them in. A brief glimpse of Krao the Apewoman's dinner – a lump of red meat raised high on a pole – and the crowd can wait no longer. *Take care, Lady! Stop that crowding there! All in good time now! They won't start without you . . .*

Inside, the country folk are overwhelmed by a hot stink of popcorn and elephant dung. The Menagerie Tent is grubbier than expected; it has a forlorn, run-down air which no amount of gloss paint or ballyhoo can conceal. There are elephants and snakes, camels and ostriches. But the greatest attraction of all is a huge candy stall, replete with every possible species of sweet and soda. Behind pyramids of salted peanuts and dairy toffee, a platoon of sharp young men dash about like acrobats, ringing their brass tills. *Big Business today*, shouts one. *Immense!* cries another. *Top Notch!* Their most popular line is Pink Lemonade, a Side Show staple for many years. (Although Barnum and Bailey wish to stress that, contrary to Circus legend, their Pink Cordial is not extracted from the laundry water of young showgirls with a weakness for red tights . . .)

No sooner have the audience taken their first soda slurp than Farally's launch into a deafening fanfare. Without further ceremony, a long line of the queerest, quaintest-looking characters troop on to a bare black platform, marching in time to a snare drum – *Da-Rumm, Da-Rumm, Da-Rumm, DUMM DUMM!* A tall, trim fellow follows them on to the stage. He wears a long dress coat with a brown suede collar, and a fine pair of pinstripe pants. The Side Show Lecturer is a cut above the Bally Man still howling away outside. He waits for his audience to settle, fixing each one of them with a mischievous glare. When it comes, his voice is theatrically slow and rich, as if he is reciting from the Book of Revelation:

Abnormalities, Ladies and Gentlemen . . . in ANY form of life never fail to excite our most extreme interest . . .

When such Abnormalities are found in HUMAN form, then our curiosity increases twice, thrice fold . . .

But before we stray down the wilder paths of God's creation, let us consider one of Mother Nature's more recent abominations . . .

A bass drum pounds mournfully. The audience draws closer.

Imagine if you will, my friends, a beautiful seaside town, set in the curve of a dazzling blue sea. A tropical paradise, no less. A PEARL of a town, so blessed with beauty and elegant sophistication . . .

BOUM . . . BOUM . . . BOUM . . .

. . . that it was known throughout our world as . . . The Paris of the Caribbean . . .

The cornet player trills a few familiar bars of the *Marseillaise*. Our lecturer bows his head.

Quite so, my friend. But no more.

For early on the morning of Thursday 8 May 1902 – barely a year ago – the city of Saint-Pierre on the island of Martinique was . . . snatched away in less time than it takes, dear friends, to boil a humble egg!

THREE MINUTES!

All that was needed for the island's long-dormant volcano, Mont Pelée, to turn this French idyll into a latter-day Pompeii!

He paces around in time to the thunderous drum, drawing lightning bolts and lava flows from an imaginary sky.

Families slain as they slept!

Children slaughtered as they skipped to school!

A calamity which has sent a thrill of terror across the entire civilised world!!!

'The Day of Judgement!' shouts a sarcastic voice.

Thank you, young man. And yet, dear friends . . .

The Lecturer pauses at the platform edge, and peers into every palpitating soul. He has no idea whether his words, perfected over a hundred hurried performances, have any bearing to the truth. But he rattles through them so rapidly, so rapturously, that the audience have no time to argue.

And yet God in his mercy DID preserve one living creature from this apocalyptic fury . . .

A HUMAN BEING who felt the full, awful effect of Pelée's wrath, and upon whose memory the scenes of this horror will be forever stamped.

The name of this Marvellous Man, Ladies and Gentlemen, is Ludger Sylbaris . . .

From the ranks of the miserable and misshapen, a stocky figure rises to his feet, wrapped in a black cape. Quite spontaneously, a round of applause spreads through the crowd. Many of the claims they will hear today are of an improbable or impossible nature. But this story, they know, is indisputably true. He is a young man, muscular and haughty. A faint grin plays across his face, as if he is somewhat amused by all this hoopla. His cape stays firmly closed.

Ludger Sylbaris, my friends.

A French negro of twenty-eight years.

A PRISONER that day in Saint-Pierre's humble jail.

Imagine — if you will — the terrifying sights before his prison bars.

Hundreds of tons of molten lava and gas flooding over the . . .

'So how'd he escape?' shouts a voice, impatiently. 'All these windy old words. You're spoutin' longer than that volcano!'

All in good time, Sir. All in good time . . .

'It's a half pound of half-baked nonsense. A high-falutin fairy tale!'

This time, a few scattered voices add their agreement. Where's the evidence, Sir. Show us your proof! The circus man smiles, familiar with such challenges. He produces a sheaf of documents from his pocket.

I refer you to all manner of affidavits and photographic evidence which confirm Monsieur Sylbaris's story.

A birth certificate . . . Is that not so, Ludger? . . .

The prisoner nods.

. . . confirming both birth and parentage.

And a letter of authentication from our consul in Martinique, Mr John F. Jewell, proving beyond a shadow of a doubt that he is unquestionably the ONLY survivor of the death-dealing Mont Pelée.

And there are photographs, too, ladies and gentlemen.

Taken of Monsieur Ludger as he lay in hospital, nursing his terrible wounds.

All FACTS, my friends, which can be demonstrably attested.

Beside the stage, a pair of reporters are scribbling busily in their notepads. They are lifting their copy, with shameless enthusiasm, straight from Barnum's own poster: *The Only Living Object that Survived in the Silent City of Death . . . Where 40,000 Human Beings were Suffocated, Burned or Buried by one belching blast of Mont Pelée's terrible volcanic eruption . . .* A ten-dollar bill usually secured their services. But on this occasion, the lecturer reflects, a bribe will not be necessary. Particularly after they see his final *coup*.

He places an avuncular hand upon young Sylbaris's shoulder.

For those who harbour the slightest remaining doubt, I offer one further proof.

Under this cape, our dear friend carries souvenirs of his frightful incarceration. A sight so gruesome, that I would advise those of a SENSI-TIVE disposition to distract their eyes for several moments . . .

With a gentle tug, Ludger's black cape tumbles to the floor like a theatre curtain, revealing a plain white shirt and cotton trousers. Slowly, carefully, he unpicks the buttons of his shirt. There are shouts and gasps from the audience.

Oh my Lord! My Blessed Goodness! Sweet Holy Mother of Jesus!

It is hard to describe the sight which greets these cheerful, small-town people, especially to those ladies who have fainted straight away or resorted to retching into their handkerchiefs. For Sylbaris's chest and arms have the rippled, puckered appearance of melted wax. Although his face is clear, every inch of his hands and feet are tricked with scars. Young Ludger displays his wounds without complaint, turning obediently from left to right at his master's instruction.

Imagine, dear ladies, the trials which this body has endured.

The miseries his heart must conceal.

Ludger Sylbaris is, without question, the most UNIQUE person upon the face of this earth!

A worthy addition, I am sure you can see, to this greatest of Human Menageries! A worthy subject of your undivided applause!

The audience agree, happy for once to have seen an authentic curiosity. A brisk glance at his pocket watch tells the lecturer he must press on. There are twenty acts in today's Side Show, and none will thank him for lingering on the Volcano Guy. But before introducing Billy Wells, the Man with a Skull as Hard as Pittsburgh steel, he has one last duty to perform for this curious, lost-looking man. Those with a passable knowledge of French, he explains, may speak with Monsieur Sylbaris in his native language, and hear more of his ordeal.

And now, ladies and gentlemen, pay your attention this way . . .

Each day, a handful of people take up his offer. Some want to touch the young man's wounds, as if that can bring them closer to this biblical calamity. Others attempt to converse, although young Ludger's soft Creole voice is hard to follow. When conversation fails, the prisoner takes a postcard from his trouser pocket. It dates from 1901, the year before the disaster, and shows a long-distance *Vue Générale* of a twinkling, crescent-shaped bay full of ships and tiny houses. It is a magical scene, far removed from the apocalyptic horror of Barnum and Bailey's poster. As he describes the lost world of Saint-Pierre – its fine Italian theatre and beautiful cathedral – Sylbaris's hand passes over the photograph like a sorcerer raising some distant spirit. In Caribbean folklore, Martinique is known as *Le Pays des Revenants*: the Land of Ghosts. And yet *Revenants* are more than simply ghosts. They are those eternal, wandering spirits – a spectral horseman, an evil temptress – who inhabit every plantation and forest upon the island. The picture postcard Saint-Pierre is full of *revenants*: Ludger Sylbaris is their last living heir.

Move Along Now, Ladies and Gentlemen.

Make way for the breath-abating sights to come!

Moments when Hearts cease to Throb and the Minds of all Visitors are Unsettled!

The Big Top show is about to begin. With a few gentle words of apology, Sylbaris's visitors get up to leave. He folds the postcard back into his pocket, a final memory, and smiles politely. There is never time to explain what he has endured, even to the most patient listener. All they ever hear is a whisper of forgotten names and places, buried far away beneath a blazing blue sea.

1901

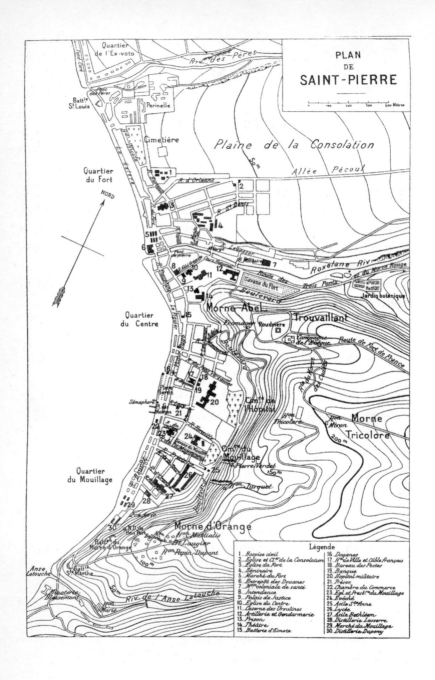

PLAN
DE
SAINT-PIERRE

Légende

1 . . . Hospice civil
2 . . . Église et Cie de la Consolation
3 . . . Église du Fort
4 . . . Séminaire
5 . . . Marché du Fort
6 . . . Entrepôt des Douanes
7 . . . M.^{on} coloniale de santé
8 . . . Intendance
9 . . . Palais de Justice
10 . . . Église du Centre
11 . . . Caserne des Ursulines
12 . . . Artillerie et Gendarmerie
13 . . . Prison
14 . . . Théâtre
15 . . . Batterie d'Esnotz
16 . . . Douanes
17 . . . H.^{tel} de Ville et Cable français
18 . . . Bureau des Postes
19 . . . Banque
20 . . . Hôpital militaire
21 . . . Trésor
22 . . . Chambre du Commerce
23 . . . Égl. et Presb.^{re} du Mouillage
24 . . . Évêché
25 . . . Asile Ste Anne
26 . . . Lycée
27 . . . Asile Bethléem
28 . . . Distillerie Lasserre
29 . . . Marché du Mouillage
30 . . . Distillerie Dupony

ONE

PETIT PARIS

THEY ARRIVE on Tuesday 8 January 1901.

After two weeks at sea, the French steamer *Saint Laurent* putters into Saint-Pierre soon after seven o'clock, its crimson smokestacks gleaming in the morning sun. Beneath its iron prow the water parts in bright blue furrows, and new arrivals remark yet again how they have never seen a sea as blue as this one, so richly shaded with turquoise and ultramarine. The passengers who gather noisily beside the embarkation rail this January morning are of all sorts and sizes: their faces are black and white and a dozen colours in between. Amid the laughter and chatter, one passenger stands awkwardly apart: a watchful, red-faced gentleman surrounded by a jumble of crates, cases and brass-edged boxes.

Fellow travellers call him The Photographer. Those crates and boxes, which have rarely left his side during the thirteen-day passage, contain the tools of his magic trade: filters and light meters, lenses and chemical potions. His plan, expounded over several Atlantic evenings, is to take photographs of Martinique's most celebrated sights, and then to market them as postcards. The cards are preserved today within the leaves of a collector's album owned by the Martinican photographer Loïs Hayot: ten black-and-white portraits by a man called 'H.K.' working for Royer and Company of Nancy. Apart from these enigmatic initials, we know nothing about their creator. He must have been a *Métropolitain*, a visitor from mainland France; a man with a keener eye than most. Like us, he is seeing Saint-Pierre for the first time, as it shimmers temptingly through the blue mist of morning.

Now the steamer bucks and twists, nudging closer to its landing stage. Ropes fly lazily through the air, the anchor plunges, a gangplank clatters down like a drawbridge. All is activity: shouting, waving, beckoning. Eyes adjust to a blaze of green after endless days of blue. Martinique is a small island: forty-odd miles long and twenty miles wide at its broadest point, a crescent-shaped link in the chain of Caribbean islands known to the French as the Lesser Antilles. It is surrounded by the British colonies of Dominica, Saint Lucia and Saint Vincent, a fact which helps explain Martinique's strident attachment to all things *à la française*. Saint-Pierre seafront is lined with immaculately shrunken imitations of French town houses, complete with white louvre shutters and wrought-iron balconies. Martinique, the buildings insist, is as French as Versailles or the *Sacré-Coeur*: a state of affairs which has prevailed – give or take a few English incursions – since the Norman duke Pierre Belain d'Esnambuc landed in 1635.

Every effort is made to ensure the islanders feel part of the Third Republic. Martinique may be five thousand miles from Paris, but their electors send two Deputies and one Senator to the National Assembly, an allegiance strengthened by three tele-graphic cables which keep Paris and Martinique's capital Fort-de-France in constant contact. Traders obtain commodity prices direct from the Paris Bourse; the Governor confers with his ministerial bosses at the *Pavillon de Flore*. For six francs and 35 centimes per word, Martinicans can be part of a modern Empire: an enterprise upheld by fear, faith and endless underwater coils of copper and lead.

A heap of steel trunks and leather cases has piled up on the quayside, along with those odd personal effects which always seem to surface at such moments: a bright red bicycle, a yellow parasol and two rusting bird cages. The passengers have had several days to acclimatise, yet the heat at this early hour is already beyond endurance. Every physical act demands an extraordinary effort: starched collars start to prickle and sweat runs from the most unlikely places. Who would have thought, the new arrivals mutter, that paradise could be so *uncomfortable*? At least H.K. has an itinerary of sorts to distract him. He will visit Le Diamant, a diamond-shaped chunk of rock about one mile off Martinique's south coast, scene of an epic nineteenth-century battle between Britain and France. Then there is the splendid cathedral of Saint-Louis in Fort-de-France, and Trois-Îlets, birthplace of Joséphine, wife of Emperor Napoléon.

But Saint-Pierre sounds the most intriguing prospect. Although Fort-de-France is Martinique's administrative centre, Saint-Pierre is seen as the country's true capital: a delightful, mythical place known as *The Paris of the Caribbean, The Pearl of the Antilles*. During their long sea journey, the passengers have heard a great deal about Saint-Pierre; its petty feuds and simpering rivalries. Some of the best stories come from a group of city merchants. To the photographer's unspoken surprise, most of these *négociants* – substantial traders in sugar and coffee, rum and grain – are coloured: as relaxed and confident in their French skins as he is in his own. They have names like Modeza, Caminades and La Touche and each of their shrewd faces is a different shade, from dark reddish brown to an almost indiscernible beige.

From their mischievous mouths come tales of poor Governor Merlin, exhausted by his tussles with the island's political bosses, and gleeful details of the court case against Hyacinthe Nicole, the sometime Mayor of Saint-Pierre who has been accused of assaulting a political rival. To top it all, there are problems at Saint-Pierre's theatre, where several recent performances have degenerated into fistfights between members of the cast. A six-month diet of stale farce and the lightest of light opera has left its mark; the director, old Erhard, is at the end of his tether. When actors are not tumbling off stage, then lumps of masonry are falling from his roof. An impossible state of affairs! The more H.K. hears about Saint-Pierre, the more he wants to see this city for himself. Perhaps his camera will capture some of its enchantment.

The next day, he starts with the panorama: *La Vue Générale*.

At the southern edge of Saint-Pierre, high above the red roofs and slender masts, a statue of Our Lady surveys her town from a small square plinth. If such a view is good enough for the Holy Mother, the photographer reasons, then it is surely good enough for him. Saint-Pierre stretches out beneath his feet in a lazy curve, curled around the natural amphitheatre of the bay like a cat in its basket. At this distance, the city reveals only its most obvious features. There is a harbour, with wooden jetties and a trim white lighthouse. To the right, he sees the twin hundred-foot-high towers of the cathedral, and, running in between, like parallel rail tracks, are the two main roads: the *Rue Victor Hugo* (formerly the Imperial *Grande Rue*) and the *Rue Bouillé*.

The streets which branch off these thoroughfares – the *rues* and *ruelles, cales, marches* and *escaliers* – house more than 26,000 people. 26,011, if one accepts the official census of 1901. Their 3,000 homes stretch over two miles, clambering one on top of another, with roofs of every pitch and pigment. The only obstacles to further communal advance are those imposed by nature. To the north lies *La Montagne* or Mont Pelée, an old volcano which towers some 4,000 feet above this busy town. Today, like most days, Pelée's summit is covered in grey cloud, loftily indifferent to its human neighbours. To the east of Saint-Pierre, a stony ridge rises steeply over the rooftops, while the western horizon is full of sea; nothing but sliding silver sheets of sea.

H.K. takes two heavy photographic plates from his case and ferrets for his light meter. The air is heavy and full of a faint, leafy scent. In a few moments the sun will tip over the brow of this hill, the *Morne d'Orange*, and throw a shaft of soft white light onto Saint-Pierre. He does not want to miss that moment. Working quickly, he kicks his tripod legs into place and tightens the brass stays. The humidity makes him dizzy: perhaps it would be better to come back later today. But then this is how life is here: the same relentless thirty degree heat, wrapped around you like a fur coat; the same un-changing weather forecast every day, predicting *Beau, Beau* and more *Beau*.

One of the local newspapers bemoans 'the monotony of our colonial life', yet every newcomer is struck by Martinique's luxur-iant variety. The photographer has never seen such a profusion of vegetation, such overwhelming vitality. Every single centimetre of earth has been overrun by forest: the pathways are dotted with mauve bougainvillea and red hibiscus; each hillside is wild with ferns, layered like feathers on a gigantic bird. Palm trees of every shape and size peer over the clearing. A handful are as straight as masts, while others bend at fantastic angles, as if on the verge of an embrace. Some are curved like bows; others rear up like snakes poised upon their tails. If one peers further into the forest, there are trees with leaves as slim as cutlass blades and some with big oval leaves on stalks, like frying pans on a scullery rail.

The photographer is also amazed by the torrent of noise emerging from this forest. He can hear the chirp of cicadas and a stately creak of timber, along with all sorts of squeaks and whistles, scratchings and snufflings. At every turn, there is a constant chatter of running water. God knows what is going on in there. He has been told to watch out for a certain kind of serpent, unique to these islands. The pit viper or *fer de lance* has a pale yellow back and a pink belly: a single bite to the leg was usually enough to kill. By the time you were aware of the pain, it was too late. The photographer is not a nervous man, yet even he feels a tremor of anxiety in this isolated clearing. This is not the tame, regimented nature he has learnt to appreciate in the botanical gardens of Paris: this is something far more wilful. Like most French citizens, his only knowledge of Martinique up to this point has come from the Parisian newspapers. He knows the island is prone to natural disasters. Hurricanes, floods and earthquakes are the most common dangers, the latter on average twice a year. Trouble could strike at any moment.

On 22 June 1890, a fire tore through the capital, Fort-de-France, incinerating many of its most beautiful wooden buildings. Thousands of rare books, bequeathed to Martinicans by their former Deputy, Victor Schoelcher, were also lost. The books were being stored in a warehouse prior to their display in the newly completed Schoelcher Library. Early editions of works by Rousseau, Chateaubriand, Stendhal and Hugo were consumed by the flames, as were more than 250 volumes of sheet music and many hundreds of books in Spanish, Italian, Latin and Greek. An entire lifetime of meditation and annotation had perished in but a few minutes.

A year later, on 18 August 1891, Saint-Pierre was visited by a similar outrage. A cyclone roared into the city, killing 420 people and injuring another 1,400. 'Martinique', wrote one French journal, 'is no longer able to count its calamities.' In theory, the islanders were citizens of the *Métropole*. At times like these, the connection felt impossibly remote.

Familiar with misfortune and afraid of being abandoned, the colonists make fitful attempts to impose order on their island. To

18 August 1891

mark the new century, a new road map is being drawn up, designed
to show all thirty-one of the *routes coloniales*. Despite decades of talk
there is still no railway line, although the island's rough relief (two-
thirds of Martinique is bare mountain rock) may have had some say
in that matter. A telephone service is in place, connecting all of the
principal towns and villages. The service can be a little erratic and
expensive. A five-minute call from Saint-Pierre to Fort-de-France
costs one franc: the average daily wage for a plantation worker. Yet
the most important point is that the exchange exists at all. Nature
can – and will – be overcome, even in these unpromising conditions. That is part of *la mission civilisatrice*.

Before leaving the hillside, the photographer pauses to appraise
the statue of Our Lady. Restless nature has been at work here as
well, eroding and corroding, taking charge. The plaster folds of
Mary's gown are full of holes and her right hand, raised in
benediction, has lost the tip of its little finger. Beneath the plinth,
there is a small plaque – *Notre Dame de la Garde, Our Lady of the*

Watch, Erected 1870 – around which tiny green lizards slither and creep.

Back at the edge of town, H.K. turns left into a high, narrow street. Like most newcomers to Saint-Pierre, he is a little lost. There are no street maps or road signs in this town; each road contents itself with a nickname, passed down from generation to generation like a folk story. The *Rue Précipice* is particularly well named.* From here it is a sheer drop down to the harbour, where yachts and steamers loll about in dazzling watery azure. It is as if a painter has washed his summer brushes in a vast jar. The photographer tries to admire the view, but his mind is elsewhere. These streets are full of traps. If he does not fall down a pothole, then surely he will tumble into a vast stone gutter. Every street in Saint-Pierre has the same extraordinary drainage system, although on days like this it is hard to believe it is ever needed.

At the foot of the precipice, he stops.

A carnival of noise fills the air: a clatter of cartwheels on cobblestone, of rum barrels rattling over sunlit yards; the see-saw music of jetties groaning under their loads of sugar and grain. There is an American energy about Saint-Pierre's trading district, better known as the *Mouillage* or Anchorage. It is renowned as the best harbour in the Antilles, and has the market stalls and warehouses to match. The biggest traders have painted their names in bold letters across the shopfronts: *J & P Plissonneau – Suppliers of Colonial Foodstuffs*; *L. T. Knight and Sons – Providers of Building Materials (Timber, Tiles, Windows, Cements)*. Far out at sea, twenty or so boats lie idle in the steeply shelving bay, as neatly aligned as verse on a page.

Most of the bustle and mayhem comes from Place Bertin, a large public square overlooking the harbour. Here at last, sheltered under

---

* And so, in the same mischievous spirit, were the *Rue Mont-au-Ciel* (The Road to Heaven), the steeply raked *Rue d'Enfer*, (The Road to Hell) and the shady *Allée des Duels* (The Path of Duels).

boughs of tamarind and breadfruit, are the people H.K. needs for his compositions; people in all their random variety. He sees young women in bright cotton dresses and madras check turbans, their bare feet swish-swishing swiftly over the flagstones, and men in loose white shirts and straw hats, struggling comically to tug tarpaulins over portly barrels of sugar and rum. It is *une vraie fourmilière*, a real hive of activity.

Dotted around the Place, like actors in a period play, are the stock characters of French authority. There is a customs inspector in a white blazer, and three *gendarmes* in slate-blue tunics and pillbox hats. At the northern end of Place Bertin stands the Customs House: a sad, somewhat dilapidated pile of wood and corrugated iron. Like many official buildings in Saint-Pierre it exudes an air of transience and decay, while the local private structures appear much more healthy. The Chamber of Commerce, at the southern end of Place Bertin, is one of the latter: a white, clapboard mansion with well-proportioned windows and a pillared verandah. An ornamental clock graces one side. It keeps better time than the Town Hall clock, which is consistently a quarter of an hour late, as if drifting back towards its Parisian home.

Yet the strangest feature of Place Bertin sits underneath the whitewashed lighthouse. For there, in the midst of all this heat and holler, is a public fountain as elegant as any you will find in the *Jardin du Luxembourg* or the *Place de la Concorde*. There is something ludicrously outlandish about the *Fontaine Agnès*, with its bronze figurines and tiers of spouting water. Perhaps it is the way the statue has been planted here like a domestic shrub, and left to fend for itself. Maybe it reminds the colonists of home, drawing them back to Paris in the same wistful way as those newspaper advertisements for *Printemps*, the grand department store on Boulevard Haussmann. And yet the sheer absurdity of this fountain must also remind them how far – how very far – they are from the *Métropole*. For the first time, a doubt enters the visitor's mind, between what this place appears to be, and what it *is*: an inspired tropical imitation.

The Métropole. Source of Martinique's strength, and prime cause of its humiliating servitude. Consider the following list taken from the *Notice sur la Martinique*, a promotional book written for the Paris Exposition of 1900. Amid a drizzle of statistics (Saint-Pierre produces '1,000 litres of river water and 200 litres of natural water per inhabitant, per day . . .'), the book shows how meticulously France fleeced its old colony. French traders were given privileged access to Martinique, exporting a wide range of goods at greatly inflated prices. Among the favoured products were:

Soap
Flour
Mules
Horses
Cheeses
Candles
Varnish
Potatoes

Umbrellas and Sunshades
Musical Instruments (pianos, harmoniums, organs, &c)

And so on. In the seventeenth century this was known as the *Pacte Colonial*; in the eighteenth century it was the *Exclusif*. Names changed, but the principle stayed the same. In return, Martinicans were allowed to export only a limited number of goods back to mainland France. They included:

Sugar – Raw and Refined
Rum and Tafia (White Rum)
Dried Pineapples
Cocoa beans
Indigo
Coffee
Nuts

The production of sugar and rum – 33.7 million kilos of raw and refined sugar exported in 1900; 26 million litres of rum – had made many quick fortunes. (In past times, French traders would boast of being *As Rich as a Creole*.) But tropical wealth often vanished just as rapidly. Hurricanes, typhoons and torrential rain could wipe out a season's sugar crop in an afternoon, and Martinique's over-dependence on sugar made it vulnerable to sudden reversals of fortune. Rival producers in Europe and Latin America were advancing every year, happy to undercut the colonial supply lines. In troubled times, an old proverb would rise again on the lips of plantation workers; a piece of folk wisdom rather than the official mystery of charts and graphs: *Misfortune*, they said, *never warns*.

Apart from France, the main exporter to Martinique was the United States, increasingly keen to extend its influence over the Caribbean. From the meat houses of Chicago came salted beef and pork; from Boston and New York, strips of timber and building stone, clocks, oil lamps and sewing machines. Now and then, the island was blessed with an automobile. Faced with these powerful trading blocs, all that Martinique and her neighbours could do was fill the gaps. From Guadeloupe came coffee, vanilla and molasses. From Guyana, the hard woods needed for furniture. France was half a world away from the Caribbean, yet it dictated every detail of Martinican life. The anger which this servility generated among Martinicans – like that of an adolescent towards its ageing parent – is easy to imagine. They called it *L'Oppression Coloniale.*

The photographer does not pick up these irritations. Instead, he sits under a burning blue sky, watching *négociants* dicker over quarts and kilos, eighths and sixteenths. He is fascinated by a sack of raw sugar, sweating syrup from every pore. The *Mouillage* feels like a southern port – Marseilles perhaps, or Montpellier – except that the smells which tease one's nose here are quite different. There is a constant reek of coal fires, of sun-roasted brick and rotten meat. An open sewer bobs unmentionably into the bay, and from every gutter comes a stench of dying fruit. Surveying these mounds of custard apple and molasses, banana and mango, the visitor concludes that life under the Antillean sun is a short affair: a frenzy of bloom and decay, beauty and deformity. Every animal labours under this frenetic rhythm: an anthill carelessly kicked has, by dusk, been carefully rebuilt. Mosquito bites heal with remarkable speed. Men notice how their beards grow faster here than at home. No sooner is one shave complete, it seems, than another is needed.

The American writer Lafcadio Hearn was fascinated by these natural wonders when he visited Saint-Pierre in the late 1880s. Mankind's efforts, embodied in the 'little red-white-and-yellow city', were as nothing compared to the 'green fire' of nature. The island's prodigious energy – the 'absolutism of green' – both enchanted and terrified him. 'You who know only the North', he wrote, 'do not know colour, do not know light . . .' Such thoughts may have inspired the premonition which Hearn describes in his book, *Two Years in the French West Indies*, published in 1890.

Walking alone in Saint-Pierre's botanic garden, he has a terrifying vision:

> You see no human face; but you see all around you the
> labour of man being gnawed and devoured by nature –
> broken bridges, sliding steps, fallen arches, strangled
> fountains with empty basins; – and everywhere arises
> the pungent odour of decay . . . it never ceases to remind
> you that where Nature is most puissant to charm, there
> also she is mightiest to destroy . . .*

H.K. has begun to find his bearings. Standing in Place Bertin, the sea behind him, Saint-Pierre divides into three districts. To the north of Place Bertin (far to his left, as it were) is the *Quartier du Fort*, the city's religious and military quarter. There, beneath the gentle folds of Mont Pelée, lies the bell tower of the *Église du Fort*. Two religious foundations occupy the same raised piece of land, known as the *Plaine de la Consolation*: a seminary college run by the Fathers of Saint-Esprit and a more modest convent for the thirty-one Sisters of Saint-Joseph de Cluny. Many of the town's oldest families – the Perinelle-Dumays, the Pécouls and des Grottes – also live in this

---

* Of all the writers drawn to Martinique, Patricio Lafcadio Tessima Hearn (1850–1904) was certainly the most remarkable. The son of a Greek beauty and a British Army surgeon, Hearn was a half-blind recluse whose omnivorous reading led his remaining eye to swell grotesquely to twice its normal size. Moving to America, Hearn's journalistic career flourished until he confessed to living with a mixed-race woman. Salvation came through literature. A meticulous writer (he once spent eight months perfecting 73 lines), Hearn's account of *Two Years in the French West Indies* was enthusiastically received. After a series of rows with his American patrons, however, Hearn moved to Japan where he married into a Samurai family. Prolific to the end, he wrote twelve books about Japan while being unable to speak the language. A tiny man, Hearn must have cut a peculiar figure on the streets of Saint-Pierre. 'The peajacket he affected was much too large and his very low collar with its black string tie much too big, giving him the appearance of a miniature but serious-minded scarecrow' – Dumas Malone (ed.), *Dictionary of American Biography* (New York, 1932).

quarter. They hide behind finely carved wooden gates, their wealth weighed in ruby and silver, amethyst and gold. The largest houses have courtyards with marble fountains and granite balconies, just like in New Orleans.

The grandest public buildings – stone built, stone flagged – stand directly in front of the photographer, in a district known as the *Quartier du Centre*. Separated from the Fort by the River Roxelane, the Centre is smarter, more sophisticated than its neighbour. Here is the Governor's second residence: the *Hôtel de l'Intendance*, Saint-Pierre Town Hall with its homesick clock, and the Head Office of the Bank of Martinique. Here too are the city's infamous theatre and local jail. This, then, is the quarter where Pierrotins come to do their official business – and where their politicians come to fight and squabble. Every six weeks or so Governor Merlin makes a formal visit, installing himself at the *Intendance* to hear petitions.

A final turn of the neck brings H.K.'s gaze back to the *Quartier du Mouillage*: the harbour district which has so diverted him this morning. Presiding over this scene are the twin towers of Saint-Pierre's cathedral, *Notre Dame de Bon Port*, Our Lady of Safe Harbour. The church's principal bell has begun its sad, low toll summoning the people to prayer. 'When it is made to speak,' writes Lafcadio Hearn, 'the effect is startling: all the city vibrates to a weird sound . . . an abysmal, quivering moan.'

Notre Dame is beautifully decorated, as fine as any equivalent church in mainland France. To the east stands a marble altar, adorned with stone reliefs of the four evangelists. Above their ageless, bearded heads there is a fresco of Our Lady ascending into Heaven upon the wings of angels. Three elaborate crystal chandeliers hang from the ceiling. Most days, the dark wooden pews are dotted with townsfolk waiting for confession. On Sundays, however, they sit according to their social rank: white landowners in front, mulatto traders close behind, followed by the town's labouring blacks.

Back outside, H.K. photographs a fleet of lighters threading from ship to shore. Once the low-slung boats have dropped off their cargo, two white-helmeted customs officers move in to pick over their contents. There is a ritual quality to their actions: something stagey and over-elaborated. But that, one suspects, is part of the point. For it is through such routines that the illusion of France is upheld. Take 14 July: Bastille Day. According to Martinique's *Bulletin Officiel*, the revolutionary holiday must begin with a salvo of twenty-one cannon rounds, fired from all the forts and batteries dotted across the island. All public buildings are ordered 'to raise the national flag from 6am to 7pm on 13 July, and from 6am to 6.30pm on the 14th'. A review of the island's infantry is to finish with each soldier being given exactly 'fifty centilitres of wine' for their pains. No wonder many people treated the *banalités antédiluviennes* of Bastille Day with quiet contempt.

★   ★   ★

Other French traditions are accorded more respect. Food, for example. Place Bertin's street market offers dozens of strange and implausible temptations. Our visitor might like to taste some strips of shark and silver flying fish, laid out neatly on a table like kitchen blades. Or perhaps he would prefer the Wine Cask fish, with its round boneless body. There are blue fish and red fish, blind fish and fanged fish; there are eels the size of pythons and sprats with snouts as sharp as needles. Another stall sells sea toads and sea snails, and the magically named Through-my-fault Crab, so called because it has one very small and one very large claw, the latter of which folds up against its body like a penitent striking his chest at cathedral confession: *Through my fault* . . . it seems to whisper. *Through my most grievous fault* . . . One has to move quickly, for Saint-Pierre is settling into its daily *sieste*, when every wooden awning is pulled down as low as an old man's fedora.

If the market fails to satisfy, then there is always the Rue Victor Hugo. The city's main street curls north for a mile or so, from harbour to theatre. Like main streets across the world, it provides a stage for all kinds of public drama: a place to shop and gossip, to drink and dawdle. Even at this hour, with the sun nearing its height, the sidewalks are full of life. H.K. watches wooden carts and beetle-black buggies juddering up and down, while on every corner, a trader sells their wares in melodious Creole:

– *Bonjou' Missié! Coument ou yé?*

– Hello Sir! How are you?

A young woman in black-and-white calico beckons, a red sash tied tight at her waist . . .

– *Ca qui le canna? – Ca qui le di pain aube?*

She has fresh duck and newly baked loaves, shaped like cucumbers. But the newcomer shakes his head and walks on.

– *He! gens pa' enho', gens pa' enbas!*

– Hey! You folks upstairs, You folks down below!

– *Moin ni bel gououôs poisson!*

It is a boy with a big and bountiful fish on his arm.

No thank you, says H.K. That is most kind, but I must . . .

– *Missié!*

An old man croaks from the shadows.

– *Ca qui le charbon?*

But the photographer does not want charcoal . . .

. . . *le bel – avocat?*

or an avocado as rich as brie cheese.

Perhaps he wants something from this pastry boy striding down
the street, chanting half in French and half in Creole:

Toujours content.

Toujours joyeux.

Oh, qu'ils sont bons!

Oh, qu'ils sont doux!

Always content, Always happy. Oh, how *good* they are, he shouts.
Oh, how *sweet* they are!

The baguettes are as rich and crisp as any you will taste in Paris. As
he eats, the photographer marvels at the Rue Victor Hugo's stone-
built three-storey houses and fashionable boutiques. It looks like a
scale model of a French high street. The colonial blueprint has been
followed so diligently that many first-time visitors imagine they are
back in France, even though every piece of evidence – the Creole
faces and the ridiculous heat – suggests the opposite. Perhaps Saint-
Pierre is not a real city at all, but an act of fevered imagination.

– *Missié! Missié!*

The traders, again.

– *Ai, Missié!*

Creole is hard to follow, even for a native French speaker. Words
drift and swirl like tobacco smoke, constantly changing shape and
meaning. They form a secret world of songs and stories, of sorcery and
legend, an invisible wall between the white landowners or *békés* and
their workforce. Stray words swim through this *gumbo* soup of African,
antique patois and mangled French. But for the most part, outsiders
find this language as closed as a clam, as mischievous as a monkey.

The voices are more insistent. Women's voices.

– *Missié! Mon ché!*

Hey Mister! My Dear!

H.K. feels a dig in his back. Before he can turn around, a platoon of young women brushes past him laughing and singing, their earrings jingling in harmony. He tries to shout back, but the women's extraordinary appearance stops him in mid-thought. Their long cotton robes are a fabulous array of reds and greens, pinks and mauves, lilac and gold. Each of them has a wooden tray perched on her head, filled with all manner of treats. These are the *porteuses*, Martinique's most formidable sales force. It is said that the women can walk barefoot up to fifty miles a day, carrying their neatly wrapped parcels through rivers and forests, over hills and ravines. Most of the trays are light enough to rest freely on their heads, although some weigh up to 150 pounds and demand a steadying hand.

There is an art to this balancing act. One lady sways from side to side, oranges as big as cannon balls rolling around her tray; her friend grips three layers of nutmeg and sweet potato, while a third rests a stick of bananas on her hip, like a rifle. When Lafcadio Hearn persuaded an earlier group of *porteuses* to unwrap their waterproof packets, he found entire storerooms upon their heads. He saw pins and needles, soaps and toothbrushes, cuffs and collars, plates and dishes, knives, forks, coffee pots and tin flutes. Another lady carried pencils, paper, envelopes and ink stands. The whole scene reminds H.K. of a circus act. Or perhaps these ladies are part of a *Carnaval* procession . . .

After all, January is the start of Carnival season in Saint-Pierre. From now until late February, the city spirals into an ecstasy of riot and misrule. If Bastille Day upholds the dry rituals of Republican France, then *Carnaval* knocks them down with a belch and a cheer. To the white establishment, it is 'the occasion of disorder, of insults . . . A carnival of provocation'. For the people, it is a burlesque revolution, a rare chance to mock their masters. After two months of weekend *charivari* the mayhem comes to a head in the four days leading up to Lent: a time when, as one visitor noted, 'the entire town is in the street'. And what a racket they make, marching to the steady *Tam-Tam-Tam* of the *Ka* drum! There are men dressed as women and women dressed as men; everyone is wearing the most ridiculous hats and wigs.

Each year, their parade follows the same route. After gathering beneath Mont Pelée in the *Quartier du Fort*, this satanic cavalcade descends into the Rue Victor Hugo and on to Place Bertin. 'A human torrent', wrote one journalist, 'inconceivably bizarre and lively; a flood of men, women and children electrified by an infernal orchestra.' Through the midnight streets they go, led by devils in blood-red masks and cloaks which glitter with a hundred tiny mirrors. As they pass beneath the windows of the good and the great, an unearthly bass bellow goes up:

Bimbolo! Zimbolo!
Bimbolo! Zimbolo!

This is the Devil's Song: a chant to raise people from their beds and souls from their graves. All are possessed by the spirit of *l'envers*: of a world turned inside out, back to front and upside down. At the front of every procession, in comic majesty, stands the ten-foot figure of *Vaval* or *Bois Bois*, the King of Carnival. Each year he represents whatever Pierrotins decide is their greatest fear. Some years *Vaval* assumes a human face, perhaps that of a politician or an adulterous husband. Other times he takes allegorical form, representing a dreaded disease like smallpox or yellow fever. On the night of Ash Wednesday, to squeals of delight, the effigy is burnt beside the sea. Saint-Pierre's carnival is the longest and loudest on the island: a symbol of its people's desire to keep going *jusqu'au bout*, to the very last drop.

Carnaval drew visitors from around the world. American and European cruisers would time their arrivals to coincide with the four days of *Dimanche Gras, Lundi Gras, Mardi Gras* and *le Mercredi des Cendres*. The French authorities were less enthusiastic. The anarchic *Carnaval* was banned altogether from the 1770s to the 1850s and only returned under strict supervision. Masks were not to be worn before midday and after eight o'clock at night; revellers who threw flour or soot at their social betters (how sweet that was!) were severely punished. The saucy custom of clanking tins and saucepans outside the houses of newly-weds had long been outlawed, but went on all the same.

Chanson de Carnaval

Satirical songs, *les chansons de Carnaval*, were also turned to mischievous effect. Any subject was suitable: a failed love affair, a political scandal, a shopkeeper who charged too much or a sailor who went too far. If one was unlucky enough to be the victim of such a song, one was expected to listen politely and with good grace – assuming, of course, the *chanteurs* had picked on the right person. In 1885, a certain Jean Fréjus was moved to write:

NOTICE

Having received last night a masked serenade, accompanied by lyrics of an indecent nature, I wish the public not to confuse me, Jean Fréjus, master-carpenter, rue Isambert, with one M. Fréjus, painter, living on the rue d'Orleans.

And everyone had heard about the lady who once ran a bar on the Rue des Bons Enfants. After hearing her virtue ridiculed in song, the woman threw herself out of a second-floor window, bounced improbably off a shop awning and landed on the street. End of story.

Carnaval begins with a series of public balls. The Rue Victor Hugo is lined with handbills for costumed balls and masked balls, dinner dances and municipal concerts. One had to choose carefully. Two weeks on the *Saint Laurent* has given H.K. a sense of the sharp social distinctions which operate in Saint-Pierre. The white land-owners – the *békés* – keep their own company in private clubs like the *Cercle de l'Hermine* and the *Cercle des Blancs*. The men of colour have responded by creating their own separate retreats: the *Cercle d'Égalité*, the *Cercle de Fraternité* and a *Cercle de Concorde*. By 1901, Saint-Pierre had eighteen societies and circles. They catered for painters and musicians, scientists and sportsmen. Women formed their own *Cercles* while more radical citizens joined a new *Cercle* called 'The Social Future of Martinique', an institution where Socialism was invoked without apology.

Younger people preferred the dance halls. At the upper end of this market is *Casino*, which promises 'well-stocked buffets at excessively good prices' with musical accompaniment from M. Médouze the clarinettist and his eight-piece orchestra. Dances are led by Messrs Nauda and Libon. *Casino* overlooks Place Bertin, its windows glimmering with paper lanterns of rose red and primrose yellow. Inside, tall mirrors give the illusion of an immense *Belle Époque* ballroom, while the walls are dressed with French tricolours. In the *Quartier du Centre, Moulin Rouge* draws a more varied crowd under the guidance of Masters Cerique and Téramene. And then there are the rougher temptations of the *Blesse-Bobo*, much favoured by sailors and soldiers. Most evenings these seem to end in what newspapers politely call *une rixe*: a bloody blaze of bottles and machetes.

This season, however, there is an added attraction.

Electric light has finally arrived in Saint-Pierre and the dance masters promise 'illumination of great brilliance and splendour'. Paris has enjoyed this privilege for several years. But that is the nature of things. Parisians have a *Métro*; Pierrotins have a tramway run by Madagascar the Mule and her two sisters. No matter: one has to accept a certain shortfall between Paris and the provinces. So far, the electricians have installed arc lamps on the Rue Schoelcher, Place de l'Église and around the Town Hall. Every step of their advance is reported in Saint-Pierre's journals: by the end of January, they say, the whole city will be beaming with light. Yet the move from oil-powered lanterns to electric arcs has not been entirely without difficulty. Turbines overheat; oil is leaking everywhere and power cuts have disrupted the telephone system. A Parisian newspaper, *La Dépêche Coloniale*, relays more selfish concerns. Older people, it says, are opposed to street lighting because it will force up prices for candles and matches. But their anger will be nothing compared to that of theatregoers, the paper warns. 'If ever the lights go out during a play at the Saint-Pierre theatre, there will be a tremendous riot.'

It has been a long day. The photographer is tired of dragging his crates and boxes around these higgledy-piggledy streets. His throat is as dry as sandpaper. At the northern end of Rue Victor Hugo there is a bar called The Central Vaults. Out of curiosity, he orders a *Mabi*: a mild local beer made from molasses and, at first taste, quite repulsive. Outside, the shadows begin to lengthen. Little *béké* boys scuttle off to piano lessons in grey blazers and white bow ties; mulatta women glide past in their check dresses, all drawn up at the waist like curtains draped under a pelmet. Their silk headscarves are knotted in all kinds of strange ways, a secret code for those who know:

One Knot: Heart for the taking.
Two Knots: Heart already taken.
Three Knots: Heart already taken . . . But still with room for another!

Shops start to close. Although few stores bother with sign boards, Saint-Pierre's shopkeepers can satisfy most needs. According to the *Bulletin Officiel* there are 204 traders here, all the way from Ablancous (André) via Ponk-Tsong (Jules) to Zamy (Marius). Some of their names seem to have been invented by Paris's famous nineteenth-century caricaturist Honoré Daumier. There is a cobbler called Emmanuel Bellefeuille, a grocer called Gaston Crocquet, a perfumier named Georges Nivalsy and a pharmacist with the incredible title of Aman Tranquillin. Like many visitors, H.K. has that exhilarating sense of a whole world laid out before him: a place which is a little like France and a little like the Caribbean, and a lot like nowhere else on earth.

That night, the photographer heads for the *Grand Café de la Comédie*, a white man's club beside the theatre. One of those sour old planters on board the *Saint Laurent* had recommended it. There were newspapers from Paris, London and Guadeloupe, he said, and the most *piquante* conversation in Saint-Pierre. Intrigued, H.K. gallops up the theatre's sweeping stairway, past a row of blazing torches. Disappointment is too strong a word, but he is certainly not impressed by what greets him at the *Grand Café*. The room is silent save for the *click* and *tchipp* of billiard balls and a sullen grumble of conversation. The men are all of a certain type: self-important whites, prating on about politics as their jowls wobble like saddlebags. Perhaps this was what Lafcadio Hearn meant when he referred to the 'mental famine' which quickly troubles the metropolitan visitor to Martinique. After one has marvelled at its landscape, and battled with its climate, there is really nothing much else to do.

H.K. finds an armchair and settles down with his vermouth. The supply of newsprint, he soon realises, is as stale as the company: five-year-old back issues of *Le Journal des Voyages* (1896!), *Le Monde Illustré* and the pictorial weekly *L'Illustration*. Soon, like many a bored traveller, he is leafing through old reports about the Paris Exposition of 1900. Symbols of Capital and Empire – the Gallery of Machines, the Castle of Water – fill the pages and from this distance they seem faintly ludicrous, arrantly presumptuous. As do the national pavilions, which served as showcases-cum-shopwindows for the 132 countries assembled beside the River Seine. Some of these pavilions are ridiculously grand. Others, like the Russian House, are filled with common *bric-à-brac*. H.K. spots a stuffed walrus, two polar bears, some fossilised fish and an igloo. They remind him of that childish game where everyone tries to memorise the contents of a tray and then work out which item has been removed.

One item is quite conspicuously missing from these pages. As he wades through the endless photographs and line drawings, H.K. can find no mention of Martinique or its Antillean neighbours. It is as if they have disappeared, or been written off the map. There are plenty of pictures of France's newer colonies in Africa and the Far East (the Algerian pavilion, all white domes and minarets, gets a page of its own). But Martinique merits no mention at all. Every day the French flag is raised, the *Marseillaise* is sung, yet no one in Paris seems to hear its distant melody. Perhaps the phrase *Paris of the Caribbean* has a more wistful sense than he first imagined.

Night has fallen. Walking carefully down those steep streets, the photographer hears a tree frog belching and a chorus of drones, gurgles and ululations unlike anything he has ever heard. Saint-Pierre was French but its soul held something quite different. The visitor recalls his first glimpse of Place Bertin and of the whitewashed lighthouse, busy with semaphore cables. It may be the drink, of course, but for a moment he senses how fragile this enterprise is, how contingent: a conjuring trick held together with wires and lights.

TWO

DEATH TO THE WHITES!

THE PHOTOGRAPHER known as H.K. took at least ten pictures of Saint-Pierre. They give a fine sense of how the city and its people must have looked at this time, capturing their daily lives in that naive, unwitting way that postcards often do and which is so hard to fake. They have also become, by the workings of fate, unconscious souvenirs of a world which has vanished completely. A year or so after the photographs were taken, Saint-Pierre and its people were obliterated so suddenly, so mysteriously, that the first rescue teams were unable to identify any of the ruined streets or houses. In the years which followed, such postcards were often the only proof that certain parts of this city had ever existed.

Leafing through Loïs Hayot's postcard collection one hundred years later, one is struck by another kind of absence. The French photographers who visit Saint-Pierre at the turn of the century studiously ignore the poverty and deprivation which surrounds them. One catches occasional glimpses of the city's celebrated *blanchisseuses*: women who stood knee deep in the Roxelane River, washing sheets for half a franc a day. Apart from these distant figures, there is nothing to upset the illusion of a white man's Eden. The lives of Martinique's blacks, of people like Ludger Sylbaris, the Most Marvellous Man on Earth, were not deemed worthy of record. Nor were the miserable conditions in which island workers had to live.

A later generation of artists, led by the poet and dramatist Aimé Césaire, were determined to rewrite this story; to ensure the struggles of their African ancestors were not forgotten. Césaire

Plantation workers. Date and location unknown.

was raised in a small town called Basse-Pointe on the northeast coast of Martinique. Born in 1913, he well remembered 'the clownings of poverty':

> . . . the carcass of wood, which I call 'our house', comically perched on minute cement paws, its coiffure of corrugated iron in the sun like a skin laid out to dry, the main room, the rough floor where the nail heads gleam, the beams of pine and shadow across the ceiling, the spectral straw chairs, the grey lamp light, the glossy flash of cockroaches in a maddening buzz . . .

Césaire's *Notebook of a Return to the Native Land* is a complex work: an act of celebration yet also an act of rejection. The poet in Césaire is excited by the sensory profusion of poverty; yet the politician in him, the laureate of black pride and *négritude*, despairs of its humiliating squalor. Later, he recalls:

. . . another little house very bad smelling in a very narrow street,
a minuscule house which harbours in its guts of rotten wood,
dozens of rats and the turbulence of my six brothers and sisters . . .

H.K.'s photographs do not record these kind of experiences. As a
white man, he cannot see them. He cannot *feel* them. Race divided
Martinique as sharply as any southern US state. The island's black
majority would know, for instance, that Place Bertin was not just a
pretty marketplace but also the main venue for state executions.
Two nineteenth-century cases still burned in popular memory. In
1822, twenty-one black slaves were sentenced to death for leading a
revolt against their white masters. By cover of night, they had
murdered two plantation owners and wounded seven others.
Retribution was swift and brutal. The plotters were hunted down
and brought to Place Bertin, where a ritual punishment had been
arranged. In full public view the men's right hands were cut off, then
their heads. The bodies were left to rot under the tamarinds for four
hours before being tossed onto a rubbish tip.

Eight years later, Place Bertin provided the spark for an even
more reckless revolt. As before, the rebels moved at night. Their first
symbolic act was to knock down the public gallows in the Place and
to leave a red, white and blue tricolour draped over railings outside
the *Mouillage* church (later to become the city cathedral). *Liberty or
Death* was scrawled on the flag. The following night, 7 February
1831, sugar fields at *Habitation Perinelle* were set on fire. The
Perinelles were one of Martinique's wealthiest families, well-known
inhabitants of the *Quartier du Fort*. Seeing their plantation ablaze, the
white planters or *békés* began to panic. White women and children
fled from Saint-Pierre. Two days later, the *Habitation* was attacked
again, along with half a dozen other plantations. By now, the revolt
was spreading south and west, and a pattern was emerging. The
rebels were attacking property rather than people; their target was
white economic power rather than whites themselves.

When order was finally restored, the revolt had taken the lives of six slaves. Another twenty-two were condemned to die at midday on 19 May. Their bravery before the gallows astonished the Governor, Admiral Dupotet. He describes how they sang Republican songs and jeered at their captors. 'We are the victims of Liberty', they shouted. 'We are dying for Liberty. Long Live Liberty! The coloured men will avenge us . . .'

These were the spirits which haunted Place Bertin.

Slavery was the constant wound, the indelible shame. Official records for 1847 classed 74,447 men, women and children as slaves. Pressure for abolition had increased throughout the 1840s, as had public awareness of white brutality. More than a hundred cases of 'excessive punishments, inhuman and barbaric treatments' were brought before Martinican courts in 1847. Many more were left unreported. Of those that did come to trial, the court transcripts record acts of pathological cruelty. Martinican historian Armand Nicolas claims a complete account of these assaults and humiliations would furnish enough material 'for a weighty book'. Instead, he details more than a dozen cases from that particular year. Among them:

I

A YOUNG SLAVE BOY called Modeste, who was forced to eat a mixture of pig, turkey and chicken excrement. The boy was then pelted in the face with human faeces and made to smear the excrement all over his body.

II

A MAN FROM SAINT-PIERRE called Augustine Genet, jailed for one month for striking a twelve-year-old girl with a baton. Genet was also found guilty of assaulting various other unnamed slaves. His assaults included: 'blows to the mouth with a shoe, tobacco thrown in eyes, boiling water poured on bare feet, burns to the neck and arms with a hot knife, pepper in the sexual organs.'

III

A SIX-YEAR-OLD SLAVE called Clémentine who was detained in her room with her hands bound behind her back. The girl was then suspended from a beam, her feet barely touching the floor. She was left in this position for an entire night. The next day she was taken to the courtyard, where her leg was chained to a block of wood.

Slavery was formally abolished in April 1848, thanks in large part to the efforts of one of Martinique's MPs, Deputy Victor Schoelcher. But two hundred years of misery, engrained deep in the flagstones of Place Bertin, would not be exorcised quite so easily. In September 1870, southern blacks and coloureds rose again. This time, the police and army were outnumbered. For two days, France lost control of its idyllic island: more than fifty plantations were torched around Rivière-Pilote, Vauclin and Sainte-Anne. Several prominent landowners were murdered.

The trigger on this occasion was an emotive court case in which a mixed-race man, Léopold Lubin, had been jailed for five years. His crime: an assault on a boorish white landowner called Augier de Maintenon. The judges rejected Lubin's claim that he was responding to an earlier, unprovoked attack by de Maintenon. Public anger increased when Lubin's sentence was found to equal that given recently to a white thug for murdering his coloured mistress. Lubin was yet another victim of White Man's Justice.

By 23 September, the rebel force had grown to over a thousand men. They were a loose band of field hands, factory workers and small farmers, armed only with picks, cutlasses and sharpened bamboo sticks. The French army were nowhere to be seen. Fields of golden cane flamed orange and red; white hot sparks twinkled in the night air. To ward off French bullets, rebels rubbed themselves in a magic lotion made up of rum and *ghombo musquée*. They thought they were invincible.

The white landowners had learnt an important lesson: *Békés* could no longer afford to rule alone. In future they would have to form alliances and work with their mixed-race neighbours, a prospect which led many whites to abandon politics altogether. Paris was consumed with talk of revolution, and Saint-Pierre was not far behind. To make matters worse, the Franco-Prussian war had left Martinique short of food and capital. Commodity prices had risen sharply and there was no money for workers' wages. The *békés'* best hope of retaining power was to make a pact with coloured merchants in Saint-Pierre and Fort-de-France. A citizen army of whites and mulattoes was hastily set up, united by a common interest in liberty, equality and the pursuit of property.

When it came down to it, the rebels' *ghombo* lotion was no match for modern rifles. Their Southern uprising was soon over. More than five hundred men, women and children were thrown into jail. Four ringleaders – by the names of Eugène Lacaille, Louis Telgard, Auguste Villard and Daniel Bolivard – were executed. Order had been restored, but at a price. Martinique had endured an all-out race war, where the words *À bas les Blancs! Mort Aux Blancs!* – Down with the Whites! Death to the Whites! – had echoed round every town and *habitation*. The revolt of 1870 soured Martinican politics for decades. Many whites feared their postcard paradise was coming to an apocalyptic end. In a letter to the Foreign Ministry, written soon after the revolt, Governor Menche de Loisne observed:

> Already in the countryside, as in Saint-Pierre, certain individuals are saying in a loud voice: 'We are going to get revenge on the whites. We are going to dispossess them.'

This was the turbulent world into which a boy called Ludger Sylbaris was born in the summer of 1874. The Most Marvellous Man on Earth arrived on 1 June, at seven o'clock in the evening. A handwritten French document records this fact, although you may prefer to imagine the scene as Martinicans do, as the hour when the sun slips gently into a silver orange sea. Ludger Sylbaris was born on

Birth certificate of Ludger Sylbaris

Habitation La Bonneau, a plantation near the fishing village of Prêcheur, five miles north of Saint-Pierre. Ludger's mother was a seventeen-year-old called Augusta Doreur. His father was a thirty-four-year-old, Eucher Sylbaris, who laboured on the same plantation. Ludger's parents were not married; a common enough state of affairs. The birth certificate fulfilled a legal need and presumably lessened the stigma of an *enfant naturel*. Their affidavit was witnessed by M. Modeste Théalist and M. Thine Toussaint, both described as 'neighbours of the child'. This brief intrusion by official France concludes with a signature from M. P. Boudet, clerk of Prêcheur Town Hall.

Ludger's home town was a quiet place, best known for being the childhood playground of Madame de Maintenon, wife of Louis XIV. Prêcheur's other claim to national fame was more peculiar. A mile or so out to sea, in the shade of Mont Pelée, there lay a stretch of water known as *The Tomb of the Caribs*. Fishermen avoided the area, claiming it was haunted by the spirits of Martinique's early settlers, the Caribs. Several hundred years ago, so the story went, French soldiers had driven these primitive people off the island, slaughtering them in the sea around Prêcheur. Seeking revenge, the tribesmen had thrown a curse on the invaders: *une malédiction.* By 1901, few Martinicans could recall the curse, let alone remember what it was about. Even so, sailors preferred not to pass through Mont Pelée's shadow if they could avoid it.

Ludger Sylbaris's early years are equally mysterious. After the birth certificate, he vanishes from the formal, written world of Imperial France and slips back into the Creole forest, an underworld of mischief and fantastic legend. Perhaps he cut cane like his father, wielding his cutlass and hoe under an unforgiving sun. Perhaps he worked the steam barges, ferrying raw sugar to the Guérin refinery near Saint-Pierre. Or maybe he was a longshoreman, idling away his days on Place Bertin, waiting for steamers to roll in. Whatever Sylbaris did, he would have been poorly rewarded. None of these jobs paid more than one franc – or twenty sous – a day, and often a lot less. When Lafcadio Hearn told his readers that *porteuses* lived on twenty sous a day, he warned them to temper their admiration for 'her economy will not seem so wonderful when I assure you that thousands of men here – huge men muscled like bulls and lions – live upon an average expenditure of five sous a day. One sou of bread, two sous of manioc (cassava) flour, one sou of dried codfish, one sou of tafia; such is their meal.'

By 1901, this seems to have been Sylbaris's lot too. Local records have him working at this time as a labourer on the *Canoville* plantation back in Prêcheur. Not that young Ludger took his duties too seriously. Saint-Pierre legend (never the best guide, admittedly) remembers him as a gambler, a boozer and a brawler; a man keener to pursue the *Ka* drum than a regular job.

Martinique's politicians had a similar sense of mischief. Although race was still the dominant issue, the sharpest clashes came from a long-running feud between two of the island's political bosses.

Amédée Knight and Marius Hurard had dominated public life here for twenty years. Knight was leader of the self-styled Radical Party: a political faction devoted to bourgeois socialism and bashing the Catholic Church. The Radicals were also part of René Waldeck-Rousseau's 'Government of Republican Defence' in Paris – a connection which M. Knight never tired of publicising, along with his own work as Senator for Martinique. Marius Hurard represented the opposite camp: a loose alliance of white landowners and conservative diehards known as the New or Progressive Party. In theory Martinique was run by Governor Merlin, under instruction from the Ministry of Colonies in Paris. In practice, real power lay with the two political parties. Nothing got done in the conservative stronghold of Saint-Pierre or Fort-de-France (M. Knight's heartland) without their approval.

Like eighteenth-century court factions, each party had a newspaper to promote its cause. Senator Knight underwrote *L'Opinion*, 'The Organ of Martinican Democracy', while the New Party's exploits were exhaustively reported in *Les Colonies* (Prop. Marius Hurard). Week after week, the two journals traded slurs, libels and insults: a spectacle rendered somewhat absurd by their dismally low circulations. Not that the propagandists seemed to mind. The low stakes only seemed to spur them on to ever-greater feats of invention. Marius Hurard's main pastime was dreaming up rude nicknames for Senator Knight. Among his favourites were:

THE CHIEF OF THE PARTY OF FAKE SOCIALISTS
THE WHITE HATER
THE SENATOR MILLIONAIRE
LE PETIT SULTAN MACHIAVELLIQUE

And, after a book of poetry had been dedicated in Senator Knight's honour:

THE MAN MOST EMBARRASSED TO HOLD A PEN.

Not to be outdone, *L'Opinion* retaliated with a few names for M. Hurard:

THE OLD HAM
THE POLITICAL NARCISSUS
THE MAN OF INSATIABLE AMBITION

And most hurtful of all:

THE EX-DEPUTY OF SAINT-PIERRE

The roots of this ludicrous tiff can be found in that final headline. Marius Hurard had indeed been the former Deputy for Saint-Pierre, before falling from grace in a most spectacular fashion. How galling it must have been for him to hear Senator Knight crowing about his powerful new friends in Paris, his close friendship with the Minister of Colonies, Albert Décrais! (A man of 'great benevolence' according to *L'Opinion*.) It was even more irritating to read about the Senator's great wealth, particularly when Hurard's own fortune had been swept away in a torrent of debt and bankruptcy. Differences of political principle had their place of course, but one senses the driving force behind the Hurard–Knight feud was good, old-fashioned jealousy.

   To judge from their portraits, Amédée Knight was the more impressive looking of the pair: a light-skinned mulatto with the brisk, plain-talking manner of a big businessman. A high collar and handlebar moustache suggest a touch of vanity, as do the red sash and silver medals added for a later oil painting. The Senator enjoyed the privileges of office: on his annual visits to Martinique he was greeted by a claque of party workers, who would shout *Vive Knight!* with practised spontaneity. *L'Opinion* also knew its place, referring regularly to 'our affectionate Senator' and his 'brilliant' boss, Prime Minister Waldeck-Rousseau.* Marius Hurard was a more complex

---

* *L'Opinion* excelled itself on 13 April 1901, referring to an 'eloquent . . . important . . . and vivid' speech made by Knight at a school prize day.

character. Beneath the pale, distracted eyes and weary expression was a man of whom great things had once been expected, and never quite realised.

Amédée Alexis Augustin Knight was born in 1852. His father was one of Saint-Pierre's first mulatto merchants, the owner of a prime warehouse site on Place Bertin importing fish, meat and building products. At sixteen, Amédée was sent to the *École Navale* in Paris, followed by the *École Centrale*, where he obtained a diploma in engineering. His final years in Paris were spent studying metallurgy and sugar refining: skills which he was to use immediately on his return to Martinique in 1878. After several years working for his father, Knight junior set up on his own, buying sugar, coffee and cocoa fields. Wealth brought political influence and a steady climb up the civic ladder via Saint-Pierre's municipal council, the *Conseil Général*, and, eventually, nomination and election as the Radical Party Senator in 1899. Knight had reached the top of his greasy pole. Election to the Senate brought a seven-year stint in the National Assembly, and unparalleled access to the ministries of Paris.

It had been an impeccable career, sealed with a town house and a country *Habitation*. Fellow Radical Jules Monnerot praised Knight's 'great knowledge of business, his competence in agricultural and industrial matters'. But others thought the Senator a little *too* good at business for a self-declared Socialist and man of the people. In short, he was a hypocrite. Knight the politician criticised factory owners for paying miserable wages. Knight the businessman paid even lower. 'Mr Knight is a singular sort of Socialist', sneered *Les Colonies*. 'He demands that other factory owners should pay their workers at two francs and above, while he continues to pay his own workers between one franc and one franc twenty-five!'

Such remarks were to be expected from a rival paper. Less welcome was the interest of *La Dépêche Coloniale*, one of France's leading titles. When Senator Knight voted in favour of a bill banning rum manufacture at night, *La Dépêche* raised an eyebrow. It seemed that one of Martinique's biggest rum producers was backing a measure which would drive small factories out of business. If that was true, then this law was surely 'one of the most anti-democratic, and most anti-economic measures which has ever been invented for a French colony'. The article went on to accuse Knight of running Martinique with a coterie of friends. It clearly hit a nerve. In a hysterical reply, Knight said *La Dépêche* had printed 'all sorts of ridiculous accusations', mainly recycled from his enemies in Saint-Pierre. But Parisian newspapers were not so easily swayed. *La Dépêche* concluded the affair with a sarcastic swipe at the 'Chief of the Party of Fake Socialists':

> The decree in question favours the rich distillers. Among them, shining on the top rung, is M. Knight, who is a millionaire (we congratulate him) and, at the same time, a socialist. He has achieved the ruin of the poor agricultural distillers. This, there-fore, is a decree with profoundly anti-democratic tendencies . . .

Marius Hurard's career had followed the brilliant but erratic trajec-tory of a firework: a sudden, noisy ascent, an ear-splitting explosion of colour and light, and an equally rapid fall to earth. The high point (as Senator Knight's camp were always reminding people) had come twenty years earlier in 1881, when the thirty-three-year-old had been elected to the National Assembly with an enormous majority. 5,641 votes out of a possible 5,662 in the northern *arrondissement* had gone to the charismatic young lawyer and newspaper editor. So popular was *le Beau Marius* at this point that voters in the southern *arrondissement* made him their Deputy as well, with 3,889 votes out of 3,892. The new Deputy, already a subject of *Carnaval* songs, toasted his victory with typical immodesty. 'Never, since the memorable election which followed the abolition of slavery,' he bragged, 'have so many votes been brought together under a single name.'

Hurard had ridden to power on the back of a single issue: Education. In the early 1880s, Martinique's schools were still run by the Brothers and Sisters of the Catholic Church. Encouraged by changes in mainland France, Hurard began a campaign for a secular *Lycée*, free from religious interference. The struggle was bitter and, on occasion, violent. But Hurard battled on. As a moderate Republican, he believed blacks and mulattoes should have the same civil rights as whites – which meant the right to a proper, state-funded education. In a speech to the *Conseil Général*, the young reformer presented his plan in revolutionary terms: 'The goal, which we have pursued for ten years, is the destruction of that Bastille called Ignorance and, with it, that incredible foolishness which one calls the prejudice of colour . . .'

Hurard's newspaper was part of the same crusade. When *Les Colonies* was launched in 1878, it described itself as 'the first journal for the coloured men of Martinique' and 'the organ of the coloured bourgeoisie'. Parisian newspapers read Hurard's editorials and concluded that a dangerous demagogue was on his way to the Assembly. 'Monsieur Hurard', wrote *Le Soleil*, 'has built his popularity by exploiting the worst passions, the most dangerous passions. That is, the hatreds of race.'

It should have been a staging post on the way to even greater glory. But Hurard's political career was not a success; the human rocket appeared to falter and then fail. Perhaps he did not like the Chamber of Deputies: the long, airless afternoons in the Palais Bourbon, listening to windbag debates. Or perhaps he found the whole business too intimidating. Maybe Paris swallowed him whole, like a shark gobbling up a sprat. Either way, Hurard soon fell into listless obscurity. The Member for Martinique (North and South) rarely cared to speak in the Chamber, or bother to vote. The newspapers now laughed in his face. 'Where, pray, is M. Hurard?' asked *Le Propagateur*. 'What, pray, does M. Hurard *do*? The idol of the blacks and the coloured men of Martinique has found in Paris the delights of *Capoue*.* He does not speak. He does not vote. And

---

* Hannibal's victorious troops wintered in Capoue in 215 BC, intending to prepare an attack on nearby Rome. But the soldiers succumbed to Capoue's earthy pleasures, and lost their will to fight.

he lets the Deputy of *another* colony deal with all his newspaper correspondence; a newspaper of which he was once editor-in-chief . . .'

M. Hurard was evidently enjoying himself. Once installed in the French capital, the new Deputy and his wife devoted much time and energy to social climbing. Readers of *Les Colonies* were given regular updates on their attempts to shin up the drainpipe of Parisian high society, as in this account of a fancy dress ball held on Saturday 21 May 1887:

SOCIETY NOTES

The ball brought together many notable political and artistic *personnages* . . . Mme Hurard was dressed as an Indian, the heavy jewels upon her arms and shoulders having been bought from the bazaars of Ceylon and the Coromandel coast. M. Hurard was robed in the splendid costume of a Maharajah.

Such antics cost money, and Hurard had plenty of that. His family rum business – under the winning name *My Hurard* – turned in huge profits during the 1880s. Deputy Hurard denied he was using his public office for private gain. But it was hard not to draw that conclusion when rivals found Hurard wines, rums and *tafias* on prominent display at the 1889 Paris Exposition. One Parisian newspaper, *La Petite France*, was appalled by this blatant cross-promotion:

On the shop front, alongside an offer of rum at ten sous per glass, is a picture of a beautiful mulatresse, her head covered with a superb madras, laden with brooches . . . Beneath the portrait, one reads the inscription: 'Let's go, Hurard. Let's go to the Assembly.'

Hurard's enemies got their revenge four years later. It was clear that the family business had grown too far and too fast, and was tumbling into debt. Without money to grease the wheels, the Parisian high life came to an abrupt end. On 25 April 1893, Deputy Hurard resigned from the Chamber. On 16 September, *Les Colonies* announced a sale of furniture and personal effects, the traditional prelude to bankruptcy. The great Hurard had fallen back to earth with a magnificent crash.

Le Beau Marius remained a dynamic figure, though he became ever more bitter and vindictive. A certain sourness entered the editorials of *Les Colonies*, along with a pronounced loathing for Amédée Knight, the Senator Millionaire. By 1901, Hurard had become a strident defender of white rule, accusing his Radical enemies at *L'Opinion* of fomenting race war. The one-time young liberal, the editor of 'the first journal for the coloured men', had turned into a middle-aged reactionary. 'There exists in Martinique', he growled, 'a political party which, while wanting to benefit from the laws of the Republic, systematically pursues the eviction of the White Race from this land . . . [They demand] the gradual eviction of one of the two ethnic elements, just like in the laws of Darwin.'

Hurard's odyssey was all the more remarkable for one singular fact. This white apologist, this prophet of race war, was himself a coloured man, the illegitimate son of a mulatto trader who only legally recognised his son when he was seven years old. Old Marius's attempts to square these facts with his opinions may help explain the blustery, excitable nature of his prose. The hired pens at *L'Opinion* loved to remind readers of Hurard's double identity. '[The man] who accuses the coloureds of hating the whites is himself a man of colour', the paper jeered. 'Is this not the best proof that race hatred does not exist?' Less determined men might have abandoned public life. But Hurard's political volte-face kept him centre stage, a man of influence within his beloved town. The people of Saint-Pierre no longer marched through the streets chanting his name. Yet he at least was determined to continue the tradition.

★   ★   ★

There was one point on which all Martinique's politicians could agree however: the incumbent Governor was always a fool, unless of course he shared your particular point of view. Thus the departure of Governor Merlin to Guadeloupe in July 1901 drew two very different responses. *L'Opinion* congratulated Merlin on his 'brilliant promotion' achieved 'despite the campaign of colonial and metropolitan reactionaries'. At *Les Colonies* they lamented M. Merlin's 'disastrous idleness and native incapacity'. In case the Governor still had any doubts about Hurard's view of him, the paper's headline was '*BON DÉBARRAS*': Good Riddance. As the bright blue waves carried him away to Pointe-à-Pitre, one can imagine Governor Merlin returning the compliment.

Political debate did occasionally rise above the level of a Punch and Judy show. There were principled differences between the two parties, particularly when it came to relations with France. To the *Métropole*, Martinique was a business: a property to be run like a farm or a factory. This attitude dated back to the seventeenth century, when Belain D'Esnambuc took the island in the name of *La Compagnie des Îles d'Amérique*. Martinique fell into private hands for a while, before being bought by the French state in 1664 for 240,000 francs (the neighbouring island of Saint Lucia was thrown in too). Day-to-day control passed to the French West Indies Company, *La Compagnie des Indes Occidentales*, who ran Martinique as a monopoly. Their Articles of Association stated that 'the company alone will conduct . . . all the commerce and navigation in the said countries for forty years'. This attitude persisted, in various forms, well into the nineteenth century.

Local politicians wondered whether there was a better way to run Martinique. After all, Algeria was treated like a part of mainland France and divided into three *départements*. Or maybe they should follow the example of Haiti, and force their independence from European colonists. These questions became more acute as Martinique's strategic value waned and its sugar industry began to fail. Although cane sugar was still the most valuable export in 1900, the total volume of trade was falling fast. 33,500 tons of sugar were exported in 1900; 5,000 tons less than in 1880. Distilleries faced the same problem. Rum production slumped from 190,000 hectolitres in 1892 to 145,000 hectolitres in 1900. The problem, as Saint-Pierre's merchants knew all too well, was that sugar could be refined more cheaply in Europe and the Far East. French capitalists were also diverting their money into vast new markets in Africa and Asia. Martinique, 'our ancient colony', was being pushed off the balance sheet.

Marius Hurard thought Paris should treat Martinique as 'an adult colony' with a degree of self-government. 'We ardently desire autonomy for our colonies', he declared on 31 January 1901. 'Let us begin by showing the greatest wisdom in the management of our finances and in our political conduct.'* *L'Opinion* wanted more independence, although it admitted such dreams were impossible so long as the island depended on France for food and supplies. 'For us,' it wrote, 'France is a mother that we are unable to stop loving, and which we will always have need of.' Every natural disaster reminded people of this umbilical link. The colonial system was humiliating, but necessary: Martinique was too vulnerable to survive on its own.

The arrival of *Le Prolétaire* in March 1901 brought a new excitement to the political game. As the self-declared 'Organ of the Workers' Party', *Le Prolétaire* was determined to bring true socialism to Martinique. Not the smug, well-heeled socialism of Senator Knight or the *de haut en bas* paternalism of Marius Hurard, but real international socialism. The Workers' Party would represent Saint-Pierre's black majority, ready to call a General Strike in order to hasten the Socialist Revolution. Race war would be replaced by class war. 'Appreciable progress', noted *La Dépêche Coloniale*, drily.

The seeds of this movement were sown in Paris by a band of Antillean socialists including Hegisippe Legitimus of Guadeloupe

---

* One could but hope. Within a week, *Les Colonies* was back to its usual adolescent tricks, accusing Senator Knight of 'hypocrisy' and 'numerous malfeasances'.

and the Martinican lawyer Joseph Lagrosillière. The Antillean
Socialist Group would spread its socialist gospel through agitation
and education. A lack of homegrown leaders meant a slow start in
Martinique. The real spur to activity – and the reason for *Le Prolétaire*
– was a bloody revolt which spread through Martinique's plantations
and factories in the early months of 1900.

The flashpoint came on 8 February 1900. A platoon of twenty-
five soldiers, led by one Lieutenant Kahn, was sent to a sugar
refinery at François on the east coast. They were ordered to
break up a strike which had started in the cane fields and spread
to nearby factories. Once more, the cry of *À bas les Blancs! Vivent les
Nègres!* was heard across the island. Accounts of that day in François
are confused, but all agreed at least ten workers were killed in a
fusillade of gunfire. Another dozen or so were injured. Kahn
said his soldiers had acted in self-defence; other witnesses said
the soldiers were never in danger. A doctor who examined
the bodies found that three of the protesters had been shot in
the back.

Horror in Saint-Pierre. Uproar in Paris. The Socialist leader Jean
Jaurès called it '*le Fourmies Colonial*': a reference to the killing of nine
miners by French soldiers at Fourmies in May 1891. 150 marines
headed for Martinique to bring the situation under control, while
the Socialists seized their moment. An office was set up at 169 Rue
Victor Hugo, complete with a *grand tableau* of the Declaration of the

Rights of Man. Trade unions or *syndicats* began to appear, although the earliest ones were soon hijacked by Knight's Radical Party. A year or so later, on 15 September 1901, the Socialists held an extraordinary meeting at Saint-Pierre theatre. Around 1,500 people heard the twenty-nine-year-old Joseph Lagrosillière outline his strategy for world revolution:

> I want you to organise in order to seize the Town Halls, so that private industry can be brought under municipal control . . . to seize the Conseil Général, so you can give direct support to your own class institutions, in order to send men to Parliament who will be your servants and no longer your masters . . .

Such talk terrified the merchants and factory owners of Saint-Pierre. They were even more disturbed when Martinique's Archbishop, Mgr de Cormont, held a Workers' Mass in Fort-de-France. A new force was making itself felt on the island, one which was beyond the control of the bourgeois men of colour and white landowners. These political tensions were aggravated by Martinique's changing racial mix. After slavery was abolished, black workers left the land in great numbers. *Habitation* owners turned to India: by 1900, around 75,000 indentured labourers had arrived from the subcontinent.

Four separate racial groups – Blacks, Whites, Mulattoes and Indians – now shared the island, each with their own needs and ambitions. Pity the man who had to govern this unruly idyll. He was, as the Creole proverb put it, *As unlucky as the fellow who sells hats to children without heads.*

THREE

LA MONTAGNE

S AINT-PIERRE'S politicians were so busy with their own private feuds that they paid little attention to the mountain high above their city. If they had, they might have noticed their old friend was behaving rather strangely. Short blasts of steam had recently been seen rising from a lake bed near the summit of Mont Pelée. On 22 June 1901, Martinique's fourth newspaper *Les Antilles* reported another odd development:

MONT PELÉE

Around two hectares of trees have been burnt by the sulphurous emissions coming from the *Étang Sec* [the Dry Lake] and its surroundings. These emissions have travelled very far, and have released a considerable volume of sulphurous gas. What is more, the Lake at the top of the summit has fallen to a level of around 0.75 metres to 1 metre [and] some openings in the soil have been noticed. This is, we believe, the first time these observations have been made.

There was nothing to worry about, of course. Pierrotins referred to Mont Pelée as *La Montagne*: an affectionate nickname for their 4,428-foot-high neighbour, the highest peak in Martinique. Man and mountain had lived together for over 350 years with scarcely a cross word between them. *La Montagne* shielded the city from the worst of winter winds, and pricked the darkest, blackest rain clouds before they stormed its streets. At some long forgotten point in the past, Pelée had been an active volcano. But as the *Annuaire* of 1901 confidently asserted, the mountain was now extinct. A relaxed volcano. *Un volcan débonnaire.*

There had been a few minor episodes in the previous hundred years or so. Yet each episode had been so trivial, so short-lived, that by 1901 they had been almost forgotten. Pelée's first recorded activity came during the French Revolution. In January 1792, clouds of ash puffed and pouted from her summit, dusting nearby palm tops and fern fronds with grey powder. According to one curious eyewitness account, published in Paris in 1796, 'much vegetation was burned and singed, and a number of opossums were killed'.

Almost sixty years later, on 5 August 1851, Pelée awoke once more. This time, the mountain was hard to ignore. Just after eleven o'clock that night, one inhabitant of Saint-Pierre reported hearing a 'muffled noise, ominous and far away' which continued throughout the night, upsetting everyone's sleep. Next morning, Pierrotins were greeted by an unearthly scene: every roof, tree, balcony, awning and pavement in their city was coated with a mantle of pale ash. The chilly tableau reminded one French businessman, M. Leprieur, of his European home. Saint-Pierre, he wrote, looked 'as if [it had been] covered by the hoar frost of the first days of autumn'. Paradise was suddenly full of alarming disorder. Earth tremors drove thousands of serpents off mountain slopes and into the city. The Blanche River, usually one of the clearest and coolest on the island, turned turbid and black.

Such portents were worrying enough for a four-man expedition to be sent up Pelée to investigate. At the summit, the men came across an extraordinary sight: an area of blackened land, almost a thousand metres wide, in which every plant and tree had been burnt or crazily uprooted. They imagined an explosion of some kind had taken place, similar to that of a bomb or a whirlwind. The air was strongly charged with a stale egg stench of sulphur, and two small fumaroles were letting out jets of white steam. There was no sign of any lava flow. The investigators – none of whom were qualified scientists – tried to reassure their fellow citizens. Mont Pelée was a 'picturesque decoration' to their city, they said; its recent activity was merely 'another curiosity added to the natural history of Martinique'.

There were no further ash falls on the city. Pelée continued to groan and grumble for another two months, leaving a steamy, sulphur-rich pool in what was once the Dry Lake. At no point, however, did Pelée threaten the city below. No one was hurt, or even mildly inconvenienced by its actions. When several fumaroles began to steam and hiss again in 1889, city dwellers were curious rather than fearful. Pelée's fits of temper had become part of Saint-Pierre folklore; another quirk of *le volcan débonnaire*. Such nonchalance may help to explain why, thirteen years later, Pierrotins refused to take Pelée's first stirrings at all seriously. They imagined events would take the same course as 1792 and 1851: a few brief rumblings, a blurt or two of ash, and then a slow, steady return to silence.

There were those, however, who recalled an older tradition – and a more sinister name for Mont Pelée. The island's first conquerors, the Caribs, knew Pelée as Fire Mountain: a wild, unpredictable spirit which could spew flame and fury from its mouth at any moment. The name had been inherited from the Arawaks, Martinique's earliest settlers, as had the ritual gifts and invocations intended to keep Fire Mountain at bay. Such beliefs were widely held in the ancient world. In Mayan, Aztec and Incan society, human sacrifices were thought to calm a volcano's temper. Every twenty-five years, a child was thrown into the mouth of Mount Conseguina in Nicaragua; another Nicaraguan volcano, the Masaya, cultivated a taste for young women. Those who felt such sacrifices were a waste of time (and of human life) were briskly dismissed. Imagine how much angrier the volcano would be, the priests argued, if these gestures were neglected . . .

The Indians of Martinique followed similar traditions. One un-named seventeenth-century visitor from Carpentras was appalled to see the polygamous Caribs worshipping puppets made of cotton 'from which the Devil speaks'. Their habit of eating human hearts and tossing severed penises into the sea did not translate too well either. In this context, one can see how the legend of Fire Mountain could be dismissed by the European invaders as yet another lurid folk tale.

Seventeenth-century French colonists may have mocked the islanders' superstitions. But these animist ideas were no more absurd, in many ways, than traditional European theories about volcanic activity. Greek and Roman writers had imagined the earth's core to be full of 'subterranean wind' which rose violently to the surface in sudden explosions. Others fancied that ash and lava flows were produced by warring Gods. In the Middle Ages, Christian writers saw volcanoes as gateways to hell: their sulphurous eruptions gave sinners a glimpse of the eternal torment down below. Famous volcanoes like Mount Etna were felt to be particularly hellish (Tudor Englanders imagined it was the final home of Henry VIII's second wife, Anne Boleyn).

By the early eighteenth century, this faith-based view of the world had been undermined by Cartesian reason and observation. Some naturalists were not convinced. In 1714, one Tobias Swinden presented *An Enquiry into the Nature and Place of Hell* to the Royal Society. After a series of projections and calculations, Mr Swinden concluded the Earth's volcanoes were too small to hold all of mankind's sinners, past and present. His conclusion – which had a certain, lopsided logic – was that the Devil's many disciples were sheltering inside the Sun, which was hotter and more capacious than the volcanic deep.

At least the myth of Fire Mountain had some basis in fact. Rock formations around Mont Pelée suggest a long history of volcanic activity in the centuries and millennia before what we call historic time. The latest deposits – those nearest to the present day – can be traced back to the tenth century, the time of the Arawaks. Historic time, measured out with clocks and calendars, makes up only a minuscule part of these histories. In geological terms, we have lived no time at all: hardly long enough to witness the smallest geological change.

The eighteenth-century British volcanologist Sir William Hamilton was one of the first to grasp this need for long perspectives. A diplomat based in Naples, Hamilton was also the famously cuckolded husband of Emma Hamilton, better known as the mistress of Admiral Nelson. Sir William spent many years watching Mount Vesuvius in eruption. Although the volcano was liable to sudden catastrophic activity, he sensed it was governed by more profound forces. In his influential study of Italian volcanoes, *Campi Phlegraei* (Flaming Fields), Hamilton rendered these observations in fine Augustan prose. 'Nature is ever active', he wrote, 'but her actions are, in general, carried on so very slowly, as scarcely to be perceived by mortal eye, or recorded in the very short space of what we call history, let it be ever so ancient.'

Back in Martinique, the French settlers were too busy to notice the slow actions of nature: there were natives to convert and land to conquer. In a calm blue bay under the shadow of the great mountain, Belain D'Esnambuc built a wooden fort spiked with cannons. He called his pioneer settlement Fort Saint-Pierre and left his nephew Jacques du Parquet in charge. Within five years, the colony had grown from 200 to around 1,000. French families from Normandy and Brittany set up rough timber hamlets along the eastern coastline. Prêcheur, home town of Ludger Sylbaris, was one of the earliest settlements; so was Carbet, a strip of sand two miles south of Saint-Pierre where Christopher Columbus had made a brief landing in 1502. As the French population increased, so too did the tensions with native Caribs. A guerrilla war raged across the island as the two groups fought for control. French villages were torched, settlers vanished on mountain paths. Seeking revenge, the French picked off Carib warriors with rifles and cannon fire. Eventually, in 1639, a peace treaty was agreed, dividing the island into two: French to the west, Caribs to the east.

It was not to last. The French zeal to colonise, to claim land for sugar cultivation, drove Caribs into ever-more desperate acts of revolt. If they were not careful, they would suffer the same fate as the Lamentin, a gentle sea mammal which had once flourished in the crystal waters around Martinique. Frenchmen were so fond of eating these amiable creatures, which looked rather like sea cows, that they soon became extinct.

In 1658, the White settlers planned a final, decisive assault on the Caribs, intent on driving them off the island for good. In doing so, they invoked a curse which was dimly recalled several centuries later as people tried to comprehend the events of 1902. According to legend, French soldiers had ambushed the native Caribs and harried them into the sea at Prêcheur. The Chief Carib was shot and left for dead in a pool of crimson water. In despair, his fellow tribesmen turned to the Fire Mountain, begging its spirit to remember their deaths and punish those responsible. *La Montagne de Feu nous vengera!* they cried. *The Fire Mountain will avenge us!* This, it turned out, was the haunting story behind the stretch of water known as *The Tomb of the Caribs*. All that remained by 1901 was a vague sense of unease and a long-held belief that the area was best avoided after dark, when it was taken over by magicians and sorcerers, the *quimboiseurs*.

Beyond this, the early colonists did not care to dwell on their handiwork or the risk of imminent retribution. By 1701, the Caribs had either fled to Saint Vincent and Dominica, or had been exterminated. 'The French', wrote one religious observer, Father du Tertre, 'burned their homes [and] killed without any consideration of age and sex all those whom they met.' The French West Indies Company had won sole possession of their beautiful island.

A New World demanded a new language. The new French name for the mountain was more familiar, less ominous than its Carib predecessor. *Pelée* in French means, literally, 'the bald one': an allusion to the mountain's bare, dome-shaped peak. To humanise nature in this way was to move one step closer to mastering it. Yet the word *Pelée* had other connotations which the new masters of Martinique may or may not have been aware of. In Hawaii, an island riven with volcanoes, Pele was the name given to a fire goddess who lived beneath the earth. A vengeful creature, Madam Pele was said to have built a permanent fire pit under her island, where she stamped about showering sparks on the people above. Variations on the word Pele appear in Polynesian and East Indian cultures. In Samoa, the fire goddess is called *Fee*. In Tahiti, it is known as *Pere*. Consciously or not, the French had chosen a word of great significance.

Pelée was a popular subject for landscape painters throughout the nineteenth century. It appears in two of Paul Gauguin's early works, painted during the artist's brief but calamitous trip to Martinique in 1887. Accompanied by fellow painter Charles Laval, Gauguin took up residence in a beach hut several miles south of Saint-Pierre, announcing his intention to 'live like a savage'. Gauguin's wish was soon granted. Within weeks, the two men were struck down with dysentery and malaria and were begging their Parisian friends to send them enough money to get home. (One senses the entire trip was somewhat under-financed. So poor were the two artists that on arrival in Saint-Pierre they sold their last box of matches to the highest bidder.) 'My body is like a skeleton', wailed Gauguin. 'My voice has gone . . . I am suffering from a martyrdom of the belly.'

The only consolation of their visit – and strangely, the only sure proof of this visit – are fourteen canvases which Gauguin produced during those wretched four months. Mont Pelée peeps from the background of two pictures, *L'Anse Turin* and *La Végétation Tropicale*. Gauguin treats the mountain as a piece of theatrical scenery: a convenient prop in his search for brighter colour and sharper light. Gauguin's excitement shines through a letter written to his estranged wife, Mette-Sophie Gad, on 20 June 1887:

It is a paradise. Beneath us is the sea, bordered by coconuts. Above us, there are fruit trees. The negroes and negresses walk around all day with their Creole songs and their eternal chatter . . . I can only talk enthusiastically about life in the French colonies, and I am sure that you would think the same.

Madame Gad was in Copenhagen at the time, looking after the couple's four children. What she made of her husband's tropical adventures is not recorded. Nor are there many traces left today of Gauguin's companion, Charles Laval. So great was Gauguin's later fame that Laval suffered the posthumous indignity of having his Martinican works passed off as inferior works by the master. In some cases, art dealers simply erased his signature from the canvas and imposed Gauguin's instead. As a result, Laval's works have almost completely disappeared: his life and work comprehensively eclipsed by that of his friend.

Stripped from its shroud of myth and invention, Pelée looked unmistakably like the home of an old volcanic crater. The mountain peak was stubby and conical, its edges fingered and thumbed like those of a giant pie crust. From the cloud-covered summit, green hills tumbled and rolled their way down to the sea, four miles to the west. If one looked closer, one could make out dozens of ravines, full of sharp plunges and extravagant vegetation. So heavy was the rainfall over Mont Pelée, that it fed over twenty separate rivers including those of the Roxelane and Blanche which flowed through Saint-Pierre. Pelée's prodigal fertility – the product of rich, volcanic soil as much as its humid climate – meant the thirty-nine square miles of mountain base supported some of Martinique's most profitable plantations. Its western foothills also housed the island's biggest sugar mill, the *Usine Guérin*. East of Pelée lay the plantation town and white retreat of Morne Rouge.

Yet the most appealing features of Mont Pelée were hidden from view: their pleasures known only to Pierrotins. Peer over the crusted peak of the volcano and you would find a large, gently sloping bowl with a clear blue lake at its base. This was the *Lac des Palmistes*, the Palmists' Lake: a popular picnic destination and a place of pilgrimage on Saints' days. A tall iron cross rises above it, a riposte to the devilish stink of sulphur in the air. A few energetic sorts might be paddling in the lake's thermal waters or sunbathing on its green banks: a just reward after their long and tiring ascent.

A visiting teacher called Louis Garaud climbed Pelée's eastern slope in 1890. After four hours battling through deep forest, often on his hands and knees, Garaud caught sight of the mountain and the sparkling ocean below, 'one of the most majestic views that one could ever hope to contemplate'. He was right to savour the moment. As the walking party resumed their ascent, the majestic view was lost once more in a haze of cloud and rain: a familiar problem for those trying to conquer Pelée. Garaud's only consolation on reaching the summit was the sight of the Palmists' Lake 'as still as a circular mirror . . . bordered by fine grass and velvety moss, and surrounded by jagged peaks like the broken shards of a gigantic vase'. But nature still had a few more games to play. So humid was the air and so damp the grass that Garaud had to eat his lunch on a tree trunk. Driving rain made his descent even more miserable. 'We finally arrived back,' he writes, 'covered with mud from head to toe, soaked to the bone, mad with fatigue, but with our heads glowing and full of the marvels we had much enjoyed.'

Three hundred metres below the *Lac des Palmistes*, on the western side of Pelée, was a smaller crater known as the *Étang Sec* or Dry Lake. Unlike the Palmists' Lake, the Dry Lake had been empty for many years and before June 1901 it had shown no signs of life. It was a forbidding sight: a lunar land of tall, steep cliffs and stark rubble. Few cared to lay out their picnics here or to pause for a devotional prayer. The most striking feature of the Dry Lake, and the one most often remarked upon by visitors, was the gigantic V-shaped notch in its southern wall. From there, one could get a perfect view of Saint-Pierre, its streets and houses laid out four miles beneath as if glimpsed through a gun sight. Such features were not thought unusual or remarkable in the ruins of an old volcano; they merely added to its beauty.

As for the forces which had created Mont Pelée, Martinicans had established several simple facts about their island and how it came into being. Moreau de Jonnès's *Geology of Martinique* (1825) correctly places the French colony within a chain of volcanic islands, most likely the oldest such formation in the world. De Jonnès speculates (quite accurately as it turned out) that the islands began life as underwater volcanoes, which had been forced up from the seabed over tens of millions of years. Each volcanic eruption added to the mountains' height and width, until they had broken free of the sea and become land masses in their own right. This was known as the 'Craters of Accumulation' theory, first outlined at the end of the eighteenth century. These elaborate processes were repeated throughout the south Caribbean: the Lesser Antilles chain stretches from the Virgin Islands to Venezuela, a distance of 450 miles. While

Lac des Palmistes

Pelée is its best-known volcano, eight others have erupted during historic times and remain active to this day.

Breaking free of the ocean, Pelée and its neighbouring peaks showed all the attributes of a volcanic landscape. Their most striking features were strange, steep-sided bumps known as pitons. There were dozens of these humpbacked creations across Martinique, the best examples being found at Carbet, south of Saint-Pierre. Even more common were rounded, pyramidal mounds known as mornes, cluttered around the island in friendly groups, or sternly solitary like the Morne d'Orange, overlooking Saint-Pierre. Martinique was a land of mountains, mornes and pitons. Wherever one went on this island, one was effectively standing on the surface of a prehistoric volcano. Not that there was anything to worry about. Islanders simply thought Pelée's life cycle mirrored that of the human world: an extinct volcano could never come back from the dead.

Such ideas may sound naive today, but they were widely and confidently held at the start of the twentieth century. Researchers were beginning to record volcanic eruptions in great detail, monitoring their effect on land formations and the earth's atmosphere. But they were no nearer to understanding why these apocalyptic events happened in the first place. In part that was because Volcanology was an obscure, rather eccentric discipline: the province of adventurers and gentlemen amateurs like Sir William Hamilton.

Typical of this breed was an English volcanologist called Tempest Anderson. As if trying to live up to his splendid Christian name, Anderson could fairly claim to have seen more volcanic eruptions than any other man on earth. His feat seems even more remarkable when one realises these hair-raising excursions were fitted around a busy professional life as an eye surgeon and sometime director of the city waterworks in York. 'For the last eighteen years', he confessed in his book *Volcanic Studies*, 'I have spent the greater part of my holidays in exploring volcanic regions, including Vesuvius (twice), Etna, the Lipari Islands, Auvergne (several times) . . . Iceland (two

long visits) and various
British extinct volcanoes
. . .' Moved to explain
this peculiar habit, Dr
Anderson wrote in the
manner of gentlemen
amateurs through the
ages. 'Very few branches
of Science still remain
available for the amateur
of limited leisure', he
wrote. 'I determined on
Vulcanology [*sic*], which
had the additional advan-
tage of offering exercise
in the open air, and in
districts often remote
and picturesque.'

Traditionalists wondered whether the study of volcanoes was
really a science at all. As scientific historian Haraldur Sigurdsson
explains in his book *Melting the Earth*, early volcano research was 'a
descriptive field, lacking rigour and on the fringes of science, allied
more with geography and geomorphology'. If this gave professional
scientists an excuse to look down their noses, then the feeling was
eagerly reciprocated. Valuable physical data on the earth's internal
melting processes – the means by which lava is created – was ignored
by volcanologists until the 1890s, despite its obvious value to their
inquiries.

Nevertheless, man's understanding of volcanoes – or at least their
external features – had advanced considerably since the Middle
Ages. The seventeenth-century Jesuit Athanasius Kircher thought
volcanic lava came from one enormous central furnace, and reached
the surface via a network of underground canals. Descartes came to a
similar conclusion. He suggested volcanoes drew their energy from

some kind of original, primordial heat deep within the earth. Another French scholar, Benoit de Maillet, took the classical combustion theory a step further in 1716, by proposing that volcanic explosions were the natural by-product of inflammable fats and oils laid down during Noah's Flood.

The first objective links between the earth's internal and external behaviour were being made. Yet it was hard for theorists to avoid the heavy hand of Christian dogma. Clerics saw volcanoes as divine objects designed to show the will (and the wrath) of God. Naturalists, on the other hand, found it increasingly hard to square religious truth with empirical fact. By the late eighteenth century, scientists had split into two camps, their differences inspired as much by God as by Geology.

On one side were the Neptunists, who accepted the literal truth of the Book of Genesis. They believed the earth's complex rock patterns had been laid down during the Great Flood. As the waters around Noah's Ark receded, so mineral deposits had been left to settle in colourful layers. Other Neptunists thought the sediments had been sieved through a primordial sea which engulfed earth on the second day of creation. The most eloquent advocate of Neptunist theory was a Prussian mineralogist called Abraham Gottlob Werner (1749–1817), who taught at the Academy of Mines in Freiburg. A charismatic lecturer, Werner influenced several generations of students, including Goethe and the explorer Alexander von Humboldt. Like many Neptunists, Werner dismissed volcanoes as superficial, local phenomena. They were relatively recent, 'post-aqueous' features, which 'arise from the combustion of underground seams of coal': a theory first proposed by the Roman philosopher Seneca sixteen centuries earlier.*

---

* Early geologists were also influenced by the environment in which they worked. As American volcanologist Fred Bullard pointed out, Western Europe (with the exception of Italy) had no recent history of volcanic activity, which led researchers to treat volcanoes as minor irritations. If geology had developed first in Latin America or the Far East, their attitudes may have been very different.

Werner's lack of interest in volcanoes was unfortunate. For it was the intense debate over the origin of basalt, the principal volcanic rock, which was to undo his Neptunist school. Their downfall was engineered by a rival group of geologists known as Plutonists. Put simply, Plutonists believed basalt was generated *inside* the earth, and came to the surface as magma or molten rock during volcanic eruptions. They reached these conclusions by the novel process of studying lava flows in action. Once exposed to the open air, magma quickly cooled and assumed the distinct porous texture of basalt.

Two French geologists, Jean-Étienne Guettard and Nicolas Desmarest, had laid foundations for the Plutonists. In the mid-eighteenth century, they correctly identified rocks from the Auvergne region in Central France as being from extinct volcanoes. But while Guettard still believed basalt had an aqueous origin, Desmarest came to a more daring conclusion. He thought the oddly-shaped hexagonal columns seen on field trips had been formed by the cooling and contraction of lava flow. It was a revolutionary idea. So revolutionary that Desmarest was unable to make the final imaginative leap and abandon Neptunism altogether. Basalt may have sprung from the mouth of a volcano, he argued nervously, but it had started off as a waterborne sediment.

Younger geologists tackled Neptunism head on. By the early nineteenth century, Werner's idea of a primordial ocean was being undermined by his own protégés, who had abandoned their lecture theatres for the natural amphitheatres of Italy and France. Coming face to face with real volcanoes, Neptunists found it increasingly hard to sustain their views. One of Werner's favourite students, a young Frenchman called Jean-François D'Aubuisson de Voisins, lost his faith in the Auvergne. Following Guettard and Desmarest, de Voisins examined ancient lava flows and came to a similar conclusion. 'The facts which I saw spoke too plainly to be mistaken; the truth revealed itself too clearly before my eyes. There can be no question that basalts of volcanic origin occur in Auvergne.'

Another acolyte, Leopold von Buch, nobly tried to fuse the two schools together. After watching Mount Vesuvius erupt in 1799, von Buch suggested that basalt had been deposited deep within the earth's crust (a nod to Neptunists) before being ejected as volcanic lava (as Plutonists suggested). But the more eruptions von Buch witnessed, the more unsteady his opinions became. In 1815, he renounced his old beliefs. Following field work in the Canary Islands, von Buch declared that all oceanic islands shared a common, volcanic origin. The implication was clear: volcanoes were not just local phenomena as Abraham Gottlob Werner had claimed, but powerful global features in their own right. Geologists had begun to sense the immense forces which created islands like Martinique, even though the inner workings of Pelée and hundreds of other volcanic peaks were still a mystery.

Neptunism had been discredited. Yet there was no coherent theory to take its place. Guettard and Desmarest had shown the value of observation over speculation. Another Frenchman, Guy Tancréde de Dolomieu, had advanced new ideas on the origin of volcanic lava. He thought the heat source for the Auvergne lava flows lay 'at great depths within or below the consolidated crust of the earth' rather than near to the surface. Italian 'volcanists' like Lazzaro Spallanzani (1729–99) revealed more about the singular qualities of basalt. No one however had found a way to draw all these diffuse observations together. When it came, the synthesis was to emerge from an entirely unexpected quarter: from the crags and cairns of the Grampian Mountains in Scotland.

For twenty years, Scottish geologist James Hutton had been examining the rich seams of rocks around his native Edinburgh. In his *Theory of the Earth* (1788) Hutton suggested that granite and basalt came from inside the earth and had intruded, in a molten state, into layers of sedimentary rock. Hutton called this process Igneous — that is, volcanic — intrusion. He had identified the earth's internal heat as a prime cause of geological change. Hutton also drew a picture of the world in endless flux, subject to eternal unrest and upheaval. 'Time,' he wrote, 'which means everything in our idea, and is often deficient to our schemes, is to nature endless.'

These theories were backed up by extensive fieldwork. They were also blighted (as one might guess from the above quotation) by an incredibly turgid prose style. It took a secondary work by his friend John Playfair, *Illustrations of the Huttonian Theory of the Earth* (1802), to bring Hutton's radical ideas to a wider audience. A Professor of mathematics and natural philosophy, Playfair did more than translate Hutton's tortuous prose; he added some ideas of his own. Playfair thought the earth's core was a superheated molten mass; its 'eternal heat' being generated by immense internal pressures. The two Scottish scientists had given Plutonists a coherent cosmology, and a terrifying sense of the turbulence raging within the earth's interior. The world was always changing. In Hutton's blasphemous words, it had 'no vestige of a beginning, no prospect of an end'.

The Neptunists sneered. There was no evidence to support such absurd ideas. An answer came from the laboratory of yet another Scottish geologist, Sir James Hall. A family friend of Hutton, Hall decided to test his countryman's theories on the molten origins of basalt. His conclusions were presented to the Royal Society in 1798. After heating lumps of basalt to very high temperatures, Hall showed the rate of cooling altered the rock's shape and texture. When this molten material was made to cool rapidly, it turned into glass. When the cooling process was repeated at lower temperatures, the molten rock reverted to the crystalline features of basalt. A French chemist, Pierre Louis Cordier, later found that the chemical composition of the mineral remained the same at each stage. There was also no significant difference between the chemical composition of recent lavas and ancient basalts.

By the early nineteenth century, then, volcanologists had made several important discoveries. They had learnt that lava was produced by melting rock beneath the earth's surface; and that it rose to the ground under high pressure, changing form and texture as it was released. Scientists were also starting to treat the earth's crust as a vast, dynamic system, constantly being built up and torn down: a model which, in general terms, still holds today.

Nature was to provide the next two lessons, with the 1815 explosion of Mount Tambora, east of Java, and that of neighbouring Krakatau in 1883. Almost 100,000 people died in the Tambora blast, when a 13,000-foot-high cone imploded on the island of Sumbawa, part of the island chain now known as Indonesia. It was one of the largest – if not the largest – volcanic eruptions in recorded history. The sound of detonations was heard over 1,000 miles away; several cubic miles of debris were blown into the atmosphere, forcing temperatures to fall by around one degree across the globe. The following year, countries as far apart as France and the United States experienced their coldest summer on record. No one drew a connection between Tambora and the freakish frosts and snowfalls; it was to be another thirty or so years before a scientific mission was sent to this remote region. When he finally reached Tambora in 1847, the Swiss botanist Heinrich Zollinger calculated that the mountain had lost 4,000 feet in the blast. But he had no detailed sense of why this eruption had taken place.

When scientists rushed back to this same island chain forty years later, they were much better equipped. The word Krakatau – or Krakatoa – has become a synonym for cataclysmic destruction, and the afternoon of 26 August 1883 explains why. After three months of fitful activity, the volcanic island of Krakatau burst into life. Within an hour, a black cloud seventeen miles high was curling over the Sunda Strait; tidal waves assailed the coasts of Java and Sumatra. A British sea captain, twenty-five miles away from the explosions, reported that the eardrums of half his crew had been shattered. No one had ever seen such a fearful show of nature's anger. But this was just a prelude. The next morning, at two minutes past ten, the whole island of Krakatau exploded. A tower of rock and ash raced fifty miles into the air; explosive detonations were heard 3,000 miles away. Without warning, a monstrous tsunami surged out from the island, reaching heights of up to 130 feet. When the waves fell back, hundreds of coastal villages had been destroyed; 36,000 people were dead. Surveying the scene, a Dutch captain declared: 'This is a scene from the Last Judgement.'

Dozens of scientists made for the Sunda Strait, which linked the Indian Ocean to the Java Sea. The equipment for measuring volcanoes had much improved, as had the theories against which to test them. Why, for example, did most of the island debris appear to be newly formed magma, rather than remnants of broken mountain? A Dutch geologist, R.D.M. Verbeek, deduced that the eruption had come from an enormous magma chamber underneath the island. When this chamber was empty, the hollow cone had caved in on itself, leaving behind a five-mile-wide crater.

Another team, based at London's Royal Society, began to collate eyewitness accounts of the volcano's aftermath. Their results were published in a 500-page report. Microscopic examination of lava particles confirmed the theories of yet another amateur volcanologist, George Julius Poulett Scrope: lava was made up of tiny, glass-like fragments made from the explosion of bubbling, gas-infused magma. British scientists also compiled a detailed account of how Krakatau's ash cloud swept across the globe, leaving eerie orange and blood-red sunsets in its wake. The phenomenon was noticed by Alfred, Lord Tennyson:

> Had the fierce ashes of some fiery Peak
> Been hurled so high they ranged round the World?
> For day by day through many a blood-red eve
> The wrathful sunset glared.

Scientists had also begun to order volcanoes into three distinct types, rather in the manner of human temperaments. In his 1825 book, *Considerations on Volcanoes*, George Julius Poulett Scrope had grouped eruptions into three categories: permanent, moderate and paroxysmal. *Permanent* eruptions were constant yet low key, like those seen at Stromboli off the coast of Sicily; *Paroxysmal* eruptions were unpredictable and much more violent, like Vesuvius. *Moderate* eruptions were equally irregular but much less violent.

By 1901, these categories had been refined by American geologist James Dwight Dana into quiet, explosive and intermediate eruptions. Field geologists now distinguished between 'Strombolian' and 'Vesuvian' stages of volcanic activity, and between the various objects ejected from mountain cones. *Quiet* volcanoes tended to release streams of lava which curdled and congealed into molten discs, like the scales of a reptile. *Explosive* types, like Krakatau, flung thousands of tons of molten rock, gas and vapour into the air. Any resulting debris then moulded itself around the volcano's main shaft (the vent) in steep-sided cones. Most volcanoes however belonged to the *Intermediate* category, being a combination of lava and fragments.

These early attempts at classification may have been vague and simplistic, but they brought discipline to the wayward science of volcanology. Geologists also hoped these advances would help them predict the course of future eruptions. What they had not reckoned upon was a catastrophe which went beyond human classification; one which was to introduce a new and terrifying form of volcanic destruction to the world.

To the people of Saint-Pierre, such risks must have seemed impossibly remote. Their island boasted six volcanic peaks, yet none of them were thought to be active. Even though Martinique was in a region of known instability, Pierrotins imagined the greatest threat came from more obvious enemies such as hurricanes, tidal waves and earthquakes, as it had done in the past. The idea of a profound link between earth tremors and volcanic activity was only faintly understood. Nineteenth-century scientists like Charles Darwin and US geologist Robert Mallet saw that earthquakes and volcanoes tended to happen in the same places; James Dwight Dana was struck by their presence around the edges of major land masses. But scientists were still several decades away from explaining this malign coincidence, or from understanding how volatile shifts in the earth's crust could shape events up on the surface.

If there had been any volcanologists on Martinique at the turn of the century, they might have taken a different view of Pelée's erratic history. The mountain's second eruption in 1851 had been more powerful than its first; the squirts of white steam seen in June 1901 hinted at furious pressures far below. Unfortunately, the dozen or so experts in this small field lived in Europe and North America. Little was known about Caribbean volcanoes, compared to those in Italy, Iceland or Indonesia. No serious studies had ever been made of Pelée; there was nothing to be gained, after all, from examining an extinct volcano.

Pierrotins blithely went about their lives, convinced of their security and remarkable good fortune. The political parties went on trading blows via *L'Opinion* and *Les Colonies*; that summer, the matter of Governor Merlin's three official carriages was greatly exercising the Ex-Deputy of Saint-Pierre. 'It is too much for such a small *personnage*', squeaked Marius Hurard, a little enviously. Saint-Pierre's leaders were never short of opinions. But real expertise, in the shape of formal scientific knowledge, was in short supply.

One exception was Gaston Landes, a renowned botanist and Assistant Director of Martinique's Botanic Garden on the outskirts of Saint-Pierre. Landes combined his work at the *Jardin Botanique* with a teaching post at the city *Lycée*, the school Hurard had fought

so hard to establish twenty years earlier. M. Landes taught natural history. One senses he was a reserved, somewhat cautious character: happier to cultivate the plant world rather than the human one. The photograph above was taken to celebrate his authorship of *Notice Sur La Martinique*, an elegant, leather-bound almanac written for the Paris Exposition of 1900. At first sight, Landes seems an unusual choice for this task. Saint-Pierre was not short of colourful writers: that was one craft the city did not want for. But perhaps the Governor needed a more reliable writer than those juvenile pro-pagandists at *L'Opinion* and *Les Colonies*. The *Notice* would be Martinique's shop window at the Greatest Show on Earth (a show which drew seventeen million visitors in its first three months), and Landes would deliver the kind of authoritative, impartial essay that was required. Evidently he was a man whose word was respected.

Landes's speciality was tropical botany, a subject he pursued with great zeal. Along with two colleagues, he revived *Le Bulletin Agricole de la Martinique*, the Agricultural Bulletin of Martinique, as a way to raise standards and improve yields. Landes also wrote regularly for one of Paris's most prestigious journals on colonial agriculture, *La Revue des Cultures Coloniales*, where he was in turn fêted as 'our distinguished contributor'. Within the *Revue*'s yellowing pages, as delicate now as tissue paper, the full range of his passions become clear. His contributions include articles on 'The Future of Sugar Cane', 'The Cultivation and Preparation of Ginger' and an analysis of 'The State of Agriculture in several

nearby colonies'. Landes, it seems, was not above stealing ideas from France's old enemy. A visit to the botanic gardens of Trinidad and Barbados prompts an article in praise of Anglo-Saxon husbandry – and the need for *La Métropole* to keep up. France, writes the school teacher, needs a proper scientific *corps* in order to fight 'against the international colonial rivals'. Despite these provocative thoughts, Landes's articles were much valued in the *Métropole*. In 1898, Gaston Landes and his *Lycée* colleague M. G. Saussine were awarded Honorary Distinctions for their work on improving the yield of sugar cane.

The school botanist was also being rewarded for his contribution to a higher cause, that of French imperialism. Colonial rivalries between the Great Powers had reached a feverish point by 1901. Like Britain and Germany, France was eager to assert its place in the world, and *La Revue des Cultures Coloniales* was not immune from this imperial virus. Agriculture, wrote Charles Naudin of the Colonial Institute, was an essential part of France's *mission providentielle*, its sacred mission to care for subject peoples around the world. Naudin's order of priorities was revealing:

What does it mean, to colonise? It is to found the nations of the future. It is to guarantee ourselves a place in the future history of mankind. It is to maintain our place among the peoples who fight over the mastery of the globe. It is, finally, a way to help those peoples who struggle painfully for their livelihoods on cramped, exhausted land . . . [France] well understands her providential mission and, by renouncing her expansionary plans in Europe, turns her wise gaze onto her colonial estate . . .

Cultivation and colonisation were important signs of national virility. The French did not take to empire building with quite the same glee as the British, but they were certainly keen to get their money's worth out of their foreign dependencies. As another *Revue* contributor Joseph Chailley-Bert put it: 'The most difficult thing about colonies is not conquering them, but exploiting them.'

Gaston Landes's work was part of this patriotic struggle. But other Martinicans were reluctant to help a motherland which had so conspicuously failed to help them. A quarter of France's overseas investments went to Russia, where they were designed to prop up a diplomatic alliance. Only ten per cent of French capital went into imperial projects, and most of that went to newer colonies in Africa and the Far East. No wonder Martinique's planter class held a grudge against their Metropolitan masters. One anonymous land-owner wrote to the *Revue*:

If French capitalists understood colonial agriculture a little better, and the income one could get from tropical land, they would not hesitate for an instant, and no longer confine themselves or their investments to the State or the railways . . .

For their part, Parisians thought Martinicans were not pulling their weight. The colony had got complacent, its economy over-reliant on sugar and state support. Not surprisingly, Landes did not

volunteer any public opinions on this sensitive matter. Perhaps he
thought such debates were best left to politicians. Reticence had its
rewards: Landes was in the rare (and fortunate) position of being
revered by all sides, a man whose opinion could not be swayed by
over-mighty politicians or newspaper editors. He was also getting
into his academic stride: in 1900, he began to research a University
thesis, based on his work for the *Revue*. When he received his
professional reward – an invitation to the 1900 Exposition – there
were no sneers or catcalls from the local press. A talented man had,
for once, received his proper reward. Landes travelled to Paris by
steamer. Ever professional, he escorted several dozen crates of
mangoes and avocados across the Atlantic in specially built ice
boxes.

As 1901 drew to a close, the gossips of Saint-Pierre turned their
minds back to politics. Like an audience trapped inside a long-
running, overfamiliar play, Pierrotins hoped several cast changes
would soon liven up their drama: a desire only heightened by the

theatre's sudden closure on 11 June that year. In an overwrought letter to *Les Colonies*, the theatre's director M. Erhard blamed actors ('Ingrates! Mediocrities!') and freeloaders (who 'filled the seats, but not the till') for his theatre's slide into bankruptcy. 'Who is the greatest victim?' he wailed. 'It is me!' *Les Colonies* did not agree. Erhard had brought disaster upon himself, the paper jeered, by embarking on a grandiose tour of Guadeloupe. What was more, his theatre was falling down. 'The cracks in the walls', it noted, 'have not been repaired for seven years.' Good Riddance, as Hurard liked to say.*

Several new distractions were at hand, however, each of them promising plenty of amusement for the coming year. A new Governor was about to arrive, to replace the much reviled M. Merlin. A new American consul, Thomas Prentiss, had settled in Saint-Pierre with his wife Clara and their two daughters Christine and Louisa, although they had not received much of a welcome. According to the *New York Herald*:

> Mrs Prentiss and her two daughters kept themselves to them-selves, and except for formal calls when they first arrived, Mrs Prentiss and her daughters saw little of the other residents.
>
> The natives seemed to have a dislike for Americans, and Mrs Prentiss told me that negroes made slighting remarks when they passed her in the street. The Misses Prentisses were actually stoned by a mob while they were walking near Morne Rouge recently. They were so badly frightened that they remained in the house unless they had a man to accompany them.

* Like most of Martinique's public buildings, Saint-Pierre theatre was not an original work. It was an imitation of a better-known building in mainland France. The blueprint on this occasion was the classical two-storey façade of the Grand Theatre, Bordeaux. So skilful was this tropical reproduction, with its high pillars and secluded arcades, that it was known as *Le Petit Chaperon Rouge*, the Little Red Riding Hood. This love of imitation continued inside the 800-seat playhouse, where a brightly painted portrait of Saint-Pierre – complete with its genial mountain – served as the scenery curtain. A rowing boat had been added at the bottom of the picture, showing actors about to disembark.

Most exciting of all, the long build up to France's parliamentary elections had begun. Martinique elected two Deputies to the 591-seat National Assembly: one for the northern *arrondissement* which included Saint-Pierre, and one for the south, dominated by Fort-de-France. The two rounds were scheduled to take place on Sunday 20 April and Sunday 11 May 1902.

Politicians knew how important these elections would be. The Radicals were desperate to keep their foothold in Government; their conservative rivals were equally determined to throw them out. But this would be a battle for spoils as well as ideology, and all the more bitterly fought for that. As Marius Hurard well remembered, the Deputy's post brought levels of power and patronage second only to those enjoyed by a Senator – not to mention a chance to make lots of money. If the new Deputies were of the Radical persuasion, they would gain access to Albert Décrais, the Minister for Colonies. This time, too, there was the added complication of Lagrosillière's Socialists. Black male voters formed an overwhelming majority in Saint-Pierre; hundreds, perhaps thousands, might defect to his party from the Radicals. Then there was the danger of electoral fraud, *le brigandage électoral*. Each party indulged in a little creative canvassing; the secret was not to get caught. At Sainte-Philomène, north of Saint-Pierre, over half the votes in a recent council election were found to be fraudulent. Electors had come back from the dead; others had voted several times over. Everyone would be on the look out for *les électeurs imaginaires*.

Governor Merlin's last months in office were relatively tranquil. The Radicals of Fort-de-France showed their gratitude to the outgoing Governor by organising an extraordinary banquet. Seven courses were laid before guests at the *Mairie*; the wine list covered thirteen different vineyards:

Madère
Saint-Julien

Saint-Estephe
Saint-Emilion
Sauternes de Bourgogne
Richebourg
Pommard
Nuits
Chablis
Beaune
Meursault
Mâcon
Volnay

Four marques of champagne:

Veuve Clicquot
Ponsardin
Moet et Chandon
Duc de Montebello

And five *digestifs*:

Rum
Cognac
Chartreuse
Anisette
Peppermint

The new Governor, M. Louis Mouttet, was greeted with similar
ceremony. His arrival on board the *Labrador* on 11 December 1901
was marked with ritual cannon rounds and flag waving. After the
open hostilities of Governor Merlin's regime, M. Mouttet tried to
establish a more approachable style. Within a week, he had intro-
duced thrice-weekly receptions at his *Résidence* in Fort-de-France.
'He is perfectly *au courant* with the needs of our Antilles', purred *Les*

Colonies. The press barons of Saint-Pierre were content. For now at least.

As Mouttet settled in, learning whom to trust and whom to avoid, he would have received a subtle education in the island's complexities. He would have heard all about Martinique's troubled economy: the slump in sugar prices, the riots at François and other factories, the tensions between *békés* and coloured merchants in Saint-Pierre. He would also have seen the island's capacity for joy, for wild pleasure. As soon as M. Erhard's financial troubles had been cleared away, Saint-Pierre's theatre re-opened for business. This time around, its bill of fare was more modish and rather more appealing: a series of phonographs and cinematographs from Messrs Filippi and Apo. The phonograph recordings were so convincing, wrote one critic, that one almost felt as if the singers were there in the theatre. One evening, the audience were so impressed with a phonograph recital by Madame Lemotte that they stood up to applaud.

Another highlight of these evenings were illuminated slides showing scenes from the great cities of Europe, and from classical history. Among these panoramic displays (occasionally halted by a lack of imported benzine from Guadeloupe) were biblical scenes and a striking re-enactment of the volcanic eruption of Vesuvius and the destruction of Pompeii. Another favourite was *The Story of a Crime* – which related various lurid stages of a 'sensational' crime from murder via absolution to execution.

There was a lot for Governor Mouttet to absorb: dozens of telegrams and memoranda, hundreds of antique orders, decrees and regulations. Amid his piles of paper, it was unlikely the new Governor would have heard anything about Mont Pelée's strange behaviour. He was too busy to bother with trivial matters like that.

1902

FOUR

ON THE BRINK OF HELL

WINTER TURNED to spring, and the season of *Carême*. Where daily forecasts had once pledged endless sunshine, they now warned of showers. The dry season was over for another year. Pierrotins adapted their business accordingly: gutters were cleared and shutters firmly fastened. In its own diffident way, *La Montagne* was part of this natural cycle: as constant as the seasons, as eternal as the lapping sea. As one American writer observed, Saint-Pierre's inhabitants were so unperturbed by Pelée's presence that they built their town facing in the opposite direction. 'The mountain was peace itself', wrote William G. Garesché. 'It seemed to provide perpetual protection.'

Little wonder then that people ignored the reports coming from Prêcheur, a few miles north of Saint-Pierre. Since early February 1902, the townsfolk had been bothered by a nauseating sulphur smell. Some days, the stink of stale egg was so bad that people had to hold handkerchiefs over their mouths to stop themselves from choking. Elderly men and women were falling ill and 'silver objects turned black inside people's houses' according to one witness. It was all very alarming. Everyone blamed *La Montagne*: sulphur jets had been seen shooting out of fissures high up on its western slopes.

From time to time, fumes would drift down into Fonds Coré and Saint-Pierre. One local merchant, Louis des Grottes, decided to investigate further. On 23 March he climbed to Pelée's highest point, the *Morne de la Croix*, and peered down into the old crater 200 feet below. Des Grottes was amazed by what he saw: the *Étang Sec* or

Dry Lake was letting out huge hissing clouds of sulphur. As he took in this hellish scene – the jets of misty white smoke, the low subterranean rumbles like the dole of a kettledrum – des Grottes decided to record what he had seen and heard, so future generations would know about Pelée's curious interlude. On the side of the Morne, he chalked a message:

Aujourd hui, 23 mars, le cratère
de l'Étang Sec est en éruption

Today, 23 March, the crater of
the Dry Lake is in eruption

Des Grottes was not the only person to realise Pelée was stirring. Gaston Landes had also heard about the strange events in Prêcheur. On Sunday 20 April, he strode up the wild overgrown valley of the Blanche River, intending to examine the mountain crater. Several hundred feet short of the summit, Landes stopped. Vast clouds of steam were roaring out of fumaroles on the mountainside, like steam from the spouts of gigantic kettles. There is no record of what Landes thought at this point, merely of his observations. Perhaps he imagined Pelée was preparing for a repeat performance of 1851. If that was the case, then debris would continue to fall several miles away from Saint-Pierre, on Pelée's northwestern slopes. The city was not in any direct danger.

Pierrotins were more interested in their forthcoming election, the latest round in that long-running scrap between Amédée Knight and Marius Hurard. An almighty battle was expected. Trapped in the middle, like a piece of meat worried by two elderly dogs, was Martinique's new Governor Louis Mouttet. After three months in office, islanders now had a better sense of his character. A late developer, Mouttet had joined the Diplomatic Service after an early career in business and journalism. There were junior postings in

Senegal, Indochina and Guadeloupe, before Mouttet became Governor of the Ivory Coast in 1896 and Guyana in 1898. It had been a slow and steady progression; nothing spectacular. Martinique was another step up this ladder: the prelude, if he kept his nose clean, to a final, sumptuous appointment in Africa or the Far East. Here, it seemed, was a man whom Paris could trust: someone who would stand up to the political factions and not be sucked into their trivial arguments.

Within a few weeks of their arrival, M. Mouttet and his wife Hélène had established a fresh style. The forty-four-year-old Governor, who had spent his youth in the smartest salons and restaurants of Paris, was touring the island's most desolate areas. Following her husband's example, Hélène Mouttet held audiences at the *Hôtel du Gouvernement* 'every Tuesday from four o'clock' according to the *Journal Officiel*. The Mouttets appeared easy with the demands of politics and protocol: as comfortable with a delegation of factory workers as with the *békés* of Saint-Pierre. Apart from public duties, there were private ones too. The Mouttets brought a young family to Fort-de-France: two daughters aged five and nine, and a son born in April 1901.

While Madame Mouttet held court, her husband visited every one of Martinique's thirty-two communes, a Prince surveying his new demesne. From Trois-Îlets to Basse-Pointe, Trinité to Case-Pilote, Mouttet saw the poverty and distress caused by Martinique's economic slump. The fall in world sugar prices (down by twenty-two per cent between 1900 and 1902) forced thousands out of work; the massacre at François was still fresh in people's memory. If Mouttet was unable to grasp the gravity of his situation, there were plenty of people ready to remind him. Within hours of arriving in Martinique the previous year, the Governor had been addressed by the Mayor of Fort-de-France, Victor Sévère. An ally of Senator Knight, Sévère outlined the Governor's task in words which were to prove prophetic. 'Your mission among us', the Mayor said, 'cannot only be one of economic progress and democracy. Our dear country has, for several years, suffered terrible hardships. Hardships which, alas, are far from over!'

Governor Mouttet took note of Sévère's words. They must have chimed with his own interpretation of the political mood in Paris. Waldeck-Rousseau's leftist coalition was rallying its supporters for a renewed attack on the Catholic Church and big business. If Mouttet was to succeed, he would have to tailor his language to a more populist style. In February 1902, he outlined his plans for economic renewal at the island's General Council. The minutes record how: 'He sketched out, for the benefit of Martinique, various projects of which he had already drawn up the main outlines, in his haste to do good.' The new Governor imagined himself a shrewd man, ready to move with the times. But shrewdness could also mask a certain weakness. Mouttet's conservative critics thought him a man of no fixed ideas, a weather vane ready to twist in whatever direction would please the party in power.

M. Mouttet's first test was political rather than economic: to steer Martinique through that year's legislative elections without stirring too much bile or bloodshed. In the Northern *arrondissement* of Saint-Pierre, three candidates had been nominated for the Chamber of Deputies:

i) **M. Fernand CLERC. The New Party**
   A white landowner and wealthy *béké*.

ii) **M. Louis PERCIN. The Radical Party**
   A local councillor and lawyer.

iii) **M. Joseph LAGROSILLIÈRE. The Socialist Party**
   A working-class socialist and lawyer.

As agreed, the first round of voting would take place on Sunday 27 April. If no clear majority was achieved, a run-off would be held two weeks later on Sunday 11 May. The importance attached to this event is shown by the immense amount of space given to electoral rules and regulations in the *Journal Officiel*, some obvious, some not quite so obvious. They included:

i) A ban on firearms in polling stations.
ii) A demand that all electoral scrutineers be able to read and write.
iii) A ban on posters in churches.
iv) The 'absolute ineligibility' as candidates 'of any members of families who have reigned over France'.

While Pelée continued to steam away, Martinicans fell into a frenzy of electioneering. Every possible wall and window was papered with posters promoting the candidates' *profession de foi*: their declaration of principles. Some carried testimonials from dutiful friends, vouching for their man's honesty and good character. Male voters – the only kind of voter allowed at this time – were lured with all sorts of treats and promises. Saint-Pierre theatre was brought back to life while

Percin, Clerc and Lagrosillière debated their policies under arcs of amber gaslight. There were serious issues to discuss: how to revive Martinique's sugar trade, the abysmal wages paid to plantation workers, and the persistent rumour that Waldeck-Rousseau was planning a further confiscation of church property: a move which would ruin the Holy Fathers of Saint-Esprit and the Sisters of Saint-Joseph de Cluny.

Such questions did not trouble Ludger Sylbaris.

The Most Marvellous Man on Earth was sitting out this year's election campaign in a squat brick building next door to the theatre, better known as Saint-Pierre jail. The twenty-seven-year-old had been sent there in mid-April, so the story goes, for slashing a friend with a cutlass in a drunken brawl. There were five separate cells in the jail complex, each one furnished with a basin of free-flowing spring water and a courtyard from where one could overhear people chattering on the theatre steps. An infantry barracks overlooked the jail's northern wall, but there was little need for any heavy-handedness: the threat of a night in solitary confinement was usually enough to bring prisoners back into line.

American papers would later depict Ludger Sylbaris as a murderous monster, but in truth his one month sentence was relatively minor. After all, street fights were a regular feature of Saint-Pierre life, particularly when sailors and plantation workers poured into the city on Saturday nights. Saint-Pierre jail was also less daunting than it appeared. The *Maison d'Arrêt* only dealt with pre-trial prisoners and those serving sentences of one month or less; more serious offenders were sent to a grown-up *Maison Centrale* in Fort-de-France. If young Ludger behaved properly, he would be out of jail in time for the election's second round on 11 May.

Four days before the first round of voting, Pelée gave Martinicans another warning. On Wednesday 23 April, Saint-Pierre was shaken by several earth tremors, each one more powerful than the last. The quakes were felt by Clara Prentiss, wife of American Consul Thomas T. Prentiss. Although they had spent less than a year in Saint-Pierre, the couple were already suspicious of Pelée, telling one relative of their fear it might erupt at any time, sweeping away everyone in its path.

Clara Prentiss's forebodings were confirmed that Wednesday morning as she sat with her fourteen-year-old daughter Christine. In a letter to one of her sisters, Alice Frye, Mrs Prentiss described hearing 'three distinct shocks'. At first, she imagined someone was at the door, but quickly changed her mind. The first report, she wrote, 'was quite loud, but the second and third were so great that dishes were thrown from the shelves and the house was completely rocked'. As people ran on to the streets, they saw a column of pure white smoke spiralling out of the mountain summit. A shower of ash and cinders danced and twirled over their heads.

Two days before polling day, Pelée sent another warning to the citizens of Prêcheur. One resident, M. Duno-Émilé Josse, was anxious enough to write to Hurard's newspaper, *Les Colonies*. 'For more than three months,' he wrote, 'we have felt the odour of sulphur which has caused considerable disquietude with the inhabitants . . . It increased steadily in force and quantity and threw us into great fear.' And then, on Friday 25 April:

> . . . the atmosphere darkened, and almost immediately it turned as if into an eclipse of the sun, accompanied by a deep growling . . . All of a sudden, a loud detonation, like the firing of a cannon, was heard: the sky appeared in places to be on fire, and there was a continuous fall of fine and white ashes which the volcano was vomiting out . . . These ashes were so abundant that at two metres distance, people were unable to distinguish each other . . .

The rain of blue-grey ashes went on for two hours. People fell to the ground as if stricken with blindness. Hundreds of tons of smoke and debris belched out of the mountain, blotting out the sun and hurling ash clouds up to a thousand feet into the sky. Many who witnessed this scene of supernatural horror rushed to roadside shrines, convinced their world was about to end.

For the first time now, Saint-Pierre took notice of what *La Montagne* was up to. But people there reacted in quite a different way to those in Prêcheur. Despite the evident danger Pierrotins still regarded Pelée's rumblings as a matter of passing interest, a distraction from their political contest rather than a reason for calling it off. According to Mgr Parel, the Vicar-General of Martinique, 'the occurrence excited everybody's wonder. Excursionists immediately set out for the crater.' At the summit, explorers found a far more fearsome sight than the one Louis des Grottes had seen a month earlier. The Dry Lake crater was no longer dry. It had cracked open like a broken bowl and, in Parel's words, 'was filling up with boiling water and emitting a sulphurous smell'.★

Two members of the French Astronomical Society, Pierre Lalung and Roger Arnoux, saw it too. They thought this crack at the base of the Dry Lake was highly significant, 'the first true opening of the volcano'. French officials saw no need to worry. The eruptions were a passing phase – and even if Pelée *did* erupt, its lava flows would stop far short of Saint-Pierre. The first round of voting would go ahead as planned on 27 April. But as Pierrotins began to vote that Sunday morning, another group of excursionists were making an alarming discovery. Six professional men, Messrs Boulin, Waddy, Décord, Bouteuil, Ange and Berté, saw that the Dry Lake was in ferment. In four days, the lake's shifting, swirling surface had grown to around 650 feet in diameter and was bubbling away like a giant's cauldron. Equally worrying was the sudden appearance of a thirty-foot-high cinder cone beside the lake. According to a later account by American geologist Angelo Heilprin, this grey-black cone 'threw out long trains of steaming vapour' from 'its brilliantly shimmering surface', while 'an almost continuous fall of water was cascading into the surrounding and lower-lying lake'. Trees around the water's edge were 'covered with black volcanic dust, and there was a film of floating cinders on the surface of the water'.

No one knew how to interpret Pelée's volatile moods. The summit lake was hot in some places and cold in others; the cinder cone might be a sign of growing activity, or it may have been a hint that the worst was over. Saint-Pierre's self-proclaimed experts split into two camps. Two members of the most recent visiting party, Messrs Boulin and Berté, thought the ash and debris ejected on 25 April had come from *inside* the cinder cone and Dry Lake. If that

★ In the absence of Martinique's Archbishop, Mgr. Marie-Charles-Alfred de Cormont (who had left Saint-Pierre in April, for business in France), Mgr Gabriel Parel became the Catholic Church's most senior representative on the island. His vivid, first-hand account of events in 1902 was used extensively by scientists and historians.

was the case, then Pelée may have exhausted itself. Gaston Landes proposed a simpler, but potentially more troubling, analysis. Perhaps the debris which poured out of Pelée that day had come from a large fissure beneath the Dry Lake, first noticed in 1851. This crack may well be growing bigger. Nobody knew for sure. As for that unearthly-looking volcanic cone, neither side realised it was the first sign of magma rising to the surface along ominous new fissures.

Such debates might have continued, were it not for the hullabaloo surrounding Sunday's election. The result, when it was declared from the Town Hall balcony that night, threw Saint-Pierre into great excitement. After a bitterly fought campaign, the two leading candidates had ended up almost neck and neck:

Fernand CLERC	. . .	4,495
Louis PERCIN	. . .	4,167
Joseph LAGROSILLIÈRE	. . .	753

Clerc had won by a narrow majority, but he had not gained an absolute majority over the other two candidates. There would have to be a second round. With Joseph Lagrosillière agreeing to step down, it looked like Radical candidate Louis Percin would now collect enough votes to win the seat. It was a similar story in Martinique's southern constituency, where a Radical lawyer called Homère Clément was expected to win the second round on the same principle. Such thoughts must have horrified Hurard's Conservative faction. Unless they got their vote out, the whole island would fall under Radical control. Only 328 votes separated Clerc from Percin; another 10,879 voters had stayed at home. With two weeks until the final round, each party was determined to increase its vote by any means possible. Nothing would be allowed to throw their campaign machines off course. Not even a volcano.

Towards the end of April, Clara Prentiss wrote a few more lines to her sister Alice in Melrose, Massachusetts:

My Dear Sister,

This morning, the whole population of the city is on the alert and every eye is directed towards Mont Pelée, an extinct volcano. Everybody is afraid that the volcano has taken it into its heart to burst forth and destroy the whole island.

For several days the mountain has been bursting forth and immense qualities of lava are flowing down the sides of the mountain. All the inhabitants are going up to see it. There is not a horse to be had on the island; those belonging to the natives are kept in readiness to leave at a moment's notice . . .

Despite official reassurance, then, Pierrotins had a fair idea of what to expect. They made plans to leave, confident they could outrun their volcano if events took a violent turn. Mrs Prentiss ends her letter with a much-quoted account of how life in Saint-Pierre had deteriorated:

We can see Mont Pelée from the rear window of the house, and although it is nearly four miles away we can hear the roar . . . The city is covered with ashes and clouds of smoke have been over our heads for the last five days. The smell of sulphur is so strong that the horses on the street stop and snort. Some of them are obliged to give up, drop in their harness, and die from suffocation. Many of the people are obliged to wear wet handkerchiefs over their faces to protect them from strong fumes of sulphur. My husband assures me there is no immediate danger . . .

Mrs Prentiss concludes with a reassuring postscript:

There is an American schooner, the *R.J. Morse*, in the harbour and will remain here for at least two weeks. If the volcano becomes bad, we shall embark at once and go out to sea.

Horses were dying and people were choking on the streets. Yet the editor of *Les Colonies* was perversely cheerful. Marius Hurard insisted Pelée posed no threat to his native town. On Friday 2 May, the paper announced a picnic at the summit:

> We remind our readers that the grand excursion organised by the Gymnastic and Shooting Club will take place next Sunday, 4 May. If the weather is fine, the excursionists will pass a day they will long keep in pleasant remembrance.

Everyone knew Hurard was a stubborn soul, the 'Man of Insatiable Ambition'. If his chosen candidate, Fernand Clerc, was to win the second round of voting, then Pierrotins would have to feel it was safe to stay in their city. The picnic was part of that insidious campaign. One also senses more than a little *amour-propre* on Hurard's part. With his great rival Amédée Knight out of action (the Senator had just arrived from France) might there not be a role for a wise old Deputy? Marius Hurard, scourge of the Catholic Church and tribune of the people; a political prodigy who lost his way in a mire of Parisian indolence. Perhaps this was the moment to redeem some of that past glory, to hear once more those excited shouts of *Allez Hurard! Allez à l'Assemblée!* beneath his office window.

Not that Pelée would have noticed. Shortly before midnight that Friday evening, the mountain let out several huge explosions. 'The city awoke to the noise of frightful detonations', wrote Vicar-General Parel, 'and to one of the most extraordinary spectacles of nature: a volcano in full eruption discharging an enormous column of black smoke, traversed by flashes of lightning and accompanied by ominous rumblings.' It must have been a horrifying sight, a picture of medieval damnation. To Clara Prentiss, it felt 'as if we were standing on the brink of Hell. Every few moments electric flames of blinding intensity were traversing the recess of black and purple clouds and casting a lurid pallor over the darkness that shrouded the world.'

When the citizens awoke on Saturday morning, they were met by a sinister winter scene. Every single surface had been coated with a thick layer of ash. Even their Botanic Garden lay buried, its palms and bamboos, rubber-trees and mangoes, giant cactuses and pink hibiscus hidden under a cloak of grey and white. The rivers which once trickled down Pelée had turned into furious torrents, full of mud and debris. Trees and boulders slid into the sea, as if uprooted by a godly hand. For the first time, small drifts of ash had fallen upon Saint-Pierre. Around Prêcheur, the downpour had been much more severe: country roads were blocked with three or four inches of fleecy grey ash. The *Journal Officiel* was moved to comment: 'It is probable that the eruptions are going to increase in ferocity. The people are very anxious.' Martinique's animals were equally disturbed. Thousands of humming birds and blackbirds were found dead in soft mounds of ash, having been poisoned or asphyxiated. As if driven by an intuition of danger, herds of cattle and sheep abandoned Pelée's slopes and made for low ground.

Heavy ash falls were noted right across northwest Martinique. Hurard felt obliged to mention them in Saturday's edition of *Les Colonies*:

> The rain of ashes never ceases. At about half-past nine the sun shone forth timidly. The passing of carriages is no longer heard in the streets. The wheels are muffled. The ancient trucks creak languidly on their worn tyres. Puffs of wind sweep the ashes from the roofs and awnings and blow them into rooms whose windows have been imprudently left open. Shops which had their doors half-closed are now barred up entirely . . .

The editor then added a sheepish note:

> The excursion which had been organised for tomorrow will not take place, the crater being absolutely inaccessible.

Those who would like to take part will be advised at a later date of the day on which this excursion will take place.

Despite Hurard's bluff assurance, Saint-Pierre was by now seized with panic. Carcasses of dead cattle floated past the harbour: a portent some said of what was to come. Schools and shops began to close; timid souls lashed their belongings to horse-drawn wooden carts and made for Fort-de-France. Others made for the cathedral; one inhabitant saw people fighting for places at the confessional. According to Mgr Parel, churches across the island were full of anxious parishioners, desperate for absolution:

> The churches remained crowded; the curates baptised, listened to confession, and attempted to sustain the courage of the terrified people. I endeavoured to reassure the inhabitants.
>
> In the afternoon there was a frightful panic in the midst of ceremonies at the cathedral. With outstretched arms the people besought the priests for absolution . . .

A city once brimming with life and colour had suddenly turned drab and grey. Boats lay low in the harbour, their white sails smudged with ash. People retreated to their homes, afraid to venture out in the suffocating air. *Porteuses* no longer swish-swished down cobbled streets; the fish market was deserted.

Even a visit from Governor Mouttet that Saturday morning failed to lift spirits. M. Mouttet had come to organise help for the hundreds of people who had fled from Prêcheur and surrounding villages. The silent white landscape and black sea which greeted him must have had a profound effect. To reassure Pierrotins, Mouttet set up a 'Scientific Mission' to examine Pelée. It would be made up of five men: Lieutenant-Colonel Gerbault, Director of Artillery; M. Mirville, Pharmacist and Army Major; M. Léonce, Assistant Engineer in charge of roads and bridges; M. Dosés, Professor of Natural History at Saint-Pierre *Lycée*; and M. Gaston Landes.

Quite what this 'Mission' was meant to achieve, or how their findings would be distributed, was unclear. Its real purpose was political: a Committee of 'Experts' would calm the situation, and stop the panic which threatened to derail next week's election. A report written by the previous team, led by Messrs Boulin and Berté, did not appear in *Les Colonies* until 7 May, ten days after they had visited Pelée's summit. Perhaps Hurard thought their findings were not important. Or maybe he realised talk of bubbling 650-foot-wide lakes would merely have driven more people out of the city.

Some of the saddest mementoes of Saint-Pierre come in the form of letters written in the days leading up to the catastrophe. The last batch of letters to be sent by steamboat to Fort-de-France include some written on Sunday 4 May. Two anonymous letters have survived, with fragments of powdery ash still trapped inside the folds of their paper. They give some sense of the city's mood that day, as church bells tolled across the bay and firemen sprayed roofs and cobblestones to dampen the rampant ashes.

The first comes from a young woman trapped at home, with 'numerous company':

> I am awaiting the event tranquilly. My only suffering is from the dust, which penetrates everywhere, even through closed doors and windows.
>
> We are all calm. If death awaits us, there will be a numerous company to leave the world. Will it be by fire or asphyxia? It will be what God wills.
>
> Tell brother Robert that we are still alive. This will, perhaps, be no longer true when this letter reaches you.

The second comes from a white married woman, writing to her brother in Marseilles:

Family group c. 1899

This unchaining of the forces of nature is horrible. The heat is suffocating. We cannot leave anything open, as the dust enters everywhere, burning our faces and eyes . . .

Fortunately, we have food, but we have no heart to eat. All the crops are ruined. It is always the same in these accursed countries. When it is not a cyclone, it is an earthquake, and when it is not a drought, it is a volcanic eruption.

A hint there perhaps – 'these accursed countries' – of how French colonists really saw their Antillean outposts. Another letter, from a man named Felix Marsan, was more pointed. 'Let us hope we will not have the same end as Pompeii', he wrote.

For a brief moment, God appeared ready to will a different ending. Sunday brought a slight reduction in ash fall. As the Governor headed back to Fort-de-France that afternoon, there was a faint hope that the worst was over. This optimism was not shared elsewhere, however. Two miles north of Saint-Pierre, workers at the Guérin Sugar Mill were facing a biblical invasion. Tens of thousands of ants and centipedes had flooded into their factory, driven off Pelée by ash falls and earth tremors. Although harmless in small numbers, these small speckled ants and foot-long black centipedes could be lethal *en masse*. Horses shrieked with pain as insects bit their legs and flanks; workers poured lubricating oil onto flagstones to repel the invaders. Housemaids tackled them with flat irons and boiling water. In Saint-Pierre itself, there was a deadlier assault. Hundreds of yellow-backed, pink-bellied *fer de lance* slithered into the city streets, arousing horror in the inhabitants. Soldiers were called out to shoot the serpents, but not before dozens of animals had died from their poison.

Les Colonies reported this disaster as if it were a suitable subject for a nature study. The sea, it reported:

[is] covered in patches with dead birds. Many lie asphyxiated on the roads. The cattle suffer greatly – suffocated by the dust of ashes.

The children of the planters wander aimlessly about the courtyards with their little donkeys, like little human wrecks. A group
goes along hesitatingly down the Rue Victor Hugo. They are no
longer black, but white, and look as if hoar frost had fallen over
them . . .

Desolation, aridity and eternal silence prevail in the countryside.
Little birds lie asphyxiated under the bushes and in the meadows the
animals are restless.

Hundreds of people had left Saint-Pierre, fleeing to the hills or to
Fort-de-France. Yet tens of thousands remained, reluctant to
leave their city until the very last moment. To aggravate matters,
they had been joined by around two thousand refugees from
Prêcheur and other outlying villages, who felt safer in the big
city. By 4 May, the population of Saint-Pierre had swollen to
around 30,000. Their decision to stay was vindicated by the
Governor's Scientific Mission, which found Saint-Pierre to be
absolutely safe:

. . . there is nothing in the activity of Pelée that warrants a
departure from Saint-Pierre . . . The relative positions of the
craters and the valleys opening toward the sea justifies the
conclusion that the safety of Saint-Pierre is completely assured.

A surprising conclusion, and one wonders whether Gaston Landes
agreed with it. From his observation post on the Perinelle plantation, he had seen Pelée's ash clouds and steaming fumaroles; he must
have noticed the increasing intensity of each day's eruptions.
Perhaps he was outnumbered, or subjected to a discreet pressure:
the Commission was meant to reassure people, not drive them into
an even greater panic. And while Landes was well-read in botany, he
did not have a confident grasp of Volcanology. He may also have
shared a belief (eagerly put around by Marius Hurard) that the real
danger to Saint-Pierre came from earthquakes rather than volcanoes.

Whatever his reasons, Landes also knew his civic duty. His job was to support the majority opinion, whatever private doubts he may have had.

Just after midday on Monday 5 May, the sky above Saint-Pierre filled with a terrible sound. Something like thunder, something like a rending of fabric and the tormented screech of a steam engine all rolled into one. By habit now, Pierrotins turned their heads to Pelée: an enormous wave of boiling mud was hurtling down the mountainside. *La Montagne descend! The Mountain is coming down!* they gasped. According to witnesses, this chocolate-brown avalanche was a quarter of a mile wide, and over a hundred feet deep. Within minutes, it had smashed into Guérin's Sugar Factory, burying workshops and outhouses. Only one solitary brick chimney – part of the Isnard factory next door – was left above the debris. From here, the avalanche raged westwards, driving waves three hundred feet back from the shore. A tidal wave was soon upon them. 'The sea receded, as if afrighted', writes Parel, 'then suddenly the ocean, rising mountain high, rushed back, breaking over the Place Bertin, and even over some of the principal streets, spreading alarm far and wide throughout the city.'

At least twenty-five people died at Guérin's Factory, including the overseer and the owner's son. Hundreds more fled Saint-Pierre, as streets were deluged with water. *Les Colonies* saw shop girls escaping with bundles of boots and corsets, 'and all in burlesque attire which would have evoked laughter had the panic not broken out at such a tragic moment'. It appeared the *Étang Sec* or Dry Lake was to blame. The swollen Lake had burst its banks, sending hundreds of tons of molten mud and debris down the mountain. 'The entire city is afoot', continued *Les Colonies*. 'The shops and private houses are closing. Everyone is preparing to seek refuge in the heights.'

Pelée had given another startling demonstration of its power, of its casual mastery over the human world. Returning to Saint-Pierre that afternoon, however, Governor Mouttet came to quite the opposite conclusion. Each successive calamity was, in his view, a sign that Pelée was hurrying towards extinction; the volcano was 'on the wane'. To reinforce this point, Mouttet decided that he and his wife Hélène should move temporarily to Saint-Pierre. Figures of authority in the city – priests, councillors, landowners – were also told to reassure people the worst was over.

In weeks to come, Mouttet's decision would be lambasted by the foreign press. 'GOVERNOR'S ORDER WAS AN ORDER THAT BROUGHT DEATH' screamed the *New York Herald*. The papers were particularly angered by Mouttet's heavy-handed efforts to stop people leaving. According to French journalist Jean Hess, soldiers were posted around the outskirts of Saint-Pierre with orders to seal off the city – a scandalous charge taken up by newspapers in Britain and America. The Governor, they claimed, had signed a death warrant for his own people, forcing them back into a city they were desperate to flee. Other historians have come to Governor Mouttet's defence. There is no written evidence of such an order having been made, writes Jacques Petitjean Roget: on the contrary, people were still free to leave the city by sea or by road.★

At worst, Governor Mouttet's presence did increase the moral pressure to stay put. It also made a certain amount of sense. French officials had seen how refugees had caused chaos in Saint-Pierre, and did not want the same scenes repeated in Fort-de-France. Looters had also begun to pick over Saint-Pierre's empty houses; people were encouraged to stay at home and protect their property.

★ The Governor's actions have also been defended by the American historian Ernest Zebrowski (*The Last Days of St Pierre*, Rutgers University Press, 2002). Zebrowski claims the telegram declaring Pelée to be 'on the wane' was written on or around 28 April, when the volcano appeared to be calming down. A second telegram, warning that 'the eruption [had] reached major proportions', was sent on 3 May. Zebrowski insists the Governor did his duty by informing Paris of the impending disaster. The fact that Paris failed to act on this information was quite another matter.

But Mouttet's main motivation may have been political. As the emblem of French authority in Martinique, he was keen to ensure the second round of voting went ahead: a mass evacuation would ruin those plans. He was also being lobbied fiercely on all sides. His political bosses in Paris were keen for the poll to go ahead, if only because victory in the two Martinican *arrondissements* would help swell Waldeck-Rousseau's twenty-five-seat majority. Cancelling the vote would also drag the Governor into a fight with one (or both) of Saint-Pierre's political factions: a fight which he had neither the time nor the inclination for. Mouttet's ability to sail with the political wind had previously worked in his favour. In the early days of May 1902, it left him looking weak and indecisive. Outsiders were appalled by Governor Mouttet's lack of leadership. The US Consul, Thomas Prentiss, took the unusual step of writing directly to his President, Theodore Roosevelt. 'To abandon the elections would be unthinkable', he wrote. 'The situation is a nightmare where no one seems able or willing to face the truth.'

One man did manage to leave Saint-Pierre.

To the embarrassment of his jailers, Ludger Sylbaris slipped out of his communal cell one night and sauntered off to Prêcheur to join a village carnival. After sleeping off his excesses, young Ludger returned to Saint-Pierre the next morning. The Prison Governor was not amused: one could take relaxation a little *too* far. Such insouciance would not be tolerated. Ludger Sylbaris was sent into solitary confinement.

Sylbaris's cell or *cachot* still exists, a rare monument in a city where most buildings only survive in photographs or scraps of memory. But there it is, crouching in a corner of the old jail yard, off the *Rue du Théâtre*. From a distance, the cell looks like a miniature log cabin. It has a gently curved roof, a tiny rectangular window and an arched doorway. Move closer, and its harsher qualities become evident. The walls are over two feet thick and as

sturdy as a castle keep; a ventilation hole pokes meekly from the roof. Even at eight in the morning, the heat of the *cachot* is hard to take. The air is stale, an old-time blend of damp and decay. This was where Ludger Sylbaris spent his days, watching beetles and cock-roaches skittle across his dusty floor. Pelée's distant rumblings must have intruded into his solitude — as did the prison guards' glib assurances that the worst was over. Ludger was ordered to spend eight days in his *cachot*; the second round of voting would go ahead without him.

Tuesday 6 May brought no respite. Pelée sulked behind veils of steam, its terrible roars and rumbles now audible on Guadeloupe, 100 miles north. The Blanche River, scene of Monday's mudslide, was still in turmoil. 'It was a roaring torrent,' writes Parel, 'rolling rocks, tree trunks and smoking mud onward in its crashing course.' This was also the day Governor Mouttet and his wife installed themselves at the *Intendance*, ready to take charge of events. A few hours later there was bad news: telegraphic cables linking Martin-ique to Saint Lucia and Saint Vincent had been cut. The avalanche which swept away Guérin's Factory had burrowed underwater, rupturing those copper threads which bound Saint-Pierre to the world. A single line, to Dominica, remained intact. With some difficulty Mouttet cabled the Ministry of Colonies in Paris, seeking advice. Based on the Governor's own complacent assessment that Pelée was on the wane, Paris's advice was clear and concise: Stay put and stay calm.

That night, an official notice was posted up around the town:

DEAR CITIZENS,

A new calamity has just hit our unfortunate country, already so sorely tested . . .

We wish to assure you that, given the immense valleys which separate us from the craters, we have no need to fear any danger.

Do not let yourself be upset by panics without foundation. Do not be discouraged . . . Return to your usual activities, in order to give courage and strength to the impressionable people of Saint-Pierre . . .

Wednesday had barely begun when Pelée made its presence felt once more. Soon after 4am, the city was roused by a roar so violent that wine glasses tumbled from tables and windows shook in their casements. Two huge craters, glowing as fierce as furnaces, had appeared at the summit. Above them, a cloud of lightning flashed and crackled. Daybreak promised a familiar scene of ash and dust. What emerged, beneath a faint grey light, was to trouble the memory of survivors for many years.

Saint-Pierre's blue harbour had gone. In its place was a waste of ash and pumice stone, on which a dozen or so boats seemed to float as if on dry land. Debris stretched many miles out to sea: a sight which drew awe and horror in equal measure. One sea captain decided to set off for France, even though his barque was only half full. Marino Leboffe was from Naples and had seen Vesuvius erupt several times. Two customs officers tried to make him stay, threatening to cable an arrest warrant to Le Havre if Leboffe did not comply. The captain's reply was matter of fact. 'I know nothing about Mont Pelée', he is reported to have said. 'But if Vesuvius were looking the way your volcano looks this morning, I'd get out of Naples.' By midday on Thursday, Leboffe and his crew were safely over the horizon.

It was unfortunate then that Wednesday 7 May was the day *Les Colonies* decided to quash all this volcano nonsense once and for all. Under a scornful headline 'The Panic at Saint-Pierre', Marius Hurard mocked those in 'mad flight' from his city:

> We confess that we cannot understand the panic. Where could one be better off than in Saint-Pierre? Do those who invade Fort-de-France believe they will be any better off there than here, should the earth begin to quake? This is a foolish error against which the populace should be warned.

Hurard's tirade was rather undercut by the reports which surrounded it. An eight-metre-deep hole had appeared near the mouth of the Prêcheur river; 'Great quantities of dead fish' were seen in the River Roxelane, while 'throughout most of the previous day, there fell in the North a fine blackish rain, which was so charged with ash as to make the carrying of an umbrella a matter of discomfort'.

But Hurard's trump card was an interview with Martinique's foremost scientist, Gaston Landes. It was a shrewd move. No one took Hurard's rantings seriously: he was a comic turn, an old ham. M. Landes was another matter. Who better to reassure the public (and support the editor's campaign) than a shy school botanist? One can imagine how Hurard's *coup* was arranged. The editor applying a little charm, some vintage guile. *Come now, Monsieur Landes. We have a duty to our City . . . Do you not agree?* Hard to disagree, at such a time. *Your Scientific Commission . . . If you think it will help calm the people, Sir, then I have no objection . . .* Yet Hurard's article leaves a nasty taste, an unmistakable sense that the scientist has been manipulated, his words unfairly distorted.

After some thoughts on the events of 5 May (Landes rightly observes that a 'mass of mud, and not lava . . . submerged the *Usine Guérin*'), the interview with *Les Colonies* turns to historic parallels. People who live close to Pelée should 'leave the neighbouring valleys and locate rather on the elevations', says Landes, in order to avoid the mudslides which overtook Herculaneum and Pompeii. Talk of Vesuvius then leads to this infamous peroration:

> Conclusion: The Montagne Pelée presents no more danger to the inhabitants of Saint-Pierre than does Vesuvius to those of Naples.

The article fails to make clear whether these concluding thoughts come from Landes or from his interviewer. Given what we know about the two characters, one suspects the latter. It looks as if Landes was cajoled into saying more than he would have liked. Or worse, that his words were twisted into a shape more acceptable to Hurard's political schemes. After all, what difference would another half-truth make, when added to the endless stream of absurdities churned out by the newspapers that year? 'It is difficult to analyse or understand the motive that prompted this appeal', wrote Angelo Heilprin later. 'Was it really given out as the expression of a personal conviction in the security of the place? Or was it, perhaps, a pennant thrown to the wind to assist in the election of a candidate to the French Chamber of Deputies, whose battle was being actively fought by the editor?'

We will never know. Perhaps Gaston Landes's sense of duty overcame his good sense; perhaps he made an honest mistake. Given the poor state of knowledge about volcanoes in 1902, one wonders whether anyone could have predicted what was about to happen. *Les Colonies* concludes its edition with a reminder that the following day, Thursday 8 May, is Ascension Day. Marius Hurard adds: 'Our offices being closed tomorrow, the next issue will appear on Friday.'

Another cause of optimism on this final day was the news coming from Saint Vincent, ninety miles south of Martinique. For several days, the British colony had been troubled by grumblings from its own volcanic peak, the Soufrière. That morning, it had exploded with an ear-splitting roar, ejecting ash over a 200-mile radius. 2,000 people died in the disaster; another 4,200 were injured. Far from alarming Pierrotins, this piece of news seemed to cheer them up. People imagined there was an underwater link between the two volcanoes: an eruption in Saint Vincent would surely release the pressure building up inside Pelée.

It also cheered Mouttet's emergency committee, which was holding its first meeting at the *Hôtel de l'Intendance* that Wednesday night. The Commission of Experts had found 'nothing abnormal' in Pelée's activity; Saint-Pierre was judged to be 'secure' from any future mudflows. In between the frenetic discussions that night, Governor Mouttet may have allowed himself a brief moment of self-congratulation. His plans were advancing well. A platoon of soldiers had arrived in Saint-Pierre to distribute food and patrol the streets; the city was calmer than on previous days, as was the mountain glowering above it. And if those scientists were right, the worst was already over.

To reinforce this point, Mouttet agreed to join Lieutenant-Colonel Gerbault on a seaborne inspection of *La Montagne*. Their steamer would leave Place Bertin at first light on Thursday and proceed north towards Prêcheur, passing through the stretch of water known as *Le Tombeau des Caraïbes*. They would arrive back in Saint-Pierre in time to greet the *Canada*, a packet boat run by the *Compagnie Générale Transatlantique*. Twice a month the *Canada* brought gifts and goods from the *Métropole* via Fort-de-France. Its presence in Saint-Pierre harbour would reassure people that life continued as usual. Thursday 8 May was also Ascension Day. City churches would fill from first light: there were services at the cathedral and the *Église du Fort* and in outlying villages like Carbet and Morne Rouge. The churches had been busy for several days;

tomorrow they would be overflowing with people, eager to give thanks for their deliverance from the volcano.

Outside Mouttet's residence, streetlamps flicker and fail; mounds of ash are clogging up the electricity turbines. Silence stalks every *rue* and *ruelle, marche* and *escalier*. There is no one around; the *Cercles* and Dance Halls have been closed for over a week now, *Carnaval* is long forgotten. The only noise (for even Pelée is quiet) comes from the harbour, where more than a dozen boats are riding at anchor tonight, their yellow lanterns bobbing and blinking under a jet-black sky.

Among them are six Italian barques: the *Albanese, Nord America, Pepho, Sacro Cruoure, San Antonio* and *Teresa Lo Vico*; two British ships, the steamer *Roddam* and the schooner *Canadian*; two big American barques, the *R.J. Morse* and *L.W. Morton*; and several ships from France and Norway. A team of engineers has also arrived on the steamship *Grappler*. Their first job tomorrow morning is to repair those ruptured telegraph cables, about eight miles out from shore. Before then there is time for everyone to drink and talk, to hear more of Pelée's antics and those of that cowardly Italian captain who cut and run. The Customs House bell marks Nine, Ten, Eleven, and still their laughter spirals up and up into the sulphurous air.

As midnight chimes, a hush falls across the bay. Even sailors must sleep. Saint-Pierre is at rest: all that remains beneath the sweep of its red lighthouse beam is a slow, steady lap of water on wood, of lanyards clanking idly on a midnight breeze. Now and then, the seamen are jolted awake by a peculiar undertow beneath their bunks, as if their boats are being dragged back out to sea. It is a little unusual, but hardly worth bothering about.

FIVE

NOT ONE ALIVE

JUST BEFORE eight o'clock on Thursday 8 May, a young man
called Raoul Lodéon received a nasty shock. Lodéon worked at
Martinique's main telephone exchange in Fort-de-France, directing calls across the tiny island. One of his first tasks that
morning was to make contact with the northern town of Ajoupa-
Bouillon. It was 7.40am. Finding no answer there, Lodéon chatted
briefly with M. Thésée, a colleague in Saint-Pierre twenty miles up
the coast. Thésée remarked, in passing, that Saint-Pierre was
'covered with a thick fog which obscured the entire town'. It
was so dark, he went on, they had turned on the lights in their
office.

Fifteen minutes later, another call to the overcast city ended in a
most unnerving manner. One of Lodéon's colleagues had to put
down his earpiece after receiving a mild electric shock. As Lodéon
discussed this strange event with his supervisor, a hail of small stones
began to fall in a courtyard beside their office, producing 'a metallic
sound on the roofs of nearby houses'. Intrigued by what he had seen
and heard, Lodéon picked up his *cornet*.

. . . I called Saint-Pierre once again. They responded after one
ringing tone.

'Hello', I shouted, three times.

It was only after the third attempt that I heard the word 'Hello'
pronounced by M. Thésée.

I swear that the uncertain tone of his voice gave me a
premonition that my colleague was greatly troubled.

No sooner had my conviction formed when, the *cornet* to my ear, and waiting for his reply, I heard a cry of great pain: it was a prolonged 'Ah!!!'

At almost the same time, I heard an incredible sound, like that of an enormous block of iron falling on a metal roof.

At this point (8.00) I too received a violent electric shock which made me drop the phone.

Within moments, every bell in the exchange was ringing dementedly and bristling with sparks. The sky over Fort-de-France had turned as black as ink, throwing its citizens into a darkness so complete they were unable to make out each other's faces. A torrent of molten rock and ash then began to fall, hissing and roaring like embers tossed from a mighty fire. As people ran for shelter, a single word formed in every mind. *Le Volcan . . . !*

Vicar-General Parel had returned to the capital on Wednesday evening. Alerted by a patter of stones on his roof and on the leaves of trees, he went outside:

> . . . Thunder pealed, pealed continuously, appallingly. The sea receded three times for a distance of several hundred metres . . . I went out on my balcony to see what was happening, and I noticed it was being covered by a hail of stones and ashes still hot. People stood petrified at their doors, or rushed distractedly through the streets. All this lasted for about a quarter of an hour, a quarter of an hour of terror.

Mont Pelée had erupted. That much was certain. And if Pelée could rain this much destruction on Fort-de-France, then it must have had a devastating impact further north. There was no way of knowing. Cable and telephone lines were down; the daily eight o'clock steamer from Fort-de-France had turned back, unable to pass through a blizzard of ash and white hot stones. 'But what was taking place in Saint-Pierre?' writes Parel. 'No one dared to think . . . The most terrible anxiety filled our hearts.'

Thursday morning in Saint-Pierre had dawned clear but grey.

Ash still fell sporadically on the city's huddled streets, and an occasional muffled detonation echoed around the sleepy bay. Soon after daybreak, several columns of white smoke were seen drifting from the summit. Beyond this, Pelée offered no clues of what it might be up to. By chance, the city's last moments were savoured by dozens of passengers and crew on board a Canadian steamer. The *Roraima* was expected in Saint-Pierre the previous evening, but had been delayed. As the 590-ton boat came within sight of Martinique, the magnificent vista must have compensated for any late arrival.

'For hours before we entered the roadstead we could see flames and smoke rising from Mont Pelée', recalled Purser Charles Thompson. 'No one on board had any idea of the danger. [Our captain] G.T. Muggah was on the bridge and all hands got on deck to see the show.' Like many others, Thompson was transfixed by Pelée's sinister grace. *La Montagne* exercised a hypnotic pull on all those who saw her, like the beautiful *Diablesses* of Creole folklore who lured men to their deaths when they least expected it:

> The spectacle was magnificent. As we approached Saint-Pierre we could distinguish the rolling and leaping of the red flames that leaped from the mountain in huge volumes and gushed high into the sky. Enormous clouds of black smoke hung over the volcano . . . There was a constant muffled roar. It was like the biggest oil refinery in the world burning up on the mountain top.

Through the ash, Thompson would also have seen hundreds of people scurrying towards Saint-Pierre cathedral: women in long cotton dresses with black umbrellas at their sides; children dressed in Sunday best white overcoats and straw hats. Every seat in the church is taken, with dozens of people gathering at the West Door. If there is a hesitancy about the priest's movements this morning, then it is shared by his congregation. Every pew is filled with frightened faces; some people have brought their animals with them, the rhythmic chatter of prayer occasionally punctuated by a baffled bleat or bark. The organist is also struggling to be heard above the various booms, creaks and crashes coming from outside. Paint is blistering from the walls. But at least they will be safe here, within the sanctuary of God's House. Here with Saint Peter, who looks down from his trembling pediment: *Tu es Pierre. Sur cette Pierre, je batirai mon église* . . .

Elsewhere in Saint-Pierre, the day is slowly forming. Marius Hurard considers how best to spend his holiday (even statesmen have to rest, on occasion); a certain solitary prisoner waits for his breakfast, smelling the sulphur-tainted air through his tiny window. Gaston Landes has risen early to observe Pelée from his garden north of Saint-Pierre, and Governor Mouttet has headed out to sea. The Governor's small boat is last seen at about quarter-past seven, sailing north towards Prêcheur with Lieutenant-Colonel Gerbault, its frail form battling against clouds of ash.

At around this time, one of Charles Thompson's fellow crewmen on the *Roraima* noticed a distinct change in Pelée's manner. 'Appalling sounds were issuing from the mountains behind the town', recalled James Taylor. 'Thunder seemed to come out of the air and up from the earth.' One man had seen enough. Fernand Clerc, the New Party candidate, decided to abandon his election campaign and leave Saint-Pierre straightaway. A premonition of disaster had come upon him early that morning: a conviction heightened by the wild flutterings of his barometer. Moving swiftly, Clerc woke up his wife and four children and ordered his horses to be brought out. 'My friends thought I was over timid and refused to leave', he said later. As Clerc passed down Rue Victor Hugo, he saw the American Consul Thomas Prentiss and his wife Clara standing on their balcony. 'They waved to me and I returned the salute,' said Clerc, 'calling to them at the same time that they had better accompany me.' The Prentisses shook their heads, and Clerc rode on.

At ten to eight, Pelée let out three or four violent explosions, as sharp and as rapid as gun shots. The crackling fusillades were quickly followed by a hideous sight: two enormous clouds of black dust bulged out of the mountainside, accompanied by a sound of tearing and grinding. Pelée was falling apart. One cloud of thick black fog raced upwards like the plume of a geyser, blotting out the sun. A second cloud shot out of the mountainside at an angle, and began to roll down Pelée's slopes in a similar way to the avalanche of 5 May.*
This time, though, the cloud moved even faster, at around a hundred miles an hour. There was another important difference too: it was heading straight for Saint-Pierre. That large V-shaped notch built into the side of the Dry Lake had found its lethal purpose: directing thousands of tons of superheated steam and hot dust down onto the city below, like the barrel of a gun. Within three minutes, this rolling cloud had struck Saint-Pierre with staggering force, destroying every object in its path.

It is impossible to imagine what these final moments must have felt like. A sense of dread and helpless panic, a search for love and shelter, the certainty of death. Everyone who witnessed Pelée's rage, and who lived to tell their tale, was haunted by the incredible noise which the volcano made as it erupted, by its chilling *otherness*. The American journalist George Kennan called it a 'rending, roaring sound'; Heilprin said it was like 'the very earth being sawed in two'; Mgr Parel likened the 'mighty, muffled detonations' to that of 'many cannons fired at the same time'. It was beyond comprehension, beyond description. For those trapped inside the cathedral, watching

---

* Accounts of what followed on Thursday 8 May are so many and so various that one has to proceed with some care. Where some witnesses saw lightning flashes and sparks of satanic colour, others insisted that Pelée only projected vast clouds of billowy, grey ash. These differences can be put down to different points of view and the vagaries of memory. They may also be a consequence, as Angelo Heilprin observed, of minds 'disturbed by events likely to affect the reason'.

chandeliers tremble and windows pucker, it must have seemed as if the end of the world was upon them.

The end came at 7.52am.★

We know this because a clock on the wall of Saint-Pierre's Military Hospital has remembered the moment, its hands welded together 'as if to mark for all time the instant at which the justice of God was meted out' (Parel). An intensely hot dust cloud swept over Saint-Pierre like a hurricane, raging through every street and shop. Heavy brick walls buckled and fell; roofs raced away like hats in a gale. So swift, so vengeful was this molten cloud that people died where they stood, in parlours and kitchens, in cramped shanty huts and marble courtyards. It was as if a gigantic black net had been thrown across the town, catching every living thing within its mesh.

Worse was to come. Within seconds of the first blast wave a second, catastrophic shock hit the city. The incandescent gas tumbling down Mont Pelée was so hot that it set fire to trees and houses, turning Saint-Pierre into a two-mile-long inferno. Hundreds of barrels of rum exploded on quays and in warehouses: rivers of flame raced across Place Bertin and into the sea. Timber structures like the Customs House and the Chamber of Commerce were swiftly consumed, along with the remains of the Theatre and Town Hall. Fire shot out from each quarter of the city, as if it had become a giant brazier, a funeral pyre.

By ten to eight, Fernand Clerc and his family had reached Mont Parnasse, a raised *morne* about two miles east of Saint-Pierre. It had been a difficult ascent, broken by several halts to rest the horses. Suddenly, they heard the mountain let out four sharp explosions. From a roadside clearing, the Clercs watched their city disappear. 'The cloud that had for so many days surmounted Pelée seemed to

---

★ Or at least it did in Saint-Pierre. The official time in Fort-de-France and its telephone exchange was 8.02am. This ten-minute time delay is explained by the Pierrotins' habit of setting watches in time to their own idiosyncratic clocks. In the interests of consistency, this account follows Saint-Pierre time.

topple over with a loud noise and tumble into the city', M. Clerc explained later. 'Behind the smoke came a sheet of flame.' As for the monstrous cloud of dust and ash, it was like 'a great torrent of black fog, accompanied by a continuous roar of half-blended staccato beats of varying intensity, something like the throbbing, pulsating roar of a Gatling gun battery going into action'.

No sooner had they seen this apocalyptic sight, than the world went dark. An inky canopy of volcanic dust swept across the heights: the only way Clerc could be sure of his wife and children's presence was to touch their trembling, tearful faces with his hands.

Another Pierrotin also watched his home town being engulfed in ash and flame. Roger Arnoux, a member of the French Astronomical Society, had left Saint-Pierre on Wednesday evening in order to get a better view of the volcano. At ten to eight on Thursday morning, he too was on Mont Parnasse, watching the terrifying spectacle unfold. Arnoux's detailed account appeared in the *Bulletin de la Société Astronomique de la France* in August 1902:

> At about eight o'clock, when still watching the crater, I noted a small cloud pass out, followed two seconds afterwards by a considerable cloud, whose flight to the Pointe du Carbet (a promontory two miles south of Saint-Pierre) occupied less than three seconds . . . thus showing that it developed almost as rapidly in height as in length . . .
>
> The vapours were of a violet-grey colour, and seemingly very dense, for although endowed with an almost inconceivably powerful ascensive force, they retained to their zenith their rounded summits, innumerable electric scintillations played through the chaos of vapours, at the same time that the ears were deafened by a frightful fracas.
>
> I had at this time the impression that Saint-Pierre had been destroyed, and I wept over the loss of those whom I had left the night before . . .

Roger Arnoux lost his mother, father, brother and sister in Saint-Pierre. In spite of this, he continued to monitor Pelée's actions, as they took a supernatural turn:

> As the monster seemed to near us, my people, panic stricken, ran to a neighbouring hill that dominated the house, begging me to do the same. At this moment a terrible wind arose, tearing the leaves from the trees and breaking the small branches, at the same time offering strong resistance to us in our flight. Hardly had we arrived at the summit of the hillock when the sun was completely veiled, and in its place came an almost complete blackness. Then only did we receive a fall of stones, the largest of which were about two centimetres of average diameter. At this time we observed over Saint-Pierre, and in the quarter which I could determine to be the Mouillage, a column of fire, estimated to be four hundred metres in height . . . This phenomenon lasted for two or three minutes, and was followed by a shower of stones and of mud–rain, which flattened the undergrowth into the ground and even some of the smaller shrubs. This torrential rain lasted for about half an hour . . .
>
> In total, these natural phenomena went on for around an hour, after which the sun broke through.

But the most vivid accounts of what happened that morning come from sailors caught in Saint-Pierre harbour. All but two of the eighteen ships anchored there were destroyed in the cataclysm. Survivors were drawn from a British steamer, the *Roddam*, and from the Quebec Line's *Roraima* which had arrived an hour earlier. Their stories must stand for the citizens of Saint-Pierre, for these horrifying, mind-numbing experiences must have been shared by tens of thousands in the town itself.

Purser Charles Thompson was on the *Roraima*'s deck admiring Pelée when, without warning, 'the side of the volcano was ripped out, and there hurled towards us a solid wall of flame'.

The Roraima *in Saint-Pierre before the eruption*

The wave of fire was on us and over us like a lightning flash. It was like a hurricane of fire. I saw it strike the cable steamship *Grappler* broadside on and capsize her. From end to end she burst into flames and then she sank.

The fire rolled in mass straight down upon Saint-Pierre and the shipping. The town vanished before our eyes and then the air grew stifling hot and we were in the thick of it. Wherever the mass of fire struck the sea the water boiled and sent up vast clouds of steam.

The fire wave swept off the masts and smokestack as if they were cut with a knife. Captain Muggah was the only one on deck not killed outright . . . He yelled to get up the anchor, but before two fathoms were hove in, the *Roraima* was almost upset by the boiling whirlpool.

Thompson survived by diving into his private cabin and burying himself in the bedsheets. Fellow officer James Taylor was equally quick-witted.

I could see a black cloud sweeping down upon us. I dived below and, dragging with me Samuel Thomas, a gangwayman and a fellow countryman of mine, sprang into a room, shutting the door to keep out the heat that was already unbearable.

The ship rocked, and I expected every moment that it would sink. Outside, I heard a voice pleading for the door to be opened. I recognised the voice as that of Mr (Ellery) Scott, the first officer, and I opened the door and dragged him into the room. When we did this the heat rushed in, blistering Thomas's face.

The fire storm lasted for no more than five minutes.

Taylor soon found the heat intolerable, and decided to step outside. He was greeted by an appalling sight.

I went on deck, to find a scene which will never fade from my mind. All about were the dead and the dying. All were covered with hot mud and with ashes.

The dying were suffering terrible torture. Little children were moaning for water. I did what I could for them, but it was very little. I obtained water, but when it was held to their swollen lips they were unable to swallow, because of the ashes which clogged their throats. One little chap took water into his mouth and rinsed out the ashes, but even then could not swallow, so badly was his throat burned. He sank back unconscious and a few minutes later was dead.

Samuel Thomas, the gangwayman whose life had been saved by Officer Taylor, was driven to the edge of madness. 'The groans and cries of the dying', he said, 'were enough to drive one crazy.' Thomas recalled seeing a woman burned to death while she shielded her baby in her arms. He also saw fellow crewmen die 'while on their knees, praying for salvation'.

Pelée had still not finished. A mass of ash and molten stones soon began to rain down on the *Roraima*, as it had on Roger Arnoux at

Mont Parnasse. According to First Officer Ellery Scott, the projectiles ranged 'all the way from the size of shot to pigeons' eggs'. After the stones came a drizzle of hot mud, of the consistency of very thin cement. Scott observes:

> Wherever it fell it formed a coating, clinging like glue, so that those who wore no caps it coated, making a complete cement mask right over their heads . . . I snatched a tarpaulin cover off one of the ventilators and jammed it down over my head and neck, looking out through the opening. This saved me much, but even so my beard, face, nostrils, and eyes were so filled with the stuff that every few seconds I had to break it out of my eyes in order to see . . .

The *Roraima*'s captain, G.T. Muggah, was not so lucky. Having bravely remained on deck throughout, he had taken the brunt of Pelée's assault. Scott goes on:

> At this time I went to the lower bridge, feeling my way along, in order to find the captain. There on the bridge I almost stumbled on a crouching figure with a hideous face, burned almost beyond recognition. 'Who are you?' I cried, for I did not know him, crouched there in the darkness.
> The man looked up, his face terrible to see.
> 'Mr Scott,' he said, 'don't you know me?'
> I said, 'My God, it's the captain!'

Muggah fell overboard, and died later of his wounds. Many other passengers and crew joined him in the seething black sea. First Officer Scott organised a firefighting team, yet only four of his crew were able to help. Several others, who had lost flesh on their hands, tried to carry buckets in the crooks of their elbows. It was hopeless.

From time to time, the sailors glimpsed Saint-Pierre through a haze of steam and wood smoke. It was impossible to imagine any survivors. Purser Thompson remembered how

> the blast of fire from the volcano . . . shrivelled and set fire to everything it touched. Burning rum ran in streams down every street and out into the sea. Before the volcano burst, the landings of Saint-Pierre were crowded with people. After the explosion, not one living being was seen on land.

Jean-Louis Prudent, a native of Saint-Pierre, was a deckhand on the Italian barque *Teresa Lo Vico*. Through great good fortune he escaped serious injury. Prudent's misfortune was to see his home town disappear before his eyes:

> . . . on shore I saw men and women rushing back and forth amid the flames for an hour. They would not run long. Then came that choking smoke and they would drop like dead flies . . . The explosion, smoke and fire all came and went in three minutes, but the city burned for three hours.

It was an agonising sight, made worse by the all-too-audible sufferings of dying passengers. Once the *Roraima*'s fires had been tamed, officers Scott, Taylor and Thompson dragged all of their survivors onto the foredeck. Cries and moans came from every corner – Water! *Water!* – which they hastened to satisfy. The internal injuries were, if anything, more grievous than those on the surface: Pelée's first wave of superheated gas and ash had invaded the eyes, ears and mouths of everyone caught in its path, scorching their throats and lungs. It was as if their insides were on fire. 'Many of the unfortunates could not drink at all', said Scott. 'When we put water into their mouths it stayed there and almost choked them, and we had to turn them over to get the water out.'

Among the wounded were several civilians. The *Roraima* had been carrying twenty-one paying passengers as well as forty-seven crew: they included a New Yorker, Mrs Clement Stokes, and her three young children. Their governess, a Barbadian by the name of Clara King, survived the disaster along with Rita, the eldest daughter. Miss King's story has an immediacy made all the more poignant by its domestic detail:

[I] was assisting with dressing the children for breakfast when the steward rushed past and shouted, 'Close the cabin door – the volcano is coming!' We closed the door and at the same moment came a terrible explosion which nearly burst the eardrums. The vessel was lifted high into the air and then seemed to be sinking down, down. We were all thrown off our feet by the shock and huddled crouching in one corner of the cabin. My mistress had the baby girl in her arms, the older girl leaned on my right arm, while I held little Eric in my right.

The explosion seemed to have blown in the skylight over our heads, and before we could raise ourselves, hot, moist ashes began to pour in on us . . . in vain we tried to shield ourselves. The cabin was pitch dark – we could see nothing . . .

When we could see each other's faces, they were all covered with black lava, the baby was dying, Rita, the older girl, was in great agony and every part of my body was paining me. A heap of hot mud had collected near us and as Rita put her hand down to raise herself up it was plunged up to the elbow in the scalding stuff . . .

[We] remained on the burning ship from 8.30am until 3.00pm . . . My mistress lay on the deck in a collapsed state; the little boy was already dead and the baby dying. The lady was collected and resigned, handed me some money, told me to take Rita to her aunt, and sucked a piece of ice before she died.

Amid these pitiful scenes, the crew of the British steamer *Roddam* were saved by a piece of incredible luck. Desperate to escape, they were given a helping hand by Pelée itself. So great was the turbulence generated by *La Montagne* that it tore their ship's anchor clean away from the seabed. Within minutes, the *Roddam* was lurching out of Saint-Pierre, flames flying from every porthole. 'It was a dying crew which took her out', said Purser Thompson of the *Roraima*. But at least they had got away. The *Roddam* limped south through foaming grey seas and thunderous skies, to Castries in Saint Lucia. There, the survivors sent news of Saint-Pierre's tragedy to the world.

Behind them, they left a roadstead brimful with burning boats and blackened corpses. As the *Roraima* dipped beneath the waves, its remaining crew jumped overboard. 'The water was almost hot enough to parboil me,' said James Taylor, 'but a wave soon swept in from the ocean, bringing with it cool water that made life possible.' With five others, he formed a 'rude craft' from stray wreckage and waited, in hope, for help to arrive.

It was several days before the true extent of destruction became known. Far from tumbling harmlessly into the sea, as Mouttet's scientific commission had predicted, Pelée had fired its toxic load with the precision of a sniper's bullet, straight into the heart of Saint-Pierre. Fires burned most fiercely in districts closest to the volcano's path: the *Quartier du Fort* and the *Centre*. The *Mouillage* took slightly less of this immediate impact, only to be levelled by the fire storm which followed. North of Saint-Pierre, the blast destroyed Fonds Coré and Sainte-Philomène. To the south, a tidal wave overcame the little fishing village of Carbet, where Gauguin had sat with his sketch books fifteen years earlier.

Scientists also noted how Saint-Pierre's peculiar features conspired to make the disaster even worse. Pelée's steep-sided slopes gave the gas clouds a fatal speed and force; the city's cramped streets encouraged fires to spread freely. Even the natural amphitheatre which surrounded Saint-Pierre seemed to turn against its inhabitants. In calmer times, these gently curving hills would shield Pierrotins from the worst of weathers. On 8 May, they provided

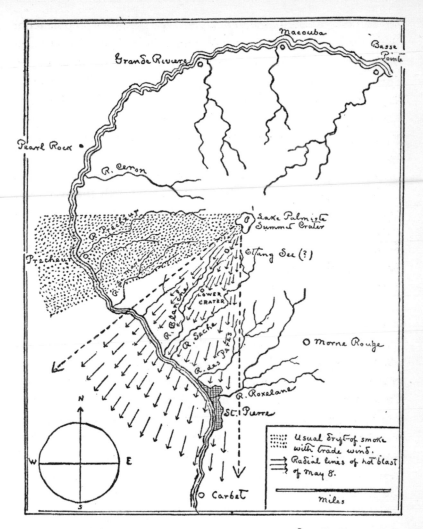

Macouba

Basse
Pointe

Grande Rivière

Pearl Rock

R. Ceron

Lake Palmiste
Summit Crater

Étang Sec (?)

Prêcheur

R. Préchent

LOWER
CRATER

R. Blanche

R. Sache

R. des
Pères

Morne Rouge

R. Roxelane

St. Pierre

N

W   E

S

:::::: Usual drift of smoke
       with trade wind.
───── Radial lines of hot blast
       of may 8.

Miles

Carbet

THE COURSE OF THE BLAST OF 8 MAY

Source: George Kennan, The Tragedy of Pelée *(New York, 1902)*

a cauldron-shaped furnace within which the city and its people were roasted to death.

The eruption of Mont Pelée was heard as far away as Dominica and Guadeloupe, another reminder of the volcano's immense power. Yet people were also struck by Pelée's strange, arbitrary nature: the way it had wiped an entire city from the face of the earth, while leaving certain people and objects miraculously intact. It was as if the volcano had a personality, a God-like presence, which gave it the power to bestow life or death.

The American journalist George Kennan relates the story of two French gentlemen whom he encountered several weeks after the disaster. Messrs Lassère and Simonut were convalescing in a hospital in Trinité. Their wounds were so curious, and their ordeal so ghastly, that Kennan decided to interview them. The resulting story, in all its macabre detail, reads like a tale by Poe or Stevenson.

Just before eight that morning, Messrs Lassère and Simonut were heading east out of Saint-Pierre when they saw a black cloud race towards their carriage, like a prognostic from the deepest pit of hell. The cloud was gaining fast, rolling and tumbling towards them with preternatural speed. Scared out of their minds, the two men lashed their mules into a gallop, hoping to escape this lethal fog. Ahead, they saw a crucifix upon a hill. But before they could reach safety, Kennan writes, they were hit by an almighty blow: 'It approached with a roaring, "galloping" sound, struck them like a mighty rushing wind; overturned and completely wrecked their carriage, setting the mules free.' The hurricane left the two gentlemen stunned, burned and half dead in their vehicle.

Both had felt an intense heat pass over them. Death, it seemed, was but a few moments away: a conviction hastened by the sudden night which fell across the island. Yet it seemed as if Pelée had decided, at the very last moment, to spare them.

Their clothing showed no signs of injury from heat, but their backs were badly burned or scalded under it; the skin at once peeled off their hands so that it hung from them in strips; and when they arrived at Morne Rouge, their shoes had to be cut from their burned and swollen feet . . .

Kennan was even more intrigued when he came across Lassère and Simonut's carriage, 'half buried in a pile of broken-off tree branches' on the road to Grande Reduit. Apart from some slight superficial damage, the vehicle was as good as new. 'The light leathern top was torn', he wrote, 'but it had not been burned, nor even scorched.' Sadly, the animals were not spared. One mule was missing; the other had been caught up in the hurricane and laid to rest beside a palm-covered shack fifty yards away.

Fort-de-France was in turmoil.

At ten o'clock on Thursday morning, the steamer *Girard* made a second attempt to reach Saint-Pierre. It returned at one o'clock with sinister tidings: the entire coastline from Carbet to Prêcheur was in flames, the heat so intense that it had been impossible to land. Another ship, the *Marin*, brought back similar news. Martinique's second city was no more. Vicar-General Parel was in Fort-de-France harbour at the time, where hundreds had gathered at the quayside for news of their loved ones. 'The news which burst upon the city at about one o'clock sounded like the death knell of Martinique and evoked an indescribable cry of horror', he wrote. 'I shall not attempt to depict such scenes; it requires the pen of a Dante, or the eloquence of a Jeremiah.'

Two more boats were dispatched: the *Suchet* and the *Rubis*. M. Lhuerre, the Acting Governor (for there has been no news of Governor Mouttet since Wednesday evening), ordered them to land at Place Bertin and to search for survivors. Fighting his way through a distraught crowd, Parel boarded the second steamer. He was joined by State Prosecutor Lubin and a platoon of thirty marines, led by one Lieutenant Tessier. 'It is impossible to believe in the reality of so terrible a disaster', Parel confided. 'We cling to every theory which permits us to hope.'

The *Rubis* leaves Fort-de-France at 2.30pm, its passengers and crew in a state of dreadful anxiety. About halfway to Saint-Pierre, they run into difficulty. The sea is strewn with wreckage and their captain is obliged to slacken his speed in order to avoid breaking the helm. As they pass Carbet, Prosecutor Lubin gets his first glimpse of the once-familiar town of Saint-Pierre:

> Saint-Pierre and its suburbs seem to us a heap of ashes and ruins. The roadstead contains nothing but an immense quantity of drifting wood . . . Not a trace of the hull of any sailing-vessel; not a boat . . . on the coast and in the surrounding country not a living soul!

Parel sees the outline of the *Roraima*, a tower of black smoke rising from its stern. Saint-Pierre harbour is studded with broken masts, the keels of overturned boats. All along the quays, fires are burning. The unalterable fact is before them.

> Its ruins stretch before us, wrapped in their shroud of smoke and ashes, gloomy and silent, a city of the dead. Our eyes seek out the inhabitants fleeing distracted, or returning to look for the dead. Nothing to be seen. No living soul appears in this desert of desolation, encompassed by appalling silence. When at last the cloud lifts, the mountain appears in the background, its slopes, formerly so green, now clad in a thick mantle of snow, resembling an Alpine landscape in winter. Through the cloud of ashes and of smoke diffused in the atmosphere, the sun breaks wan and dim, as it is never seen in our skies, and throws over the whole picture a sinister light, suggestive of a world beyond the grave.

Presently, the engines are halted. Soldiers remove their caps and bow their heads. In this unearthly silence, Parel makes a sign of the cross. The priest is standing on the boat's prow, facing the distant, ashen town. His vestments flutter nervously as he leads his *confrères* in prayer.

'Beloved and unfortunate victims!' he cries. 'We weep for you, we the unhappy survivors of this desolation; while you, purified by the particular virtue and the exceptional merits of this horrible sacrifice, have risen on this day of triumph . . .'

The *Rubis* rolls gently.

'This day of triumph with Him and to receive from His own hand the crown of glory. It is in this hope that we seek the strength to survive you!'

Amen.

And then silence.

A dispirited mood falls upon the company. There is no one left to save here. Corpses float freely around the harbour, as if strewn across a battlefield, and seagulls have begun to circle. A dozen or so survivors from the *Roraima* have already been picked up by the *Suchet.* They are heading for Fort-de-France. But in Saint-Pierre itself, there is nothing. More in hope than expectation, the *Rubis* edges closer to shore. Prosecutor Lubin lowers a boat into steamy water and, with Lieutenant Tessier and Ensign Hébert for company, rows towards the *Mouillage.* They land near the cathedral, whose right-hand tower is still wondrously intact. A stench of burnt flesh – acrid, nauseating – fills their nostrils, and makes them giddy with fear. From memory, Lubin finds Rue Bouillé, the busy market street which runs parallel with Rue Victor Hugo.

Here, they come across the first recognisable bodies – and the first mystery. Many of these corpses are badly burned, but others are relatively intact. 'In this neighbourhood we found bodies scattered everywhere', writes Lubin. 'Some of them [were] distended by gases and not carbonised; as to those who regained their homes, they seemed to be completely charred . . .' Death came suddenly and inexplicably, as if an evil spell had been cast over the city. Unable to reach Rue Victor Hugo, for 'to do so would be to walk over a glowing brazier', Lubin and his party re-embark and land at Place Bertin. The same ghastly sight greets them. 'There, too, are bodies swollen by gas, but not carbonised. The hands are not shrivelled; death seems to have been swift and free from suffering.'

Prosecutor Lubin had come across a mystery which would trouble volcanologists for months to come: how exactly the people of Saint-Pierre had died. Some had been burnt alive, but most appeared to have suffocated. No one knew of a volcano which had behaved quite like that before. Traditionally, volcanoes acted in one of two distinct fashions. They either poured molten lava onto their surroundings, or hurled huge dust clouds into the sky. Pelée was different. If the sailors' eyewitness accounts were to be believed, then it had combined *both* sets of features at the same time. Hundreds of tons of gas and debris had belched into the atmosphere. But an even greater proportion had slipped, like lava rolling down a hillside, onto the unwitting city below: Pelée had produced a gas cloud which had acted like a lava flow. Few who witnessed it would ever forget it.

Overcome by suffocating heat, Lubin returned to the *Rubis*. The streets of Saint-Pierre were still too hot for a detailed study. In a report to Acting Governor Lhuerre, the Prosecutor volunteered some tentative thoughts on how the disaster might have happened:

> From our examination of the ruined city, I conclude that the phenomenon which destroyed it was produced with such suddenness and intensity that there was no chance of escape . . . The city must have been asphyxiated, the fiery spout having exhausted all the air that could be breathed. Perhaps there was a mingling of explosive gas, for at Fort-de-France we heard loud detonations. I returned to the capital with the conviction, I may say with the assurance, that not a single resident of Saint-Pierre could have saved himself . . .

Dusk was coming. There was nothing more to do. With empty hearts, the crew of the *Rubis* turn back to Fort-de-France. No sooner have they left Saint-Pierre, however, than they encounter another distressing scene. As they pass Carbet, they see white flags and shirts being waved frantically from the beach. Four hundred villagers are gathered on the shoreline, including about thirty wounded. 'New sensations and indescribable scenes awaited us there', wrote Vicar-General Parel:

> Here, in a single house, are heaped up fifteen bodies. In another spot are dying men, horribly burned. Women and young children, their flesh tumefied and falling into shreds, die as they reach the ship. Fathers mourn their children, wives their husbands. Many of these are returning from the country, ignorant, as yet, of the horrible truth. We wished to hide it from them, but they divined it. The cries which ring out break the heart. Many lost their reason . . .

The evacuation takes four hours. Soldiers and sailors ferry the most desperate cases across what Parel calls 'a dismantled sea', to the safety of their steamship. Two other boats join the rescue operation: the *Suchet* and a cable layer called *Pouyer-Quertier*. The plan is to take only the most seriously wounded to Fort-de-France, but soon they are overwhelmed with people, all begging to leave the disaster zone.

After a long and arduous journey, the boats reach Fort-de-France at 10pm. A journalist at *L'Opinion* witnessed their return. 'When the *Suchet* arrived with around thirty wounded', he wrote, 'a crowd gathered on the Esplanade, in the lanes and neighbouring streets, hoping to meet someone dear who had been rescued at the very last moment.' Many were to be disappointed. Yet they refused to give up hope. 'Long after the last military truck had taken its funereal load to hospital', the paper continues, 'the crowd remained on the quays, its heart filled with indefinable sadness.'

Soon afterwards, the *Suchet*'s Commander, M. Le Bris, sent a cable to the Maritime Ministry in Paris:

HAVE RETURNED FROM SAINT-PIERRE. TOWN COMPLETELY DESTROYED BY FIRE STORM AT AROUND EIGHT O'CLOCK IN THE MORNING. PRE-SUME ALL POPULATION ANNIHILATED. HAVE BROUGHT BACK THIRTY SURVIVORS. ALL BOATS IN HARBOUR INCINERATED AND LOST. AM LEAV-ING FOR GUADELOUPE TO LOOK FOR SUPPLIES.

News of the disaster had already reached Paris, thanks to a brief cable from M. Lhuerre; Captain Le Bris's communiqué confirmed the worst: one of France's oldest colonies had suffered yet another calamitous misfortune. The first physical confirmation came at five o'clock that afternoon, when the British steamer *Roddam* crawled into Castries harbour in Saint Lucia. It must have presented a pathetic sight. Six inches of ash coated its deck. According to one news report, the boat was 'unrecognisable – grey with ashes, its rigging dismantled and sheets and awnings hanging about torn and charred'. Only four members of Captain Freeman's crew of twenty-two were to survive. When asked what the eruption had been like, one sailor simply said he had seen 'glimpses of hell'.

By Saturday 10 May, Saint-Pierre's annihilation was front-page news. A 'thrill of horror', as Frederick Royce put it, had passed around the world. Reading details in their morning papers, the people of Paris and Rome, Chicago and New York must have been struck by the awful *suddenness* of this cataclysm, by its fantastical speed. In three minutes, all was over. A world had passed away in less time than it took to boil a humble egg, or to perform one's daily shave.

And, with this loss, came the end of a certain, exuberant way of life. There would be no more *Carnaval*, no more picnics on top of *La Montagne*; no more extravagant lunacies at M. Erhard's theatre – and no more elections, either. Among the dead were counted Governor Mouttet and his wife, and all but one member of his scientific commission. Marius Hurard – the man who had confessed in *Les Colonies* that he could not understand what all the panic was about – had perished too, the end of 'a life full of adventures' as one obituarist put it.*

It was clear tens of thousands of people had perished. Most had died immediately, with little sense of what had overcome them. But those who had been caught on the edge of Pelée's fatal cloud were not so lucky. Among these unfortunates was Gaston Landes, struck down in his garden while he watched the eruption. Soon after nine that morning, a woman called Madame Montferrier was racing past Landes's house when she noticed a body lying face down in an ornamental pond. The botany teacher was atrociously burned, his eyes completely closed, his clothes reduced to black rags. It soon became clear Landes was not the only victim: four young children and two maids were also lying around the garden, pleading for water. The two maids were bleeding from their mouths and noses and shouting, 'We are going to die.'

For three hours Madame Montferrier and her husband tried to save their friends, only to see them die one by one. Another passer-by called Léon Chantel came in to help. He saw a man slumped beside the house, barely breathing:

> On the steps of this house, a man was rolling around, crying in agony. Madame Montferrier had not told me this was M. Landes . . . I went over to try and help him [but] his body was inert . . . He fell from the steps into the garden and died a moment later in my presence . . .

* Adventures which would pursue Hurard beyond the grave. According to friends, *le Beau Marius* died as he had lived – with three duels and several lawsuits still outstanding against his name. The most recent was a successful libel action brought by Victor Sévère, Radical Mayor of Fort-de-France. Hurard had been ordered to pay a staggering 3,000 francs in damages.

How heavy the grief, how deep the despair of those who escaped. As the storm clouds lifted that Thursday morning, Fernand Clerc made his way back into Saint-Pierre to look for survivors. All life and colour had drained from this most lively of cities; everywhere was black and grey. The cathedral where so many people had gathered that morning, sure of safety and salvation, had been crushed into a heap of stone as if struck by a giant fist.

Clerc took no pleasure in being proved right. For days he had been calling for a formal evacuation, and been rebuffed by Governor Mouttet and his own political allies. He had met a similar resistance that morning, as he rode down Rue Victor Hugo. 'Tongue or pen can never describe what I saw', Clerc said later. 'About me everywhere were my relatives and friends burning. I saw I could do no good – all were dead – not one alive.'

SIX

A MIRACLE

WHEN RESCUE parties finally reached Saint-Pierre, they came across a remarkable sight. One of the city's most famous landmarks, the stone statue of Mary, Our Lady of Safe Harbour, had been plucked from her marble plinth and thrown fifty feet across the Morne d'Orange. The Holy Mother had come to rest in a clearing directly above the road to Carbet. The statue weighed three tons. Mary's right hand was severed at the wrist; her patient, merciful face was burnt and black. People removed their hats as they passed, as if paying respects to yet another of the dead. Others saw the Holy Mother's deposal in even starker terms: as a sign that God had for ever abandoned the wretched, sinful people of Martinique.

There were more extraordinary scenes in the city itself, now turned into *une nécropole*. Pelée's aerial battering ram had reduced Saint-Pierre lighthouse to a heap of brick and wilted metal; Fontaine Agnès, that fabulous oddity, had lost its figurine-clad fountain. Amid the ruins, rescuers stumbled over ten-foot-long artillery guns, wrenched from their emplacements in the *Quartier du Fort*. They found stout old trees with upturned roots pointing in accusation towards Mont Pelée. Most unnerving of all was the cathedral graveyard, where funeral vaults had cracked open as if the Day of Judgement was upon them. Iron railings looped and festooned around the plots like strands of rope; six-inch slate slabs were torn apart as easily as scraps of paper. Many of Saint-Pierre's grandest families had sought eternal rest here, away from the common people. It may have been some comfort to the poor and excluded to know that in its final, cataclysmic moment, Pelée had treated them all in the same way.

Some curious objects had survived. As the two gentlemen of Grande Reduit had learnt, Pelée's deadly cloud followed an erratic path. In the wreck of the cathedral, rescuers found two silver chalices: the larger one contained the ashes of what had once been the Host. The smaller one was full of wafers, not one of which had been charred. When another team broke into the blackened vaults of the Bank of Martinique, they were amazed to find that every coin, bank note and paper security was still intact. In a house on Place Bertin, corked bottles of water were found pure and untainted; a row of long-stemmed clay pipes was retrieved, unmarked, from a chemist's counter. An equally curious discovery was made at the *Lycée*: to judge by the tattered remains of school books, the pupils had recently received a lesson on the destruction of Pompeii.

Among the first visitors that Friday morning was Martinique's Senator, Amédée Knight. Party quarrels were forgotten, not least because the Senator had himself lost several family members in the disaster, including his father. In an article written for Paris's *Le Figaro*, he described his astonishment at finding no trace of Saint-Pierre's market hall, built entirely of iron. 'We looked, searched, for two, three, four kilometres from its site. Nothing!' he wrote.

While thousands of humans had been incinerated, some insects had outsmarted the storm. George Kennan recalls entering a 'pretty, two-storey country house' in the outlying village of Trois Ponts or Three Bridges. 'We explored it from top to bottom', he writes, 'but found nothing alive in it except a huge black tarantula, four or five inches across . . .' Later, in Saint-Pierre, he spots more than a dozen ant colonies, 'building little mounds of volcanic ashes around their holes'. Life, of some sort, had begun again. Most animals had suffered the same fate as their masters. On a wealthy estate in the Roxelane Valley, Kennan found a wooden cage containing the remains of two pets: a mongoose and a small bantam chicken. 'Both

Rue Victor Hugo

had been killed, doubtless, by the heat of the blast; but the feathers of the chicken had not been scorched, and the cage, although covered with ashes, had not been broken or burned.'

But miraculous tales did not reassure families still living beneath Fire Mountain. In the weeks following 8 May, Pelée continued to puff out gas and ash. Thousands of people from nearby towns and villages like Grand' Rivière, Macouba and Basse-Pointe decided to flee. Every day, they could be seen heading south along the impeccable *routes coloniales*: barefoot men in rough cotton shirts and patched-up trousers, driving their oxen up ahead with sharp sticks; the women have pinned brightly coloured pictures of the Virgin Mary over their hearts to protect them from Pelée's anger. On their heads they carried all kinds of possessions: clothes and bedding, pots and pans, oddments of furniture. And beside this odd procession came little children, hugging pet chickens, kittens and puppies in their arms. Most of these people were making for Fort-de-France, where food was already in short supply. But anything, they believed, was better than staying under the shadow of Pelée. They walked in perfect silence, stopping only to whisper prayers at roadside shrines. 'All confidence in the future of Martinique has gone since Thursday's eruption', wrote Fernand Clerc. 'The populace are convinced that God is angry with the island and means to scourge it with fire and then sink it into the ocean. Unreasoning fear possesses all classes.'

Place Bertin

Not everyone felt that way, however. Looters and scavengers were soon scouring the streets of Saint-Pierre. Corpses were stripped of jewellery – a watch here, a necklace there – and family safes cleared of their heirlooms. Rescue teams were astonished to see thieves rowing off with armfuls of gold plate and antique china, their tiny *canots* bulging with stolen treasure. But in truth there was no one to stop them. For several days after the disaster, a state of near anarchy existed in Northern Martinique. 'As a result of the loss of the chief magistrate of the colony,' wrote Vicar-General Parel, 'and of so many other civil and military officials, the Government is in a state of disorganisation.'* By 19 May, matters had improved. A troop of *gendarmes* was patrolling the three-mile-long 'Zone of Annihilation', as it became known, and seventy people had been arrested.

Slowly, steadily, a proper list of casualties was drawn up. The number of dead was beyond comprehension: initial estimates went as high as 40,000, a quarter of the island's population. These were soon reduced, as a more sensible appraisal was made. The French volcanologist, Professor Alfred Lacroix, calculated that around 28,000 people had died on 8 May. His figures were based on ship manifests from the week leading up to the disaster. Although 1,500 or so of Saint-Pierre's 26,000 population had left by boat between 1 May and 7 May (and an unknown number by road), several thousand more had taken their place from Prêcheur and Morne Rouge.

Vicar-General Parel drew up his own 'moral balance sheet'. Twenty-four priests were missing; thirteen reverend Fathers of the order of Saint Esprit; twenty-eight Sisters of Saint Paul de Chartres and thirty-one Sisters of Saint Joseph de Cluny, as well as all but five teachers at Saint Pierre *Lycée*: 'Dignitaries, magistrates, merchants, honourable and Christian families all . . . fallen before the destructive scythe.' Some of the greatest crowds – perhaps up to three thousand people – were discovered around the cathedral. Black, white, coloured and Indian: all were there, 'GIVING THANKS AS DEATH CAME', as one American newspaper put it. Rescue teams agreed that no one beneath this cursed earth could have survived.

On the afternoon of Sunday 11 May, four days and three nights after Saint-Pierre was destroyed, a group of young men by the names of Léon Danglis, Georges Hilaire and Maurice Nirdé were walking through the ghostly streets when they heard a voice crying for help. It came from a pile of ruins next to the theatre, which they

---

* But not enough to cancel the second round of voting in Southern Martinique. The 11 May poll led, as predicted, to victory for Radical candidate Homère Clément.

recognised as Saint-Pierre jail. According to a report written by Father Jean Mary, parish priest of Morne Rouge, the disembodied Creole became evermore insistent: '*Messiés! Messiés!*' Gentlemen! Gentlemen!

Scrabbling through ash and rubble, the three men tracked this voice down to a solitary yard at the back of the prison. Beneath them was a small concrete shell or *cachot*, coated with ash yet apparently untouched by fire.

> – *Messiés! sauvez-moi pour l'amou Bon Die* . . .
> – Gentlemen! Save me! For the Love of God . . .
> – . . . *Vini sauve un pauv prisonnier!*
> – . . . Come and save a poor prisoner!

Someone was inside – he must have heard them talking . . .

The prison door was fixed with two heavy padlocks, the badge of solitary confinement. With great excitement, Danglis, Hilaire and Nirdé smashed the locks and dragged out a half-dead figure. He was a man in his mid-twenties, heavily built, and with the worst burns they had ever seen.

> – *Messiés, moin pas save ca qui rivé oti toute*
>   *mounn la geole* . . .
> – Gentlemen, I do not know what has happened,
>   or where the other prisoners have gone . . .

The prisoner was babbling breathlessly. It was clear he had no idea of the calamity which had overcome Saint-Pierre. Reluctantly, they told him the truth.

> – *Pa ni geole, tout Saint-Pierre brûle.*
> – There is no more jail. All of Saint-Pierre has burnt
>   down . . .
> – *Alors, Messié, conduis-moin, s'ou plaît au*

Prêcheur, dans famille moin.
 − Then take me to Prêcheur, to my family.
 − *Pa ni Prêcheur, pa ni Carbet, pa ni enien . . .*
 − There is no more Prêcheur, no more Carbet,
   no more anything . . .

At this point, Father Mary takes over the story.

His first encounter with the unnamed prisoner is at 6.30pm that Sunday evening. Returning home after prayers, Father Mary finds an excited mob on his doorstep. He has a visitor. 'A man of about twenty-five years', he writes, '[is] artlessly retelling his story to the crowd which surrounds him.' Father Mary hears this man is from Saint-Pierre jail, and has been brought to Morne Rouge, some four steep miles away, by his three rescuers. Further questioning establishes that the man 'covered all over in burns' is known as Louis Cyparis (*née* Sylbaris), a labourer from Prêcheur, a 'sometime sailor, sometime *cultivateur*'.

Steering the poor, confused man indoors, Father Mary listened carefully to his fantastic tale. On the morning of Thursday 8 May, Sylbaris explained, he had been lying in his solitary cell, waiting to be fed. What followed had the beauty of a miracle. The priest continues:

> It was eight o'clock, he said, no one had yet come to give me my daily food ration when suddenly an appalling noise broke out, everyone was shouting 'Help! I'm burning! I'm dying!'
>
> After about five minutes no one was crying any more, apart from me . . . smoke was rushing in through the little window in my door. This smoke burned so much that for a quarter of an hour, I leaped about from right to left, anywhere to avoid it.
>
> After a quarter of an hour, there was a ghastly silence. I listened, I cried out for someone to come and save me, no one replied. All of Saint-Pierre must have been destroyed in the earthquake, in the fire . . .

It was an extraordinary tale, too good to be true. It was impossible to believe anyone could have escaped Pelée's lethal cloud, let alone someone so close to its main impact. Yet Father Mary fell back on the evidence of his own eyes. The man facing him was horribly burned across his back and legs, his feet and hands. He was fortunate to be alive. Sylbaris's wounds appeared to confirm his dramatic story; the priest could well imagine how the young man had leapt around his cell, as clouds of hot gas seeped through a tiny grille. His merciful escape was a sign of God's mercy, of hope beyond boundless sorrow.

After tending to Sylbaris's wounds, Father Mary passed his new charge to the Holy Sisters of his parish church, *Notre Dame de la Délivrance*. The next day, Sylbaris was installed in a wooden house on Morne Rouge's main street, where he was nursed by an elderly woman and visited regularly by the astonished priest. So debilitating were the injuries, that Father Mary worried whether his patient would ever make a full recovery. Day by day however the prisoner's strength returned, and with it an eternal gratitude to those who had saved him. Father Mary concludes his report with the news that Sylbaris has asked to become his domestic servant – in recognition of all the kindness he has received.

News of Sylbaris's adventures spread rapidly.

Within days, Morne Rouge was swamped by journalists, diplomats and the plain curious, all eager to see and hear from the Lone Survivor of Saint-Pierre. American reporters questioned him repeatedly, trying to find loopholes in his story. One French journalist, Jean Hess, was incredulous: How, he asked, could anyone have survived the asphyxiating gas which engulfed the city? 'All those who were breathing; all, absolutely all of those who lived in Saint-Pierre died immediately', he wrote. 'No cellar could have sheltered any creature whatever – rat, dog, human – because every cellar was penetrated by the gas.'

Hess went further. Ludger Sylbaris was a fraud, a trickster who had gulled Father Mary and the Holy Sisters of Morne Rouge. It was impossible to believe that a man so badly burned had been able to stagger from Saint-Pierre to Morne Rouge, an uphill walk of several miles. Most likely, he was a common thief who had been scavenging in the empty houses of Saint-Pierre when Pelée erupted. The whole absurd story of his incarceration had been dreamt up to avoid being arrested:

> The actions of Auguste Sybaris [sic] seem to me like those of a thief who, surprised by the fire while trying to crack a safe, wanted to explain away his burns . . . The negro imagination turned all these scraps into the extraordinary history which we have just read . . .

Hess's indignant report had a certain circumstantial truth: looters and pilferers were busy in Saint-Pierre before 8 May. But he could not explain how Sylbaris had managed to get into his solitary *cachot* to start with: a trick which would have foxed the Great Houdini. Nor could he account for those singular burn marks across Sylbaris's body.

A more measured account came from that industrious American, George Kennan. Passing through Morne Rouge, he paid a visit to Sylbaris's lodgings. The man whom he had earlier dismissed as 'the product of some newspaper man's imagination' was, in fact, revoltingly real:

> We found him in one of the bare, fly-infested rooms of an abandoned wooden dwelling-house on the main street, which the curé had turned into a sort of lazaret . . . the air of the small, hot room was so heavy and foul with the offensive odour of his neglected burns that I could hardly force myself to breathe it. He was sitting stark naked, on the dirty striped mattress of a small wooden cot, with a bloody sheet thrown over his head like an Arab burnoose and gathered in about the loins. He had been more frightfully burned, I think, than any man I had ever seen . . .

At Father Mary's prompting, Sylbaris repeated his story. A few more details were added – the fact he was wearing a hat, shirt and trousers at the moment of annihilation – but in essence, his original testimony was unchanged. Once again, Kennan was struck by the perplexing order of injuries inflicted by Pelée. Sylbaris's clothing had not caught fire – yet his back was severely burned under his shirt. A mixture of hot air and fine ashes had crept in through his door grating, yet 'he heard no noise, saw no fire, and smelled nothing except "what he thought was his own body burning" '. The intense heat lasted for a few moments, during which time Sylbaris held his breath.

Kennan's methodical questions – and Sylbaris's detailed replies – were greatly appreciated by scientists who came to study Pelée. They helped form an accurate picture of what happened at ten to eight that Thursday morning. Sylbaris had not smelt any perceptible odour of gas or sulphur; the molten dust 'came in through the door grating without any noticeable rush or blast'. Beyond that, he had seen nothing of any interest: no explosion, no fire.

Newspapers continued to scoff. The *New York World* remarked that even though Sylbaris's yarn was a howling fake, it was 'so picturesque, that it would be strange if it were not incorporated in the permanent records of the disaster'. But Kennan and Father Mary were insistent. 'He answered all our questions simply and quietly,' writes Kennan, 'without making any attempt to exaggerate or to heighten the effect of his narrative by embroidering it with fanciful and marvellous details.' Before leaving Morne Rouge, the American journalist and his colleague A.F. Jaccaci arranged for fresh supplies of aseptic bandages, linseed oil, lime water and phenolic acid to be sent to the festering patient. Returning several weeks later, Kennan reported happily that 'there seemed every probability that he would live'.

Which is where Ludger Sylbaris, *aka* Louis Auguste Cyparis, once more slips from view. If there was another side to the Sylbaris story, then he chose not to share it. As the newspapers predicted, his picaresque tale soon took a prominent place among the myths and mysteries surrounding Saint-Pierre, but not before one final attempt was made to untangle fact and fiction.

The French geologist Alfred Lacroix weighed up the evidence in his 1904 study of *Mont Pelée and its Eruptions*, and concluded that Sylbaris was . . . telling the truth. His argument was threefold:

i) Contrary to Jean Hess's claims, Sylbaris *was* a resident of Saint-Pierre jail on the night of Wednesday 7 May: a fact confirmed, in the absence of any legal records, by the President of Martinique's Court of Appeal, M. Lacourne.

ii) That the *petite* grille in Sylbaris's cell faced south, 'that is to say, in the opposite direction to the volcano'. This meant it had escaped the direct, blistering force of Pelée's eruption. (It may also explain why Sylbaris failed to hear Pelée's opening fusillade.)

iii) That, despite everything, Sylbaris's *cachot* was still intact. The prisoner had been saved by its stout wooden door and thick stone walls.

Professor Lacroix concluded: 'There is, therefore, nothing improbable in the idea that a man locked up in this little cell was able to survive, because he did not receive the direct shock of the dust cloud: the ash and burning vapour only reached him in small quantities and without much force.' And that, it seemed, was that. The extravagant claims made for Sylbaris by Barnum and Bailey – 'The Only Living Object that survived in the Silent City of Death' – had proved to be correct.

Well, almost.

The Caribbean had been hit by two volcanic disasters in two days: first, Saint Vincent, and now Saint-Pierre. Relief ships were dispatched from every island, relaying food and basic supplies to their

stricken neighbours. On the morning of Friday 9 May a Danish ship, the *Valkyrien*, made a brief stop at Place Bertin, but the heat was too intense for further exploration. The *Rubis* was busy delivering supplies of flour, biscuits, beans and cod to survivors in Carbet and Case-Pilote. One of its passengers, a French official called M. Lange, did manage to set foot in Saint-Pierre, but added little to what Prosecutor Lubin had seen the previous afternoon.

The first proper chance to explore came on Saturday 10 May. It was a clear day: the fog of ashes which had shrouded Martinique since Thursday morning had begun to lift. But far from restoring this island to its habitual beauty, daylight served only to expose the most unspeakable horrors; to unveil sights which would derange the reason of all who saw them. Among the first to arrive that day was Britain's Vice-Consul in Guadeloupe, J.E. Devaux. His handwritten dispatches are held at the Public Record Office at Kew. Reading through them today, one gets a sense of the claustrophobic dread which must have overcome the search party as it neared Saint-Pierre.

Several miles from shore, Devaux's senses are assaulted by the smell of corpses – 'a horrible, nauseating odour, impossible to describe or forget'. But an even more repulsive sight awaits him. As the pale grey outline of Martinique steals into view, Devaux notices dozens of bloated and disfigured bodies in the water, their entrails eagerly picked over by seabirds and ravenous sharks. If there is a Hell upon this Earth, then surely he is about to enter it. Furious blasts of wind smite the Vice-Consul's face: now hot, now cold, followed by waves of stinging ash and mud. Soon they pass Prêcheur, and the magical city of Saint-Pierre, Paris of the Caribbean, is before them:

> The whole scene was one of the most utter desolation. Right and left stretched long rows of ruined walls plastered to one tint by the awful volcano. Mud, rising amid heaps of volcanic matter, and charred and twisted trunks of giant trees. Not a sound was heard from that vast, hideous, dull, grey amphitheatre of death.

Worse was to come. When Devaux lands at Place Bertin, the sheer scale of death and obliteration overpowers him. The traditionally staid language and metronomic rhythm of diplomatic dispatches collapses completely:

> . . . and then the full realisation of this most gigantic of world misfortunes was realised. It was not merely the silent shattered remnants of walls of the once beautiful and prosperous city but the

frightful ubiquity of death in its most hideous form by fire. Every-where dead bodies met the sight; muscular negroes, delicate wo-men, tender children twisted in shapes of indescribable agony, most with the face downward as though they had been smitten down instantly or had sought to bar ingress to the asphyxiating fumes.

In many places tens and scores of victims could be counted in a single mass of intertwined bodies eloquently telling of the awful death agony . . . So hideously transformed are these poor human remains that of all the tens of thousands not one has been identified. Over all towered Pelée, its head enwrapped in clouds and still expelling vapours and ashes punctuated sometimes with huge stones . . .

Devaux had another difficult task to perform.

A British family, the Japps, had been reported missing. Mr Japp was the British Consul to Martinique; he had lived in Saint-Pierre since 1897 with his wife and two daughters. Devaux was ordered to find their bodies.★ A lengthy search brings no success: the Vice-Consul can find no sign of Mr Japp or his family. 'Hours of search

---

★ The only record of James Japp's life in Martinique is a series of peevish letters and telegrams to the Foreign Office in London. Most of this correspondence concerns Consul Japp's miserable allowances: the bane of Foreign Office outposts through the ages. Our Man in Saint-Pierre is particularly upset at having to advance money to impecunious Britons from his own pocket: 'The constant call of distressed subjects for a little assistance forms an item which I cannot very well afford under present circumstances, but which I cannot refuse', he writes on 1 June 1900.

Japp's campaign reaches its climax with a personal letter to the Prime Minister, Lord Salisbury, supplemented with testimonies from happy, spendthrift subjects. No reply is recorded.

Mr Japp's death is announced in similarly terse fashion, in a cable dated 10 May:

VOLCANIC ERUPTION DESTROYED SAINT-PIERRE + NO NEWS CONSUL JAPP

Beneath it, a neat business card is attached with a rusting pin. It belongs to Alex Japp, 156 Hainault Road, Leytonstone. A mandarin hand casually adds: *Mr Japp's brother has been making inquiries at the office as to whether we have any information, and we ought to clear up the doubt . . .*

failed to permit identification of the British Consulate', he wrote. 'So hideously transformed are these poor human remains that of all the tens of thousands, not one has been identified.'

Saint-Pierre left Devaux in a desolate mood – although not desolate enough to forgo an application for his late colleague's job. The last three paragraphs of his dispatch are devoted to puffing his own achievements, and a request to 'take into favourable consideration my respectful application for the Consulship of Fort-de-France'. Like ants making fresh homes in volcanic dust, Devaux showed a fine grasp of life's imperatives.*

Yet the Vice-Consul had drawn attention, once again, to one of Pelée's greatest puzzles. Many of the bodies he encountered were lying face downward, or in ruptures of agony. Had these people died in the initial gas cloud, or had they perished during the fire storm which came in its wake? Nicola Parravacino, the Italian Consul in Barbados, also visited Saint-Pierre that day. He was searching for his daughter. Sig. Parravacino noticed how 'a very large number of bodies had burst at the abdomen; all spongy, cellular tissues were greatly distended, and many skulls had parted at the sutures, without any indication of external injury'. The Consul suggested these grisly sights may have come from 'a sudden removal of atmospheric pressure'. Sig. Parravacino never found his daughter.

There was another puzzle too. No lava flows had been seen on 8 May. Instead, several eyewitnesses had reported seeing sparkly, twinkling lights inside the towering clouds which rolled down Mont Pelée. It was as if the avalanche was *glowing*. The key to these mysteries would emerge in months to come, as volcanologists examined Fire Mountain in unprecedented detail.

Before this work could begin, Pelée gave islanders another reminder of its might. At around 5.30am on Tuesday 20 May the mountain

---

* A copy of Devaux's letter, with its graphic first-hand account of Saint-Pierre, was passed to the Royal Society. The final three paragraphs were unaccountably left out.

erupted once more, sending a gigantic cloud of incandescent ash onto Saint-Pierre. The whole island shook: 'Everyone thought their final hour had come', said one witness. In Saint-Pierre itself there was nothing left to destroy save for the cathedral's second tower, which crumbled into dust. As on 8 May, the dark clouds spread as far south as Fort-de-France. When he arrived there on 22 May, Jean Hess noted how 'all the food tastes of ashes; on all the furniture, on the beds, on the curtains, there are ashes and always ashes'.

Hess also relates the story of a sea captain who arrived in Saint-Pierre on the night of 24 May. Having been at sea for almost a month, the captain knew nothing of Mont Pelée, or Saint-Pierre's sudden disappearance. As a result, when the captain awoke the next morning, he was convinced they had landed on the wrong island. Slowly, the truth was revealed to him:

> The darkness lifted. The land appeared more clearly. And the Captain no longer asked whether he was dreaming, but rather if he was mad. The tip of the island, he recognised that, there was no reason to doubt it . . . But in the place of Saint-Pierre, there was no longer Saint-Pierre . . . And a scene of terrible devastation was emerging from the shadows. He saw the ravaged mornes. He saw the ruins . . . And the mountain which continued to smoke and to grumble. And he understood. And he set his boat to Fort-de-France, where he arrived 'sick with emotion'.

The last of Saint-Pierre left an overwhelming impression on all who saw it.

Some found traces of God in the sepulchral ruins. Others found no God at all. One of the most haunting *rêveries* came from Remy Saint-Maurice, a feature writer for *L'Illustration*. As he walked through the city streets, past skeletal shops and churches, his mind turned to Empires: their rise and their fall. Saint-Pierre seemed as old as the Roman Forum or the temples of Athens. 'For how many centuries has this town been dead?' he asks. 'Does the debris not already seem like the ancient relics of a civilisation from before the Caribs?' Saint-Pierre was a modern Pompeii, a spectacle of 'horrible beauty'.

This hallucinatory moment seemed to hold time future as well as time past. It was as if Saint-Maurice had stumbled several centuries into the future, to a time when France's Empire has disappeared, like so many before it. To a time when the Imperial frenzies of flag and drum, trumpet and tricolour were long forgotten. He mourns the people of Saint-Pierre. But he also grieves for the totems of French power, so casually erased by brute nature: 'Only a solitary piece of the cathedral's façade allows one to guess that the city was built by Europeans – most probably the French – in the last 250 years . . .'

Saint-Maurice was haunted by another fear. One too foul to mention within earshot of his Martinican hosts. For all his eloquence, he knew that Parisians were already bored of Saint-Pierre. 'I know the soul of my compatriots too well', he writes, 'to doubt that Martinique is already "Old Hat". A loss of three or four hundred million [francs]; a shattered colonial elite – these are not subjects which impress Paris for too long.'

On this count, at least, Saint-Maurice was right.

SEVEN

THE GREAT SECRET

NEWS OF Saint-Pierre's tragic end took several days to pass around the world, transmitted by telegraph and telephone. Yet scientists soon learnt that this natural cataclysm had passed *through* the earth itself within seconds, sending shock waves right across the planet. Magnetic needles from Athens to Honolulu twitched furiously for several hours after the eruptions of 8 May and 20 May; electromagnetic disturbances were even felt at the Zi-ka-Wei Observatory in China, whose instruments were 'agitated' for around eight hours after the first blast. The Chinese episode seemed yet more remarkable when geologists realised that Zi-ka-Wei was on the meridian directly opposite Saint-Pierre; that is, halfway around the world from Martinique. By contrast, Krakatau's eruption in 1883 had barely troubled the station's instruments at all.

No seismic disturbances were recorded on 8 May, either on Martinique or elsewhere. What most intrigued observers were the beautiful cloudy afterglows generated by the volcanic dust from Mont Pelée and Saint Vincent's Soufrière.* Though less intense than those of Krakatau, these nomadic clouds of pale orange and ruby red, brilliant pink and creamy yellow, were seen right across the world. They would emerge soon after sunset, throwing a bright

---

* Volcanologists today believe Soufrière was the dominant influence. Its ash clouds contained more sulphur than Pelée's and were thus more liable to produce atmospheric effects. There were also at least nineteen other volcanic eruptions in the first six months of 1902. Later cloud formations may also have been influenced by the awakening of Santa Maria in Guatemala on 24 October 1902 – an eruption twice as powerful as that of Mont Pelée.

loom of light over the evening sky. Sometimes a wondrously vivid lilac shade would appear, at other times a bold, emerald green. There were strange visual effects: one visitor saw five great 'shadow beams' of purple light bearing down upon Martinique, like giant pillars propping up the sky. Another, in Morges, Switzerland, saw a radiant disc of fine yellow-white light above the sunset, like an enamelled plate.

Apart from their eerie beauty, the afterglows gave scientists a chance to trace the path of Pelée's dust cloud. By late June, it had graced skies above Los Angeles and Bombay, Berlin and Milan. So brilliant was the spectacle in Switzerland that it appeared 'as if the whole of the west of Switzerland was on fire and the flames reflected in the sky'. On 22 June, Professor A.S. Herschel came to a similar conclusion as he watched the night skies over southern England fill with 'an almost terrifying resemblance to [a] reflection in the sky of an immense distant conflagration'. It was as if these clouds carried a faint memory of the destruction which had brought them into being.

At their height, Pelée's afterglows spiralled thirty or perhaps forty miles into the sky. On this count, Krakatau proved the more powerful force. Ash clouds from the 1883 blast had swirled around the world at higher altitudes and faster speeds. While Pelée's glows took ten days to reach Honolulu after 8 May, Krakatau's ashen clouds had arrived at the same spot in just twelve days, despite having to cover twice the distance. Yet there was no doubting Pelée's terrible impact. Spectacular light shows continued well into August and September, and amateur scientists were still reporting kaleidoscopic glows over Boston, Baltimore, New York and Philadelphia in mid-November.

Scientists were determined to put their observations to good use. For the first time, they could study the global impact of two near-simultaneous eruptions in the same volcanic chain. There was a striking synchronicity between the twin peaks: Pelée's second explosion on 20 May had been prefigured once again by Saint

Vincent's Soufrière, which had erupted two days earlier. Geologists were also intrigued by reports of glowing ash clouds and the marked absence of lava flows. No one had ever heard of a volcano behaving like *that* before. Mont Pelée had catapulted volcanology from antiquarian obscurity into a subject of urgent, worldwide importance. New theories and new categories were needed to explain the disaster, if only to help try and prevent it from happening again.

The terrible events of 1902 also drew dozens of journalists to the tiny Caribbean island. There were quick, lurid turnarounds like William G. Garesché's *Complete Story of the Martinique and St Vincent Horrors* and Frederick Royce's *The Burning of Saint-Pierre*. Royce enticed readers with:

A GRAPHIC ACCOUNT OF THE GREATEST
VOLCANIC DISASTER IN THE HISTORY OF THE WORLD

Garesché went straight to the point:

DEATH! DEATH! EVERYWHERE!

Galvanised by such thoughts – although more delicately expressed – rival teams of geologists began to gather in Paris, London and New York. Each team was keen to examine Mont Pelée and Soufrière at close quarters. The Americans were first off the mark. With great verve and *oompah*, the *National Geographic Magazine* dispatched 'the most important and best equipped Commission ever sent out to study volcanic action'. For once, their boast was justified. When the US cruiser *Dixie* left New York early on Wednesday 14 May, its cabins held some of America's finest geologists: Dr Robert T. Hill of the US Geological Survey, Dr Thomas A. Jaggar of Harvard and Dr Edmund O. Hovey of the American Museum of Natural History. They were joined by Carsten Borchgrevink, a Norwegian explorer best known for the singular achievement of enduring an entire winter at the South Pole. While there, he had seen two of the world's most southerly volcanoes: Mount Erebus and Mount Terror. *National Geographic* had no doubt about the difficulties their team would face. 'Theories abound as to the cause of volcanic action,' it boomed, 'but of causes we know little.' A state of affairs which, it confidently believed, would soon change. This would be the most comprehensive volcanic study ever attempted.

Another formidable American was also heading for Martinique. Angelo Heilprin, forty-nine-year-old President of the Geographical Society of Philadelphia, was renowned for his exotic – if somewhat reckless – field trips to Alaska and Mexico, Morocco and the Arctic Circle. While most academics preferred the comforts of a lecture hall, Heilprin seemed happiest when observing a volcano or peering over the edge of a yawning ravine. The son of Hungarian and Polish immigrants, Heilprin was a man of unusual talents. Aside from his academic career at Yale, he was a self-taught landscape painter and mountaineer. Quieter moments were spent dreaming up household inventions: in 1882, the Geology Professor patented a device which turned the leaves of music on a piano; eighteen years later, he won a second patent for inventing a 'ventilating railroad-car window'. Shrewd, tenacious and with a taste for high adventure, Heilprin found it impossible to resist the lure of Pelée. Newspaper reports of renewed volcanic activity stoked his interest, and on Sunday 18 May he left New York for Martinique on board the cruiser *Fontabelle*.

The energetic American would find a kindred spirit in Tempest Anderson, Britain's most intrepid amateur volcanologist and full-time eye surgeon. For his latest picturesque diversion, Anderson was joined by John S. Flett, a member of the Royal Society. Most of their time would be spent on Saint Vincent, collecting details on Soufrière. But the two men were also intrigued by Pelée's death-dealing clouds. Anderson may have been a humble amateur, but in one respect – the art of photography – he was an acknowledged expert. During his travels, Anderson captured every distinctive lava flow and crater formation, and was keen for Mont Pelée to join his collection.

The third team, led by Professor Alfred Lacroix of the French Academy of Sciences, took a less frenetic approach. They left Saint-Nazaire on 9 June and arrived in Fort-de-France two weeks later. Like the Americans and Britons before him, Lacroix was struck by the awful sadness which hung over Martinique. 'I brought back an unforgettable impression,' he wrote later, 'not just of grandiose and terrifying phenomena, but of the misfortunes and tragic spectacles I witnessed.' An unshakeable despair overcame the islanders after 8 May, as if they had been seized by a collective nervous breakdown. When Pelée erupted a second time on 20 May, hundreds fled to Trinidad, Saint Lucia and Guadeloupe, fearing their own island was about to sink into the sea. Saint-Pierre, that rough and rowdy celebration of French power, of French *permanence*, had vanished so quickly that it seemed to undermine people's faith in the entire colonial enterprise. An illusion built up laboriously over several centuries, through the daily incantation of words and phrases, prayers and protocols, had disappeared with alarming ease.

Out of this collapse came a new and bitter sense of the colonial trap; the illusion revealed in all its distasteful, exploitative reality. Yet Pelée was to impart a more hopeful lesson too. Over time, the disaster would help Martinicans grasp what literary critic Edward Said has called the 'initial insight': that moment of illumination when a colonised people realises, for the first time, that it is being held prisoner within its own land.

In public, at least, the French authorities did their duty. A memorial service was held in Paris on 18 May; flags were hung at half-mast and books of condolence were opened in every town hall. A public fund was set up, bolstered by a personal donation of 20,000 francs from President Émile Loubet and 500 francs from each Cabinet minister. Within a month, the appeal fund had reached 1.15 million francs. For a brief period, the tragedy of Martinique touched every soul in France. Grief was greatest in western cities like Brest, Nantes and Bordeaux, the original homes of some of Martinique's oldest families. The Minister for Colonies, Albert Décrais, declared: 'Never has the *Métropole* felt with such force the strong ties which have bound us for centuries to these old and loyal Antillean colonies.' Amid dozens of condolence letters in the colonial archive at Aix-en-Provence, there are curious, heartfelt offers of help: M. G. Gadenne volunteers a choral work, 'The Martyrs of Martinique'; the Society of Cobblers donates boxloads of hardy footwear; the Eiffel Tower theatre raffles two seats for its summer *spectacle*.

But as Remy Saint-Maurice had predicted, public interest in Saint-Pierre soon waned. Politicians were distracted by their own selfish concerns: despite winning a bigger majority, Waldeck-Rousseau stepped down on 4 June and was replaced by Émile Combes, a devout enemy of the Catholic Church. Senator Combes immediately launched into a fresh round of anti-clerical measures: crucifixes were torn down from law courts, around 20,000 men were thrown out of religious orders and 10,000 church schools shut down. Martinique's distant cries for help barely registered. It was not until 8 July, a full two months after Pelée's eruption, that the Chamber of Deputies voted through a one-off credit of two million francs for the devastated island. The first formal debate was held in December. American journalists in Paris were amazed by this apparent indifference. 'Paris seems to care little about stricken Martinique', wrote one on 16 May. 'The people flock to their usual resorts, attend the races, fill the theaters, none of which have been closed; no "extras" have been issued, and there is no demand for them.'

Naturally, stories about heartless European colonists (were there any other kind?) went down well in the New World. They also compared unfavourably with America's own vigorous response to the disaster. Within days of Pelée's eruption, President Theodore Roosevelt had pledged $500,000 in immediate aid. Congress haggled him down to $200,000, but a standard had been set.* Roosevelt's generosity was soon repeated across the United States,

---

* European leaders followed in their own fashion. King Edward VII and King Victor Emmanuel III of Italy sent $5,000 each; Pope Leo XIII donated $20,000.

boosted by lurid press accounts of 'the Caribbean Pompeii'. In Philadelphia alone $16,000 was collected in one week. According to France's Vice-Consul in the city, donations reached such a prodigious level that much of the money had to be given back. Yet dollar bills kept rolling in: by August, the city's Martinique surplus had climbed to $40,000.

Roosevelt's impulsive action allowed the cruisers racing south to stock up with incredible amounts of food: enough, it seemed, to feed the people of Martinique several times over. Geologists on board the *Dixie* shared their cabins with, among other things:

65,000	pounds of bacon
516	gallons of vinegar
1,468	can openers
995,500	pounds of rice
14,400	boxes of safety matches
4,800	tins of beef and chicken soup

Americans were so generous, in fact, that French officials began to suspect an ulterior motive. Martinique was within America's sphere of influence; perhaps food parcels were Roosevelt's crafty way of worming America into the hearts of disaffected Martinicans. France's Ambassador to Washington, Jules Cambon, certainly thought so. In a dispatch to his Foreign Ministry, dated 14 May 1902, Cambon interpreted Roosevelt's $200,000 aid package as part of this grand conspiracy:

> One can only assume that the generosity of the American authorities . . . was more or less inspired by the spirit of hegemony which drives this country in respect of all the colonies of the New World, whether or not they are still controlled by a European power . . .

But France was doing a pretty good job of alienating its Martinican subjects without any help from America. Mont Pelée had inflicted the worst destruction on a French territory for over a century, the island was slipping into anarchy – and yet Paris barely seemed to notice. A ministerial visit was cancelled. '[M. Décrais] had decided to go himself to Martinique to distribute emergency supplies and the necessary consolations', explained the *Journal Officiel*, 'but the pressing duties of his position, the importance of the measures to be taken, which required his presence in the capital, triumphed over his ardent desire.' In his place, Décrais sent Maurice Bloch, a senior civil servant at the Ministry of Colonies. By all accounts a cold and rather pompous figure, Bloch was told to take charge of the relief operation. To this end, he left Brest on 11 May with half a million francs in cash – a gesture greeted with great enthusiasm in Fort-de-France. Perhaps the *Métropole* was going to match American *largesse* after all.

Martinique's political leaders might have been less welcoming if they had known about Bloch's extraordinary terms of employment. He was to be paid 200 francs per day; a staggering amount of money to the people of Martinique. Bloch was supported by two secretaries, engaged for a further 80 francs per day. If one adds officers on board the cruiser *D'Assas*, the daily salary bill for this cavalcade came to over 350 francs – enough to pay the wages of some three hundred plantation workers. Assuming a mission of around six weeks, the French authorities would be left with a bill of around 15,000 francs. To compound the offence, Bloch's salary – and those of his colleagues – was to be paid out of the 500,000-franc *crédit*. If Martinicans wanted further proof of France's casual indifference to their fate, then they would find it in the dour, well-endowed features of Maurice Bloch.

Imperial rivalries seeped into the scientists' work too.

First to arrive, on Wednesday 21 May, were the *National Geographic* team on board the *Dixie*. Like detectives at a crime scene, Hovey, Hill and Jaggar wanted to examine every detail of the disaster. They began by calculating the exact dimensions of Pelée's 'zone of annihilation' with a measuring device called a planimeter. Several days of trotting up *mornes* and down *vallées* produced an astonishing figure: eight square miles of earth had been completely razed, along with every living creature within it. A further thirty-two square miles beyond that were badly charred. The geologists noticed a sharp demarcation line at the edge of this zone, as if Pelée's dust cloud had been cut short with a knife. 'When we first arrived at Martinique', wrote Edmund Hovey, 'the line between the scorched and unscorched areas was strikingly sharp, and was still very noticeable six or seven weeks later. In many places the line of demarcation passed through single trees, leaving one side scorched and brown, while the other side remained as green as if no eruption had occurred.'

Hovey was also intrigued by a supernaturally large boulder – as big as a two-storey house – which he found lying on a mud plain north of Saint-Pierre. The rock remained in a near-molten state, more than four weeks after Pelée's last eruption. 'When I inspected this block on 25 June,' Hovey went on, 'I found it too hot on the surface to bear the hand upon it for long at a time, the great mass was cracked in several directions and steam and sulphurous gases were emanating from the cracks.' Smaller versions of this rock were scattered around the outskirts of Saint-Pierre, measuring from one inch to three feet across. Hovey called them 'bread crust bombs' on account of their gnarled, crusty surface.

Toiling away in their thick cotton shirts, bow ties and maroon braces, the Americans must have looked an odd sight. Now and then a deep bass *grondement* rolled around the distant hills, a reminder that Pelée's tantrum was far from over. Venturing into Saint-Pierre, Hovey and Hill found piles of bodies massed around road junctions. The tattered remains of election posters – VOTE CLERC! VOTE PERCIN! – flapped uselessly from nearby walls. People had died at their breakfast tables, hands welded to sugar bowls and coffee cups as if in a *tableau vivant*. It was enough to try the reason of any man. Despite this, the two Americans deduced that Pelée's tempest had swept across Saint-Pierre in a roughly north to south direction, like a tornado. Houses which stood in the way – those facing east to west – had been flattened, while those pointing the same way (like Sylbaris's prison cell) were left relatively intact.

Then there was the question of temperature. To judge by the weirdly deformed wine glasses and perfume bottles found in people's homes, the blasts and subsequent fire storms had been hot enough to melt glass (1,292 degrees fahrenheit). On the other hand, Saint-Pierre's telephone cables remained intact, suggesting they had not been quite warm enough to melt copper (1,981 degrees fahrenheit). Volcanologists now suspect these figures may have been exaggerated, either due to lack of knowledge or faulty instruments. Some of the more spectacular examples of Pelée's handiwork however are on display today in Saint-Pierre museum. Shorn of their history now, they look like surreal works of art: a box of nails fused together in rusty strands; a bowl of rice, grains as black as beetles; a four-foot-high church bell, massively dented, as if a giant's thumb has been pressed against it.

Remains of Sugar Refinery

Hovey, Hill and Jaggar collected a great deal of data on the volcano's physical impact. Yet they were unable to solve the mystery of *how* Pelée had erupted. It was as if the mountain had engulfed them in dense cloud, hiding all but its most obvious features. Before leaving Martinique, however, the Americans did experience a little of what Pierrotins had endured in their final days. Edmund Hovey was exploring the *Lac des Palmistes* when he was overcome by gusts of steam and sulphur:

> The sulphur gases made the atmosphere difficult to breathe, but the most uncomfortable sensation was due to the irritation caused by the fine, angular dust getting into the respiratory passage and the eyes. Such a mixture, raised to a high temperature, and containing a large amount of dust and a considerable percentage of sulphur gases, would be almost instantaneously fatal to life.

Robert Hill's encounter was more alarming. Visiting Morne Rouge on Tuesday 27 May, he saw a minor version of the 'glowing cloud' which had rolled over Saint-Pierre several weeks earlier. All at once, the sky above his head turned into a 'black sheet':

> Through this sheet, which extended a distance of ten miles from the crater, vivid and awful lightning-like bolts flashed with alarming frequency. They followed distinct paths of ignition, but were different from lightning, in that the bolts were horizontal, not perpendicular . . . This is a most important observation, and it explains in part the awful catastrophe. This phenomenon is entirely new in volcanic history.

Yet Hill was no nearer to explaining how these bolts had been produced. He thought Pelée's blast had come from a new volcanic vent halfway down the mountain's southern flank. From there, it had spread in 'radial directions' over the northern *Quartier du Fort*. It was a plausible theory, and one which squared with the pattern of damage across Saint-Pierre. But as Hill conceded, the 'great secret' of Pelée had eluded his team: its mysterious blast had no name and no identity.

Angelo Heilprin was determined to do better. Soon after arriving in Fort-de-France on 25 May, the adventurer–cum–academic announced his intention to do battle with Pelée. Only a direct encounter, he reasoned, would banish the mystery and fearful superstition surrounding *La Montagne*. Heilprin's brisk, no-nonsense approach extended to Martinique itself, a land of 'decadent misfortunes'. Not for him the lush, overripe prose poetry of Lafcadio Hearn; such romantic reveries were an 'extreme idealisation' of reality. Far from despoiling an island paradise, Pelée had merely exposed the squalor beneath its surface. 'The island before us', wrote Heilprin, 'was not a tropical paradise, but a withered piece of the earth that seemed to be just emerging from chaos. Everything was grey and brown, sunk behind a cloud which only the mind could penetrate; there was nothing that appealed restfully to the eye.'

Heilprin had little interest in Martinique's black workers or mulatto *bourgeoisie*. As for the whites, they were crude 'points of reference' in this alien landscape: objects of pity who promenaded around the *Savane* in vain pursuit of *la vie Parisienne*:

> Here, late in the afternoon of almost every day, may be seen what there is of the fashion and wealth of the city, the little gatherings of French men and women, their promenades, salutations and dress, recalling in miniature the life of Europe. Necessarily, these gatherings are only of nutshell dimensions, and however they may take of the atmosphere of true France, they give one only the feeling of being exiled, for the life that surrounds it is foreign in every way.

Heilprin applied the same sceptical eye to Mont Pelée. Its activities had a rational, scientific explanation and were not, as superstitious folk insisted, a side effect of introducing streetlights to Saint-Pierre.

Surveying the ruined city, Heilprin compared Pelée's impact to that of heavy artillery. 'We seemed to be wandering through a city that had been blown from the mouth of a cannon', he wrote, 'and not one that had been destroyed by any force of nature.' The dust cloud had borne down like a missile or a cannon ball, hitting Saint-Pierre with devastating force. Thomas Jaggar came to a similar conclusion. The Harvard geologist likened Pelée's blast to a 'blowpipe effect' which had 'shot the death-dealing billows of falling hot sand and gravel down the mountain slopes in the direction of Saint-Pierre'.

Both scientists agreed that gravity had given the glowing clouds their awesome momentum. Jaggar thought Pelée's clouds had at first risen upwards, and then been dragged down by the force of gravity, a 'deflected, descending cloud of volcanic ejecta'. As it fell back towards the crater it had 'encountered matter in ascension, and was deflected in a horizontal direction'. Heilprin's theory was even more complicated. The initial blast, he suggested, had been caused by a catastrophic collapse in one part of the crater floor. The wave of rising steam and air had then been forced downwards by its sheer weight. But without seeing Pelée in action, such theories were highly speculative. To judge from its sullen groans and grumbles, the volcano might erupt again at any moment. Rather than wait around, Heilprin opted for a riskier course. On Thursday 29 May, the Associated Press reported that he had left Fort-de-France with three guides and a photographer. Heilprin was determined, the wire went on, 'to attempt the ascent to the top of the crater'.

The French authorities left Heilprin to his own eccentric devices. There were more urgent matters to attend to. Most worrying of all was the mutinous mood of their people. On Friday 30 May, an angry crowd of refugees massed outside the *Hôtel du Gouvernement* in Fort-de-France. They raged against the Acting Governor, M. Lhuerre, and scuffled with soldiers keeping nervous guard. Conservatives detected the hidden hand of Victor Sévère, Radical Mayor of Fort-de-France, and behind him, the Millionaire Socialist himself, Amédée Knight. But it would be wrong to dismiss this protest as a phoney, staged event. Around 25,000 people had fled their homes during the May eruptions, and were still too frightened to return. At least 15,000 refugees were living around Fort-de-France, sleeping rough in schools and seminaries, on the stone flags of Fort Saint-Louis and at a local casino. Their food rations were miserably small: 500 grams of bread (about half a standard loaf) per person per day, along with 130 grams of cod and 100 grams of dried vegetables: barely enough for a few mouthfuls. Most of these supplies had come from America. France's national appeal had reached 3.55 million francs, but Martinicans claimed the money was not getting through. The *Métropole* was not doing enough.

All the old racial antagonisms were rushing back too, and with a sharper edge than before. When a delegate from the French Chamber of Commerce in New York descended with 25,000 francs of cash aid, he was accused of favouring black districts over white. 'A sectarian spirit hangs over this distribution', wrote the Paris paper *La Patrie*. 'Because the Negroes are Radicals and the Whites are Republicans, the first group has been favoured at the expense of the second.' *La Patrie* went further. M. Crassous de Medeuil, the New York delegate, was secretly siphoning money into Radical Party campaign funds. From this distance, it's hard to establish the truth about this acrid affair. Each racial group was sensitive to the smallest slight, and the charges against de Medeuil may have been exaggerated. One senses a certain *parti pris* quality, for example, to the account published in the pro-White *Journal Officiel*: 'M. de Medeuil confirms under oath that the funds sent by the United States have been used to make election propaganda . . . The [Radical Party] Committee will be particularly responsible for these iniquities.'

Martinique's disorderly state also left people prey to all kinds of scams and rip-offs. French newspapers were outraged by the case of Clara King and Rita Stokes, the governess and young girl rescued from Saint-Pierre's boiling sea on 8 May. Deeply traumatised by their experiences on board the *Roraima*, the two survivors were taken to Fort-de-France hospital. At the end of their one-month stay, they were stung with a bill for 350 francs. While Parisian papers puffed indignantly, French officials tried to smooth things over. According to a barely believable report in the *Journal Officiel*, hospital staff claimed they had mistaken the two women for Americans. After learning they were both English (a realisation no doubt hastened by abusive press coverage), the hospital bill was withdrawn. 280 francs were returned to Ms King and a clarification sent to the editor of *L'Illustration*.

The greatest scandal however centred on Maurice Bloch, the civil servant charged with distributing half a million francs' worth of emergency aid. When this florid, white-haired gentleman stepped gingerly off the *D'Assas* late on Thursday 22 May, he was met by an eager crowd. Mont Pelée had just erupted a second time, and there was a desperate desire for reassurance. To start with, Maurice Bloch seemed the man to provide it. His first weekend was spent visiting hospitals around Fort-de-France, assuring helpless, bandaged victims of *la profonde sympathie de la France*; on Monday 26 May, he braved Pelée's rumblings to visit Saint-Pierre. Victor Sévère hoped Bloch now understood 'the immensity of our misfortune'.

But it soon became clear that M. Bloch's *sympathie* did not extend very far. After this initial burst of activity, Bloch withdrew to his official quarters in Fort-de-France. It was as if a gangplank, hastily swung down, had been drawn up again just as rapidly. During his two-and-a-half-week stay on the island, Bloch distributed a grand total of 24,100 francs: less than five per cent of the funds available, and only 9,000 francs more than his *entourage* were paid for their entire Caribbean excursion. Of the money that was handed out, Bloch gave grants of between 500 and 5,000 francs to town halls and parish priests; smaller sums of two to three hundred francs were given to sixteen named individuals. A further 100,000 francs (beyond the meagre 24,100 agreed by Bloch) was left in Governor Lhuerre's hands, to be spent as and when appropriate. As for that outstanding sum of 375,000 francs, Bloch insisted it be locked up in a bank vault and released only with the permission of the French Government five thousand miles away.

Enthusiasm turned to incredulity, hope to despair. How dare a Parisian civil servant treat his fellow citizens in such a callous, high-handed fashion! In case Paris had forgotten, Governor Lhuerre drew up a Bill of Losses. With the help of his Radical allies, Lhuerre submitted a bill of 200 million francs. It was a ludicrous, absurdly inflated sum. But it made a point:

COMMISSION OF LOSSES
(as of 17 June 1902)

		Francs
Buildings	Military	1 m
	Colonial	7.44 m
Communal and Government		15 m
	Other Public offices	1.95 m
	Factories, Refineries &c	5.75 m
Houses of Saint-Pierre		
and surrounding areas		60 m
	Rural properties	17.3 m
	Sub Total	108.44 m

Furniture &c		
Furniture, clothes, jewellery		
and Industrial equipment		50 m
	Merchandise in shops	20 m
	Losses in harbour	5 m
	Sub Total	75 m

Total: 183.44m

If one added damage to other parts of the island, writes Lhuerre, then the final (all-too-convenient) figure was two hundred million francs. Even allowing for a degree of exaggeration, for figures which were doubled, trebled or cheerily quadrupled, then it was evident that Bloch's 24,100-franc-donation was somewhat inadequate.

Bloch's off-hand manner didn't help either. By his own admission, the *haut fonctionnaire* spent most of his seventeen-day stay in Fort-de-France, preferring to conduct business through his secretaries. Martinique's two leading politicians (or mischief makers, if you will) were so outraged by this behaviour that they submitted details in a Parliamentary Report.* According to Knight and Clément, Bloch's 'lack of benevolence and humanity' deterred all but the most determined visitors. If refugees came to his *Résidence*, Bloch would send a secretary to 'go out and see what those people want'. As for his 'scandalous allowance', it reinforced their view of a man keener on his own comforts than those of others. 'In Martinique', they wrote, 'the memory of M. Bloch remains engraved in every mind as that of a man who passed through [our country] with his hands tightly closed to all the accumulated misery of a disaster which has upset the entire world.' Maurice Bloch was the physical embodiment of French *ennui*, of a Government which 'remained indifferent to the sad fate of Martinique'. Through his actions, Bloch also showed how little Paris trusted Martinicans to run their own affairs. They were being treated, once more, like little children.

L'Affaire Bloch left a nasty taste.

To get a sense of Bloch's misjudgement, one need only record the rapid flow of funds after his departure. The 100,000 *tranche* left with Acting Governor Lhuerre was spent within six weeks; a further 150,000 francs was released on 30 July, and another 100,000 francs at the end of August. A fresh eruption of Mont Pelée on 30 August put the finances under renewed strain: by 11 September the new Governor, M. Lemaire, had to inform Paris of 'the complete exhaustion of the 500,000 franc fund brought by M. Bloch'. But

* Amédée Knight and Homère Clément: *Rapport fait sur l'emploi des fonds de Secours mis à la disposition de la Martinique par l'État*. Chambre des Deputés, No. 2371, 6 April 1905.

this belated admission of need could not efface that first, damning impression. Homère Clément felt Martinicans had become victims twice over: the first blows had rained down from Pelée, the second round had come from that arrogant pen-pusher at the Ministry of Colonies. When Maurice Bloch got back to Paris on 25 June, he submitted his own personal bill for the relief mission. That *sécheresse de coeur* – dryness of heart – which he had exercised in Martinique had been forgotten. Bloch was paid 8,100 francs for his forty-four days' work.

Bloch himself saw events very differently. To his neat, administrative mind the strictly controlled *tranches* of money made eminent sense: a stockpile had been laid for unseen emergencies and for any future rebuilding of the island. There was no point spending money on food and clothing when there was already a glut. In reply to Knight and Clément's criticisms, Bloch claims that 'from the moment of the mission's arrival and throughout its stay, there was no shortage of money, food, or clothes'. Food was in such plentiful supply, Bloch goes on, that people were selling off fruit and vegetables before they went rotten. 'The best approach was to put aside the Treasury Funds until the time when food supplies fell short, and in view of the temporary accommodation of the disaster victims, to defray expenses on public works and the purchase of building materials.'

More controversially, Bloch feared that if his funds were dispersed too quickly then politicians would end up fighting over the spoils, as had happened to the unfortunate M. de Medeuil. A slow, steady release of money lowered expectations and discouraged people from making false claims. This may explain why only half of Bloch's original grant was given to local *Communes* (10,500 francs out of 24,100) while the rest was divided between parish curés and individual families. Perhaps Bloch thought they would handle their money more wisely than local councillors.

Bloch's blunt approach won him few friends in Martinique. He did however gain the support of one individual. The Ministerial archive contains two extravagantly written letters from one Étienne-Just Soumba, a self-styled 'Conservative Negro' and supporter of white landowner Fernand Clerc. M. Soumba praises Bloch for standing up to Amédée Knight's political *clique* which included Governor Lhuerre among its number (which may help explain the exaggerated figures put on his *Commission of Losses*). 'The wise M. Bloch certainly understood what was going on', Soumba tells the Foreign Ministry, 'and took the precaution of setting aside a portion of the money sent by the Minister.' Martinique, he went on, was gripped by an anarchy *sans pareille*. 'At this critical moment, ambition, hatred and vengeance are shown in all their grandeur. Things are going from bad to worse.'

Whether Maurice Bloch deserves credit for outsmarting the political bosses, or condemnation for his airy indifference, depends on many factors. The letters of a Conservative sympathiser cannot entirely restore the balance; after all, one wonders who persuaded M. Soumba to write these letters in the first place, and what purpose they were meant to achieve, beyond boosting M. Bloch's reputation at home. The best one can do, at this distance, is to treat *L'Affaire Bloch* as a parable; a story which can be seen from many shifting points of view. Both sides mistrusted each other, and acted accordingly: coloniser and colonist, trapped in an embrace of mutual suspicion.

As dawn broke on Saturday 31 May, a small, silent group of men could be seen threading their way through the cane fields of Vivé. They moved briskly, taking their cue from a tall white man in a pale yellow linen jacket and straw hat. Angelo Heilprin's first encounter with Pelée had been widely publicised. The brave American intended to find the fount of *La Montagne*'s anger, its original working crater. Heilprin hoped this would give some clue as to what Pelée was up to – and what it might do next. Behind him, a line of ungainly silhouettes trudged and stumbled over the ashen fields: a photographer called Leadbeater, a box camera strapped to

Pelée in eruption

his waist; three teenage guides and a pair of unbiddable donkeys. All felt the full weight of expectation – and trepidation.

At first, the signs were hopeful. Dawn was bright and clear; gentle, white clouds puffed from Pelée's remote peak. For several hours, the explorers traced an erratic path through open meadows and grey, deserted villages. A little after nine o'clock, they emerged on Pelée's lower slopes. To his right, Heilprin saw a thin, narrow ridge spiralling westwards towards the summit. To his left, far down below, he could see 'the blue ocean dashing its white surf against the vertical cliffs of the coast'. But he could not find the new crater which Robert Hill had identified as the prime cause of Pelée's activity. Perhaps it was higher up – or hidden behind another of the mountain's massive folds.

From here, the climb became steadily more difficult. As a veteran mountaineer, Heilprin had few problems ('The ascent', he bragged, 'presented nothing more difficult than the long slopes of our Appalachian peaks'), but Leadbeater was soon struggling for breath.

And then something happened which dented even Heilprin's *braggadocio*. A slow, hard rain began to fall, turning the ground underfoot into thick grey mud. A heavy mist swirled around the party. It was as if Pelée had detected these intruders on its flanks, and was trying to force them back. 'In a short half-hour', writes Heilprin, 'the parting line between the land and the sky had been blotted out, and the balance of our ascent was made in cloudland. A discomforting rain fell upon us and when we finally reached the summit of the mountain, shortly before eleven o'clock, the weather was decidedly nasty.'

Among Angelo Heilprin's many gifts, one should not forget his great gift for understatement. Like a mythical creature guarding its lair, Pelée was pelting its unwelcome visitors with every weapon in its armoury: torrential rain, a clammy mist and a growing rumble of thunder. According to Heilprin's aneroid barometer, they were now at the approximate height – 3,975 feet – of the *Lac des Palmistes*. Through the mist, Heilprin could see the faint outlines of this ancient Lake, which appeared to be surprisingly intact. 'It was evident at a glance', he wrote, 'that the old "crater", contrary to general belief and scientific report, had not been blown out. It remained where picnic parties, seeking its beautiful waters, annually found it to be . . .' The original vent, the source of Saint-Pierre's annihilation, was clearly elsewhere. As Heilprin continued his search, an awful rumbling filled the sky:

A crash of thunder, that seemed to rend the very heart of the mountain, broke the storm upon us, and silenced all other sounds. In an instant more a second crash, and the lightning cut frenzied zigzags across the blackened cloud-world of quivering Pelée. Then a third and a fourth, and the pitons rolled the echoes to one another like artillery fire . . . it was a strange sensation this, sitting not knowing exactly where and having as an unseen neighbour one of the mightiest destroying engines of the globe.

Rain fell in pitiless torrents, lightning slashed and flashed across the sky. The teenage boys pleaded with Heilprin, and with 'silent tears' begged him to end his mad experiment. Pelée was about to explode, they cried. The ground trembled, the sky shook. But their American professor would not be distracted. By shielding his compass and barometer beneath his coat, Heilprin was able to take readings even though 'our clothing, so far as protection to ourselves was concerned, might almost as well have been in the sea'.

And still it rained. It rained so hard that when Leadbeater placed his camera upon the ground and lay across it, the rain seemed to pass through his body, to soak the camera underneath:

> Those frightful minutes when I lay on the ground shielding my camera, with the rain descending in perfect floods of water − I never knew it could rain as it did then − with the appalling thunder-charged flashes playing incessantly about me and the very air quivering with the rapidity of the detonations, and but a few feet away the seething, sweltering crater of the most destructive volcano the earth had ever seen, will always stand out in my memory as a weird and horrible dream . . .

After forty-five minutes of thunder, wind and rain, Heilprin decided he had seen enough. 'It was perhaps the most trying of any like period that I had, up to this time, experienced', he wrote. But however 'storm-beaten and mind-beaten' he might be, Heilprin was determined to try again. Pelée was proving a more powerful opponent than he had imagined, but it would not get the better of him. The original vent was tantalisingly close, hidden behind waves of mist and rain. Heilprin and Leadbeater slipped back down the mountain, through sheets of mud and water. They returned to their base at Vivé with some relief, and more than a little frustration, for 'that for which he had climbed the mountain had eluded us . . . and yet could hardly be more than a stone's throw away'. That night, Heilprin spent several minutes on his balcony, staring at the

mountain in all its 'grand and unconquered magnificence' and
vowed to try again the next day.

This time, he was joined by reinforcements. George Kennan,
Special Correspondent of *The Outlook*, and his illustrator George
Varian expressed an interest in seeing the summit, as did a fellow
magazine writer, A.F. Jaccaci. A somewhat larger cavalcade left Vivé
that second morning; more than half a dozen attendants and carriers
laboured along the plantation paths of Vivé and Morne Balai. Their
ascent, this time around, was more arduous too. A night of heavy
rain (the storm in which Heilprin and Leadbeater had experienced
the opening salvos) had left the slopes soft and treacherous. The sun
was more trying and intense than previously, without any hint of a
breeze. It was soon too much for Mr Jaccaci, who suffered an attack
of vertigo and had to abandon his ascent. The others made steady
progress, with occasional stops for breath.

After a solid three-and-a-half-hour climb, Heilprin's party reached
the *Lac des Palmistes*. Once more, it seemed as if Pelée was going to
frustrate them. 'The aged mountain had again buried its head in cloud
and vapour', he wrote, 'and growling thunder reverberations held out
little hope that we should be able to accomplish more than we had
already done.' A squally rain swept over the mountainside, accompanied by stray rolls of thunder. Small puffs of steam could be seen
rising from several surface vents. But the grand spectacle still eluded
them. There were murmurs of disappointment. To have come so far,
and yet to have failed a second time!

Heilprin advised patience. The cloud would lift in a while, he
insisted. And then, as if to prove his point, the white mist parted
briefly: 'Below the mountain's clouds we could clearly mark out the
ascending column of steam, with its flocculent whorls rolling in upon
themselves and upward. The position of the crater had been located,
but alas! it was hardly more than an instant.' No sooner had this hard-
won revelation appeared, than it vanished once more into the mist.

A bitter cold wind and rain resumed; the show was over. Pelée
had tempted its visitors with a brief glimpse of its soul, only to steal it

away. Or so it appeared. At the very moment when Heilprin was ready to give up, a gust of wind swept away the clouds, and illuminated Pelée's summit. Directly across the Lake bed, they could see ascending columns of steam. Scrambling, running over mountain scree and ash, Heilprin raced to the edge of the giant vent, finally revealed, and gazed into its mouth with childish joy:

> We were four feet, perhaps less, from a point whence a plummet could be dropped into the seething furnace, witnessing a scene of terrorising grandeur which can be conceived only by the few who have observed similar scenes elsewhere. Momentary flashes of light permitted us to see far into the tempest-tossed cauldron, but at no time was the floor visible, for over it rolled the vapours that rose out to mountain heights. With almost lightning speed they [the vapours] were shot out into space, to be lost almost as soon as they appeared.

About two hundred and fifty feet away from this cauldron, Heilprin saw several huge cinder cones, which he recognised from his night-time observations of Pelée. They had reached the epicentre of the volcano, its majestic heart:

> The spectacle was a stupendous one – like a wild tempest raging everywhere. We stood silent, overawed in its presence . . . A low rumbling detonation, broken at intervals by louder bursts, crept about the hidden floor of the interior, from which also issued the sounds of clinking, falling and sliding cinders, the hissing of the emerging steam-sound which one would fain describe were it possible to do so.

All the circumstantial evidence supported Heilprin's discovery. The crater pitched steeply downward, its mouth pointing in a direct line towards Saint-Pierre. It also occupied the same position as the narrow rift or *Fente* blamed for the 1851 eruption. A strange mixture of feelings overcame Heilprin, a blend of fear and awe. Before hastening back down the mountain (for they did not feel inclined to stay any longer than necessary, peering over its great mouth), Heilprin reflected on what he had discovered. 'I felt', he wrote, 'that finally I had stood over nature's great laboratory, and been permitted to study some of its workings. Many years before on Vesuvius I had gazed into the crater funnel, and watched the molten magma of the earth rise and fall, but the scene was one that could not compare with this, grand and inspiring as it was.' It was a religious experience, an epiphany – and well worth the wait.

A few days later, the Associated Press reported Heilprin's achievement with the animation normally reserved for the discovery of an ancient river source or a new mountain peak. The report gave due credit to Heilprin's bravery and tenacity:

THE ASCENT OF MONT PELÉE BY PROF.
ANGELO HEILPRIN

. . . amid a thousand dangers Professor Heilprin reached the summit and looked down into the huge crater. Here he spent some time in taking careful observations. He saw a huge cinder cone in the centre of the crater. The opening of the crater itself is a vast crevice 500 feet long and 150 feet wide.

While Professor Heilprin was on the summit of the volcano several violent explosions of steam and cinder-laden vapour took place, and again and again and again his life was in danger . . . He still persisted in his observations however, and twice more was showered with mud. He learned, as had been suspected, that there were three separate vents through which steam issued.

The first part of Pelée's mystery had been solved.

EIGHT

GLOWING CLOUDS

A FEW WEEKS after Heilprin's discovery, an old but familiar slogan appeared on the classified pages of *Billboard*, America's entertainment weekly. After five years in Europe, the Greatest Show on Earth was coming home to America. Or, as Barnum's press department would put it, with typical understatement:

> HOME AGAIN
> After having received the HOMAGE OF THE REIGNING MONARCHS OF THE GLOBE, whom all, together with their Courts and Ministers bowed down before the Great and Mighty Potency and Widespread Influence of this Representative American Show. A GREAT LESSON TO OTHER COUNTRIES OF THE GREATNESS AND GRANDEUR OF AMERICA.

But such patriotic bombast was only half the story. The real reason for Barnum's return was ruthlessly commercial. Rival circus operators, particularly the Ringling Brothers, had taken advantage of Barnum and Bailey's long European absence to take over some of their most profitable 'stands'. They had also bought up some of the best acts. By 1902, the Ringling Brothers' opening stand in Chicago had become as much of a showbusiness fixture as Barnum's first night at Madison Square Garden. There was one other niggling matter. So successful were the Ringling Brothers at duplicating this Big Top formula, that they had taken to calling themselves *The World's Greatest Shows*: a cheeky echo of

Wanted for the Concert and Side Show Departments of the

BARNUM and BAILEY
Greatest Show on Earth

For the travelling season of 1903 on the Continent of America. **Human Curiosities of every description, Novelties and conspicuously high-class attractions.** Specialty, Character, Sketch, Vaudeville, Comic, Serious, Dramatic, Pantomimic, Musical and other Artists of the highest merit of either sex. **Also wanted.** experienced and competent Side Show Orators. Reliable and trustworthy persons lib rally dealt with.. Address **GEORGE ARLINGTON, Superintendent of Privileges.**

Also Wanted Several Experienced Elephant Trainers

Those capable of teaching and performing preferred. Sobriety and reliability on the part of applicants will be considered as of the first importance, and when accompanied with good temper, fair appearance, exemplary conduct and deportment at all times, will insure employment by the year, if desired, at adequate compensation. Suitable persons may begin an engagement on or before the first of next September. Address **J. A. BAIL Y, Managing Director Barnum & Bailey Show, 3 Crosby Square, London, E. C. England, or Room 504, Townsend Building, 1123 Broadway, New York City, U. S. A.,** from which addresses all letters will be forwarded.

Barnum's own, fiercely protected catchphrase. Clearly, it was time for America's Finest Amusement Institution to reclaim its crown. To James A. Bailey, there was only one way to fight back: an imperious, imperial spectacle which would match the spirit of the age, a show which was *Marvellous in size and Amazing in features.*

The *Billboard* ads, with their call for *Human Curiosities of every description*, were part of that imperial ambition. Barnum agents scoured every fairground and music hall for new acts, the more peculiar the better. Among their finds was an intense-looking Italian called Vito Basile, a man 'without a rival on Earth in carving fancy flowers from vegetables' ('The Vegetable King') and Louise the Leopard Girl, a young girl from Louisiana whose hair and skin were marked into stripes of black and white. Several old stagers – Billy Wells, the Hard Headed Man, and J.W. Coffee, the Living Skeleton – were also pressed back into service.

As for Ludger Sylbaris, it's not clear when or how he was invited to join The Greatest Show on Earth. The *idea* of exhibiting the Lone Survivor of Saint-Pierre may well have taken root in the spring of 1902, during Barnum's European odyssey. On the day Mont Pelée erupted, the circus was in Narbonne, halfway through a French tour enlivened by tent blowdowns, missed dates and an occasional riot. News of the 8 May disaster clearly touched every performer. A few days later, they put on a benefit performance in Toulouse which raised six thousand dollars for the Martinique relief fund. As a showman as well as a businessman, James Bailey's interest would have been heightened by Sylbaris's growing celebrity. Details of his incredible escape appeared in every American paper, often exaggerated to the point of incredulity. At some point in July or August, Sylbaris was sent to Fort-de-France hospital, where he was snapped by an American photographer. Soon afterwards, Barnum and Bailey made their own independent attempts to check his story: the official *Book of Wonders* for 1903 includes affidavits from American Consul John Jewell and from two of the men who rescued Sylbaris from the ruins of Saint-Pierre jail. All appeared to be in order. *THE GRANDEST GATHERING OF LIVING HUMAN WONDERS* had found an extraordinary new recruit.

Back at Barnum's New York office, plans were being laid for a show of quite unprecedented scale and ambition. A gigantic twelve-centre-pole canvas was ordered from Lushbaughs of Kentucky, lit by over a thousand electric lights. Impressed by the luxury of European theatres, Bailey also ordered thousands of cast-iron seats with fitted footrests. Then there was the show itself, a three-ring affair with dozens of clowns, acrobats, elephants and bareback riders all performing at the same time. (One of the standard grumbles about Barnum's extravaganzas was that you came away having

✿ ✿ THE LARGEST TENT EVER MADE. ✿ ✿

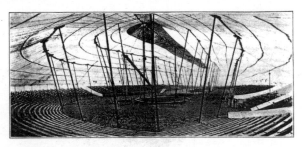

MANUFACTURED BY

WILLIAM LUSHBAUGH,
COVINGTON, KY.

All Kinds of Tents Made to Order.   A LARGE NUMBER OF TENTS, NEW
AND SECOND-HAND, ALWAYS ON HAND

missed most of the show.) As if these attractions were not enough, the time between Side Show and Big Top shows would be filled with a historical spectacle called *The Tribute of Balkis*, 'a glorious illuminated page from Ancient History'. It is hard to understand the appeal of such ludicrous events today, yet circus spectacles worked on the same grandiose principles as a Hollywood blockbuster, or grand opera. The idea was to lay on an awesome 'eye feast' of colour and costume which, if the posters were to be believed, simply *had to be seen*. Like the Freak Show, the Spectacle was a sure-fire way of luring 'natives' through the door. Once they were inside, of course, it was too late to complain.

Barnum's 1903 production involved more than four hundred characters dressed up as Philistines, Phoenicians, Egyptians, Africans and Arabians, 'the whole forming a brilliant kaleidoscopic vision of animated and iridescent splendours'. It was directed by a Hungarian, Mr Bolossy Kiralfy. The Kiralfy family had some form in these matters, having previously staged such low-concept productions as 'Nero, or the Destruction of Rome' and 'The Dawn of Christianity'. All seemed set for the most ambitious, most spectacular circus tour America had ever seen. 132 separate dates in twenty-three states; a travelling town of eighty-eight railway carriages and five steam trains; performers from every corner of the globe. It was as if James A. Bailey was trying to create his own empire, to stamp his mark upon every continent of the world. 'The immensity of the Barnum and Bailey show is simply dumbfounding', wrote *Billboard*. 'Every day some new, costly or big innovation or plan is disclosed. The wonder is when it will end.' Or, the doubters added, whether it would work.

In Martinique, meanwhile, the British geologists Tempest Anderson and John Flett had learnt an important lesson: one should never *ever* stand around to watch an active volcano.

After spending several weeks on Saint Vincent, the two Britons had reached Saint-Pierre early in July 1902. Their near-death experiences in the shadow of Mont Pelée – related with laconic brevity in the Royal Society's *Transactions* for 1903 – gave scientists their first detailed account of what was going on *inside* Pelée's cloud of glowing ash. They also gave future readers a terrifying sense of what it must be like to come face to face with an angry volcano.

Anderson and Flett's adventure began early on Wednesday 9 July, when they set off to explore the ruins of Saint-Pierre. It was a clear, sunny day. Tempest Anderson indulged his photographic habit by taking pictures of Rue Victor Hugo and the *Mouillage*; John Flett strode through cane fields, looking for volcanic rocks and boulders. Both men were struck by Pelée's relative tranquillity: the last major eruption had been over a month ago on 6 June, and all that emerged now were occasional spurts of steam which were 'so beautiful, so large, so perfectly formed that we perforce had to halt in our wanderings through the city and gaze on their varied formations'.

Pelée's apparent calm encouraged the two Britons to sail north towards Prêcheur, where they could get a closer look at the mountain's western flank. As Anderson busied himself with photographic plates and light meters, Flett noticed white clouds beginning to rise with greater frequency, 'so that one interfered with the isolated development of that which went before'. It was an intriguing sight, but hardly an ominous one. The geologists were planning to climb Pelée the following day, and saw no reason to call off their excursion. With this in mind, their tiny sailboat, the *Minerva*, ran down to Carbet to pick up supplies.

Soon after reaching the fishing village at around 6pm, 'clouds of pale slaty vapour' began to emerge from the fissure that Heilprin had identified six weeks earlier. From their new vantage point, one and a half miles south of Saint-Pierre, Flett and Anderson watched excitedly as a long, black scarf of ash unfurled from Pelée's summit and rolled out to sea. They could not quite believe it. *La Montagne* appeared to be performing one of its periodic throat clearings, and they were lucky enough to have front-row seats. Quickly, eagerly, the two men pitched their camp chairs on the *Minerva*'s deck and waited for the next act of this unexpected drama.

Light was falling fast now. Slate grey puffs emerged more frequently, turning the dusky sun into a disc of pale greens and yellows. Anderson and Flett were discussing the odds of an ascent the next morning, when they noticed that one cauliflower-shaped cloud was behaving in an odd manner:

> It did not rise in the air, but rested there, on the lip of the fissure, for quite a while as it seemed, and retained its shape for so long that we could not suppose it to be a mere steam cloud. Evidently, it had been emitted with sufficient violence to raise it over the lip of the crater, but it was too heavy to soar up in the air like a mass of vapour, and it lay rolling and spouting on the slopes of the hill . . .

One can imagine the studious chatter which must have passed between Anderson and Flett at this point. The cloud appeared as solid as a boulder, and just as immovable. And then, with a growing sense of dread, they saw that this was not the case at all.

. . . slowly we realised that the cloud was not at rest but was
rolling straight down the hill, gradually increasing in size as it
came nearer and nearer. We consulted together; it seemed so
strange and so unaccountable, but in a minute or two suspicion
gave way to certainty. It seemed that the farther the cloud
travelled the faster it came, and when we took our eyes off it
for a second and then looked back it was nearer and still nearer
than before. There was no room for doubt any longer. It was a
'black cloud', and was making directly for us . . .

Academic detachment gave way to panic. Flett and Anderson
helped the sailors to raise anchor and set the head sails. They had
to get out of Pelée's path as quickly as possible. By the time their
mainsail had been hoisted, the ash cloud had gone through a
'startling' transformation. It had swollen enormously and streaks
of lightning played across its boiling, pillowy surface. Silhouetted
men could be seen running south along the cliffs, pursued by pulsing
black shapes. But then, to everyone's relief, the grey cloud seemed
to lose speed. It stopped abruptly at the shoreline and lay 'almost like
a dead mass on the surface of the sea'.

It was twenty to eight. Anderson and Flett were exhilarated. They
had seen Pelée's rolling, tumbling clouds at first hand and also
confirmed Heilprin's theory about the active fissure: all in all, a
highly satisfactory day's work. As they sailed south to Fort-de-
France, they kept a close watch on *La Montagne*. Soon, the black
cloud began to clear and Pelée's distant summit came back into
view, with a 'faint red glare above the fissure from which the cloud
had come'. From time to time, red hot stones flew out of the gash
and rolled down the hillsides.

The *Minerva*'s crew were nervous. They had visited Saint-Pierre
several times since 8 May and had never seen anything like this
before. Their fears increased when the *Minerva* came to a standstill
about thirty minutes down the coast. They had hit a patch of dead
calm; all they could do was wait for a fresh breeze. Flett and

Anderson made the most of this delay by resuming positions on the foredeck, cameras and notebooks at the ready. Pelée's red flares appeared to be a postscript to its earlier performance, but then a sudden yellow glow lit up the clouds above the summit. 'It was like the lights of a great city on the horizon, or the glare over large iron furnaces', they wrote. It was followed by a long moan, 'like the sullen growl of an angry beast'. Pelée's tantrum was far from over:

> Then in an instant a red-hot avalanche rose from the cleft in the hillside and poured over the mountain slopes right down to the sea . . . Its velocity was tremendous . . . The red glow faded in a minute or two, and in its place we now saw, rushing forward over the sea, a great rounded, boiling cloud, black and filled with lightnings. It came straight out of the avalanche, of which it was clearly only the lighter and cooler surface, and as it advanced it visibly swelled, getting larger and larger every minute. The moonlight shining on its face showed up the details of its surface. It was a fear-inspiring sight, coming straight over the water directly for us, where we lay with the sails flapping idly as the boat gently rolled on the waves of the sea.

Trapped on their tiny boat, Anderson and Flett watched hopelessly as the black cloud, thick as 'a mass of ink', barrelled towards them. Its 'ebony mass' was round and globular; the bulging, pullulating surface boiled with furious energy. While sailors fell to their knees in prayer, the two scientists tried to keep their nerve:

> Nearer and nearer it came to where our little boat lay becalmed, right in the path of its murderous violence. We sat and gazed, mute with astonishment and wonder, overwhelmed by the magnificence of the spectacle, which we had heard so much about and had never hoped to see.
>
> In our minds, there was little room for terror, so absorbed were we in the terrible grandeur of the scene. But our sailors were in a

frenzy of fear, they seized their oars and rowed for their lives, howling with dread every time they looked over their shoulders at the rushing cloud behind us. Their exertions did little good, as the boat was too heavy to row, and fear gave place to despair . . .

For a moment, it seemed as if Flett, Anderson and their crew were to suffer the same fate as Saint-Pierre. But then a sharp puff of wind blew in from the southeast, enough to let the *Minerva* drift out of danger. Fear was now replaced with wonder. Pelée's massive cloud had halted once again about a mile from Flett and Anderson's foredeck, where it hung splendidly in the air like a velvet curtain:

> It now lay before us nearly immobile, a gigantic wall, curiously reflecting the moonlight like a pall of black velvet. Its surface was strangely still after the turmoil it had exhibited before, and great black rounded folds hung vertically like those of an enormous curtain . . . Soon it became evident that the base was darker, and the paler summit was rising in the air and soaring obliquely upwards and forwards. The dust was sinking and the pale steam set free from entanglement with the heavier solid particles, was following its own natural tendency to ascend, while still impelled forwards by the great onward impetus it had received.

Flett and Anderson had discovered the secret of Pelée's speed and direction. The cloud had not spread out laterally, but had powered forwards in 'surging masses'. As it moved closer it appeared to get paler, with lighter particles floating off into the air. Clearly, a separation of sorts was going on within the cloud. Heavier pieces of dust and debris were falling away all the time, allowing lighter pieces to carry on unimpeded. This idea was soon confirmed by a strange sequence of events. As the steam cloud passed over their boat, the geologists were pelted by a series of smaller and smaller objects: a hail of pebbles, pellets, moist grey ash and then dry grey ash 'which got into our eyes and felt gritty between our fingers'.

Each successive wave carried lighter debris, as if the vast overhead cloud was thinning out as it passed. At this point, a fresh breeze got up, and the *Minerva* resumed its voyage to Fort-de-France.

It had been a remarkable and terrifying display. In just over an hour, Pelée had shown off some of its most striking features: the black clouds of 'hot sand' which rushed downhill at dizzying speed; the lightning sparks which made those clouds 'glow'; the shower of debris which fell in order of size and weight. As thunder clouds chased them back to Fort-de-France that night, there was much for Flett and Anderson to think about. They were struck by how Pelée's dust cloud had propelled itself along the ground, a trait not picked up in earlier scientific reports. Indeed, one of the American geologists, Robert T. Hill, had seen quite a different effect. Observing Pelée on 24 May, he saw a cloud 'fall suddenly, flatten, and float out horizontally into the sky like an aerial river'. But Flett and Anderson were adamant: the blast of 9 July had swept along the ground like an avalanche, and if the various eyewitness accounts collected on 8 May were reliable, then Saint-Pierre had succumbed to the same kind of blast.

But what gave these clouds their incredible speed? On Thursday 8 May, Pelée's avalanche of ash had raced across Saint-Pierre in three minutes, reaching speeds of over a hundred miles per hour. 'The fundamental question remains', wrote Anderson and Flett. 'What is the source of energy which drives the cloud along?' Heilprin, Hovey and Hill had likened this propulsive force to a gun or a cannon. The British geologists had a more prosaic theory: simple gravity. 'The motive power', they wrote, 'is supplied by the weight of the mass . . . [It] proceeds to flow downward in obedience to the law of gravitation.' A theory developed, you might say, from their own uncommonly close observation. That night, Pelée's cloud

> . . . did not start its rush down the slopes at once, but rolled and tumbled, squirted and seethed for quite a perceptible time. Then it began to move with greater and greater speed down the hillside.

Faster and faster it came till it struck the sea, when its velocity began to diminish, at first slowly, and then more rapidly. It was like a toboggan on a snow slide. It was not the blast of a gun, it was the rush of an avalanche. Gravity did the work and supplied the energy.

Thursday 9 July was a day which neither man – nor their weary crew – would forget for a long time. They had survived an encounter with Fire Mountain, and learnt a great deal about how it worked. The mystery of Saint-Pierre was slowly being solved. Angelo Heilprin had found the source of its destruction; the two Britons had seen enough to speculate on *how* the town had been destroyed. By keeping their nerve, they had given scientists a richly detailed account of the incandescent clouds; a phenomenon so new that no one had yet come up with a name for it.

Anderson and Flett left Martinique on 11 July, after one final tour of Saint-Pierre harbour. Tempest Anderson had seen volcanic eruptions all over the world, but few could have matched the sheer stomach-churning terror of Mont Pelée. On their return to England, the two men quickly prepared a report for the Royal Society. Given all they had endured, the report's *précis* is a masterpiece of Edwardian understatement:

> The night of 9 July was marked by one of the major eruptions of Pelée, and we had the exceptional good fortune to be in Saint-Pierre that day, and to have a magnificent view of the eruption, while we escaped entirely unscathed . . .

There was only one man who could match these adventures, and in August, he came back for more.

Angelo Heilprin returned to Fort-de-France on 22 August, glad to see the island had recovered a little of its old colour. A new Governor, M. Lemaire, was installed at the *Hôtel du Gouvernement*; a new journal had been launched, borrowing the name *La Colonie* from Marius Hurard's old standard, *Les Colonies*. In Saint-Pierre,

Heilprin saw that looters had been busy among the ruins. Skeletons, or parts of skeletons, lay around Place Bertin, and 'at a few places, some few signs of a systematic excavation after treasure were noticeable'. Most striking of all, clumps of banana trees and sugar cane were sprouting from heaps of ashes. Life in all its splendid and selfish forms had started again; even Pelée's lower flanks had broken out in brilliant green.

But Heilprin's real interest lay higher up the mountain. Undeterred by his experiences in May, he was ready for a second assault on Pelée. Since 9 July *La Montagne* had been quiet. But soon after Heilprin's arrival, Pelée began to growl and grumble once more, as if it had sensed his return. The second ascent was set for Saturday 30 August. This time, Heilprin was joined by a photographer called Julian Cochrane, three assistants and seven volunteers, who seemed to draw courage from the American's presence. As they strode through sunlit fields of cocoa and swaying cane, Heilprin was delighted to see new life all around him. The sky was full of blackbirds and flycatchers, while hundreds of green-and-black caterpillars were munching their way through fresh vegetation.

Pelée was not so welcoming. A storm cloud swirled above their heads, accompanied by what Heilprin describes as the most appalling roar: 'Were it possible to unite all the furnaces of the globe into a single one', he writes, 'and to simultaneously let loose their blasts of steam, it does not seem to me that such a sound could be produced . . . The mountain fairly quivered under its work, and it was perhaps not wholly discreditable that some of us should have felt anything but comfortable.' Heilprin pressed on, reassuring his anxious party. After all, nothing could match the torrential assault he had experienced in May . . .

At three thousand four hundred feet, Heilprin changed his mind. A whistling sound, like that of a bullet or a missile, shot over his head, closely followed by a second and then a third. They were being bombarded by molten rocks. 'We were in battle,' he writes breathlessly, 'the bombs and boulders coursing through the air in parabolic curves and straight lines, driven and shot out as if from a giant catapult.' Retreat was the only option. Scrabbling and scrambling through thick fog, Heilprin fell back behind a high rock about one hundred feet down. The volunteers had seen enough. Ignoring Heilprin's pleas, they raced down the mountain to safety.

Heilprin had a choice. He could join his fleeing colleagues or continue this life-threatening mission on his own. A sane, sensible person would have turned back at this point. Fortunately, Heilprin possessed neither of these qualities. Pelée had beaten him once; he was determined it would not defy him again. With great *sang-froid* he writes: 'Not wishing to incur any responsibility in a call for company in what appeared to be a rather hazardous enterprise, I made a second attempt by myself, keeping my body as close to the ground as was possible.' The volunteers vanishing into mist far below fancied their mad American friend was touched with good luck. They would soon find out if that was true.

Crouching like an infantryman under sniper fire, Heilprin resumed his ascent, shielding his face with a raised arm. Pieces of hot rock, which he called 'bursting bombs', shot past on both sides. 'The roar of the volcano was terrific – awful beyond description. It felt as if the very earth was being sawed in two.' After about fifteen minutes, he reached the *Lac des Palmistes*. All was as it had been three months earlier, the summit engulfed in steam 'as if in a surging sea'. Heilprin lay flat on the dusty ground, but to no avail. He had risked his life for nothing. 'It was useless to remain longer in the open fire', he writes despairingly, 'and I descended to join my associates.' Pelée had one final joke to play on the Americans. Heilprin and Cochrane were standing together on the hillside when a bursting bomb landed ten feet away from them, soaking every thread of their shirts, jackets and pants. *La Montagne* had defied Heilprin a second time.

That night, Pelée laid on a firework display of such wonder that Heilprin and his companions quite forgot the disappointments of the afternoon. From a balcony at the *Habitation Pécoul*, they watched a black-and-purple sky fill with electric flashes of great intensity. 'Scintillating stars burst forth like crackling fireworks, and serpent lines wound themselves in and out like travelling wave crests.' Ash rained down, in the order already noted by Flett and Anderson: particles the size of peas, then lentils and then sand. The only worry in Heilprin's mind was the fiery red glow hovering above Morne Rouge. 'No flame was visible, but it was only too evident that fire was devastating somewhere.'

It was not until the next morning that these fears were confirmed. The villages of Morne Balai, Morne Capot and Ajoupa-Bouillon had been destroyed by a dust cloud even bigger than the one which overran Saint-Pierre. Morne Rouge was no more. Heilprin encountered harrowing sights at every turn: cattle and horses lying on their backs, 'with their legs rigidly extended into mid-air'; a young woman of thirty years 'rolling in agony in one corner of a dark room, her flesh terribly burned and hanging in places from the bone'. Less than four months had passed since the catastrophe of 8 May, noted Heilprin, and the tragedy was being enacted all over again. Yet private grief fought with a guilty sense of relief; yesterday's storms had clearly been a prelude to this much greater catastrophe. The Americans were lucky to have escaped.

Over a thousand people died in the eruption of 30 August. Among them, Father Mary, friend and nurse to Ludger Sylbaris. Like many of his parishioners, Father Mary had only just returned to Morne Rouge, believing Pelée's danger had passed. Heilprin finds consolation in his final moments:

When the presbytery was on fire he sought the shelter of the church, but was struck by the hot blast before that building could be reached. He succeeded, however, in dragging himself into the interior, and, with terrible suffering, stretched himself upon a bench. Here he was found at four o'clock the following morning, still fully conscious and expressing anxiety for his flock. He was removed to Fond-Saint-Denis, and thence to Fort-de-France, where he expired at eleven o'clock of the morning of September 1 – a man honoured by all.

Notre Dame de la Délivrande, Morne Rouge

A wave of misery swept across the island. Just as Martinicans had begun to get their lives back in order, *La Montagne* had reminded them that their situation was hopeless, beyond repair. Geologists now conceded there was a real risk that Martinique's northern half might crumble into the sea; the colony would have to be abandoned. To make matters worse, Martinique's politicians were falling back into their old habits. The petty politicking of Saint-Pierre – which many blamed for the 8 May disaster – had returned, much to the dismay of Governor Lemaire. Each day his mansion was surrounded by noisy crowds, shouting against 'the apparent indifference of the *Métropole*' as he put it. Lemaire knew these protests were being orchestrated by the island's leftist faction. After all, he was a Conservative, well disposed towards Fernand Clerc and his *clique* of white landowners: a stance guaranteed to enrage Amédée Knight's Radical Party.

To start with, Lemaire reported the protests sympathetically. People were depressed after the eruption of 30 August; Maurice

Bloch's pot of money was fast running out. 'I cannot hide from you', Lemaire told Paris on 11 September, 'that the progressive part of the population, along with some elected representatives, mayors and councillors, have been struck by a real sense of discouragement.' The solution, wrote Lemaire, was for Paris to send more money. 'Although the new catastrophe has increased our difficulties, I estimate that with the *Métropole*'s help, the situation is not irremediable . . . This help must appear immediately.' But as the weeks wore on and difficulties mounted, Governor Lemaire came under immense strain. It was impossible, he realised, to please Paris and Fort-de-France at the same time.

One can trace this process through Lemaire's increasingly exasperated dispatches to Paris. 400,000 francs were spent on public relief in September 1902: a marked improvement on Maurice Bloch's ill-judged 24,100 francs in June. Yet by the end of September, Governor Lemaire felt his efforts were being frustrated at every turn. Food rations had been cut by a third, because people were using false names to extort extra supplies; refugees were refusing to work because they thought Paris was holding back millions of francs in public donations. 'Their general theme', wrote Lemaire, 'is this: "There are 8 million francs for us in France, that should be given to us. When that has been used up, we shall decide what to do. If the government cuts off our rations, then we will march *en masse* on Fort-de-France."'

Lemaire placed his faith in public works. Two new settlements were built to house refugee families, and to provide paid employment. The *Tivoli* at Fort-de-France would hold 180 families; *La Démarche*, near Case Pilote, almost double that number. But even these initiatives could not defuse the animosity between Lemaire and his Radical enemies. By 31 November, the Governor had had enough. 'In this town [Fort-de-France], I have met with an inertia and a systematic hostility which I am unable to define', he spat. All food aid, except for emergency relief, had been halted. In the privacy of a ministerial dispatch, Lemaire railed against his fellow citizens in quite extraordinary language: 'There is a native apathy and indolence in the population. Most of all, there is an immense credulity which is exploited by some (political) leaders and some parasites in search of easy popularity . . .'

It was a familiar enough trajectory. Lemaire was not the first Governor to rage against Martinique's political schemers. Nor would he be the last. But were his private frustrations – expressed in startlingly bigoted language – at all justified? Certainly not, screamed the Radicals. They were the victims, not the poor, pampered Governor. French policy was driven by 'Negrophobia', by a deep suspicion of black or mixed-race politicians. As Senator Knight's mouthpiece *L'Opinion* put it on 9 September:

EDITORIAL

There comes a time when one's thoughts reach breaking point and when, far from clearing up, the horizon only seems to darken around us. When we see our brave brothers sighing in vain for help which they have merited ten times over, when finally, a new disaster comes to add still more to the horror of our situation, we should find our silence to be criminal. Let us, therefore, protest at this hour . . .

The message was clear. A volcanic explosion should lead to a political explosion, in which France and Martinique established a more 'adult' accord. Not that anyone knew how this would work, or when it would start. 'The battle of politics was again being hotly waged', wrote Angelo Heilprin sadly, 'and with the same intensity and personal feeling as at the time of the destruction of Saint-Pierre. It seemed as if the volcano had already been entirely forgotten.'

The political storms stirred up by Mont Pelée took several years to subside. French MPs were still arguing over Governor Lemaire and the Bloch mission in 1905, when a special debate was held on the issue. Time had done nothing to reduce the sense of hurt and neglect. The former Minister for Colonies, Gaston Doumergue, insisted that France had done all it possibly could for Martinique. Which French *département*, he sneered, had ever received quite so much state support as the Antillean island? The Deputy for Southern Martinique leapt to his feet. Homère Clément's words resound down the years, full of rightful indignation:

> I beg to ask him in which period of history did a misfortune similar to the one which has desolated my country hit any part of mainland France? I ask him – where and when did an entire town disappear so suddenly, where and when were 35,000 inhabitants annihilated in the space of a second, as in Martinique . . . ?

While politicians squabbled, geologists were transfixed by a strange new phenomenon. A huge white slab of lava had begun to sprout from Pelée's summit, growing at up to fifty feet per day. The white obelisk was around five hundred feet wide at its base, and glowed at night with red veins of light. Scientists and locals alike called it the Tower of Pelée, but no one had any idea how this striking object had been formed, or why it continued to grow. By the end of November 1902, the Tower had reached 800 feet above the surface; by March of 1903, it had risen to 1,020 feet. Nothing like it had ever been seen before.

One geologist in particular became obsessed with the lava monolith. Professor Alfred Lacroix, of the French Academy of Sciences, had made a short visit to Martinique in July 1902, and returned again after the second disastrous eruption of 30 August. 'Of all the phenomena produced during the eruption', he wrote, 'the most important from the point of view of the history of volcanism . . . consisted in the creation of an andesitic dome in the crater of the

The Tower of Pelée

Étang Sec.' Lacroix and his assistant, Captain Perney, became so intrigued by *L'Aiguille* (the needle) that they built an observation post high up on Pelée's flanks at Morne des Cadets. From here, Perney drew a series of pencil sketches of the Tower's daily progress. Some days it shot upwards. Other days it lost height and width as chunks of molten rock peeled away like skins from an onion.

The Tower was not an entirely new feature. An earlier version had crept over the lip of Pelée's summit in early summer, only to be destroyed in the eruption of 9 July. As far back as 1 June, Heilprin and Kennan had reported seeing 'a central cone of volcanic debris' deep inside Pelée's crater, a sight later confirmed by Thomas A. Jaggar and by the British team of Flett and Anderson – although the Britons had mistaken Pelée's budding Tower for a crag of rock. To Alfred Lacroix, the White Spine presented two separate, but equally absorbing mysteries. First, there was the Tower's chemical composition, and its habit of changing colour from deepest brown to roseate pink, purple and white. Then there was the question of *how* it had been formed. It was as if the lava was being gently squeezed out of the summit crater like toothpaste from a tube. Or perhaps the dome served another function altogether. Either way, Lacroix hoped it would help explain why Pelée had erupted on 8 May. The Tower had set his brain working in quite a different way to his American and British colleagues. And it was this intuitive leap which was to lead to the greatest and most lasting discovery about Pelée.

For six months, Lacroix and his wife scoured Pelée's lunar slopes for clues. Mme Lacroix, an enthusiastic amateur geologist in her own right, took many of the photographs. From time to time, she makes a guest appearance in front of the camera: peering here into the mountain's steamy crater alongside her husband. The linen jackets and parasols may look somewhat amateur – better suited to a summer picnic than a tussle with a volcano – but their approach was formidably professional. When Lacroix's epic study of *La Montagne Pelée et ses Éruptions* (647 pages, plus plates) appeared in 1904, it made previous scientific studies seem rushed and superficial.

Lacroix's first discovery was a relatively simple one. Yet it had been missed by everyone else. During his daily walks, Lacroix noticed that debris from the May eruptions had gathered in unusual places. Logic suggested that rocks and stones would have raced down the steepest slopes. But Lacroix found that most of the ejected material had rolled down much gentler gradients. Gravity alone (Flett and Anderson's theory) could not account for these movements; there must have been some other propulsive force *inside* Mont Pelée which had helped to give these objects their momentum. Heilprin and Hovey's theory of a lateral blast, shooting debris out of Pelée's side like a cannon, may have had something to it, after all.

Lacroix's second breakthrough related to Pelée's ash clouds. Like Anderson and Flett, the French geologist was lucky enough to see one of these clouds in action, and promptly gave this new phenomenon a proper name. Lacroix called them *Nuées Ardentes*, or Glowing Clouds. On 16 December, he was in Saint-Pierre harbour on board the French cruiser *Jouffroy* when a lengthy grumble came from the mountain top. A wall of ash and flame up to 4,000 metres high raced downhill, engulfing a tiny yacht moored beside the shore, and then trailing off into the sky. Lacroix had initially thought of calling these cauliflower-shaped clouds *dense* rather than *glowing*, but having seen them in action, he changed his mind. As for their structure, Lacroix thought the *nuées* were 'an intimate blend, a sort of emulsion, of solid materials suspended in water vapour and gas, carried together in a high temperature'.

These internal dynamics explained, in turn, the *mélange* of debris held within the cloud. British and American geologists had already noticed the order in which rocks and particles fell away from an advancing cloud. Lacroix suggested this was due to their peculiar composition. He asks us to imagine the cross section of a *nuée ardente*:

> At the base, one finds the highest temperature zone, in which solid materials predominate . . . Above this, and overlapping with it, one finds sections in which the proportions and the dimensions of solid objects diminishes more and more.

At the base of the *nuée*, Lacroix also noticed a wedge of black debris protruding like a tongue. This 'base surge' appeared to give the cloud its implacable speed and momentum. Drawing together eyewitness accounts and geological samples, the French professor was now tentatively able to explain how Saint-Pierre had met its end, under the assault of a massive *nuée ardente*. 'It constituted, in effect, an enormous mass of gas and vapour, carrying a great quantity of scorching hot material, [and] preceded in its departure by incandescent rocks . . . this curving, opaque mass rolled along the surface of the soil, with a much lower tip out in front, then it had expanded and obscured the sky.'

Which left the question of why this glowing cloud had rolled down onto Saint-Pierre with such ferocity, killing almost everything in its path. The answer, it turned out, was staring Lacroix in the face. What if the Tower of Pelée was not the paste in a toothpaste tube, he wondered, but the stopper holding that paste in place? Perhaps these constant upward lurches were a response to pressures *underneath* the lava bloc? This simple idea led Lacroix to a revolutionary conclusion: that Pelée's white monolith was in fact a giant plug of solidified lava, which was blocking up the volcanic vent like a cork in a bottle. When pressure within the mountain became too great, as on 8 May, steam and gas escaped from the summit's weakest point. On this occasion, that meant the fissure noted earlier by Angelo Heilprin. This sudden, catastrophic release of pressure had given the lethal cloud its momentum. It also explained the terrifying sight witnessed by Flett and Anderson on 9 July, when the 'rolling and spouting' clouds had appeared to swell faster than their minds could comprehend. Lacroix explains: 'The form and dimensions that [the cloud] presents at the moment of release from the dome's carapace shows that it was subject to a formidable compression, because after several seconds, it occupied a volume many thousands of times greater than it had possessed during its release.'

Lacroix's theory incorporated elements from all his predecessors. From Hovey, Hill and Heilprin he took the idea of a huge, propulsive force firing itself laterally from a weakness in the mountain wall, like a cannon or a gun. From Anderson and Flett, he absorbed the notion of gravity as an important motive force driving the *nuée* downhill. And from the Tower of Pelée he had drawn ideas taken from his own diligent observation. Lacroix spent a year poring over the ruins of Saint-Pierre, measuring every possible aspect of its destruction. The only previous sighting of a *nuée ardente* had been in the Azores in 1580 and 1808. But Pelée's eruption had been of a quite different order. By the end of his study, Lacroix could confidently declare that the world had witnessed the birth of an entirely new kind of volcanic action. Such outbursts in future would be known as *Peléan* eruptions:

> Instead of always being thrown vertically, as with normal erup-
> tions, the *nuées* roll with great speed down the slopes of the
> mountain. In the case of weaker eruptions, gravity has the
> predominant influence on its progress; while with great parox-
> ysms, they are driven by a much more rapid movement, due to
> the accumulated force of the initial projection and to the gravity
> acting in the same direction. With Mont Pelée, the position of the
> exit point had a decisive influence on its direction.

Lacroix's inspiration, the Tower of Pelée, lasted until the autumn of 1903, when it collapsed under its own overbearing weight. But not before leaving a mark on the people of Martinique. To them it represented, as Angelo Heilprin said, 'nature's monument dedicated to the 30,000 dead who lay in the silent city below'.

On Survivors &c

Before leaving Martinique, Alfred Lacroix met the Lone Survivor of
Saint-Pierre, establishing to his own satisfaction that Ludger Sylbaris
was telling the truth about his remarkable escape. There was a
problem, though. A little *incongruity*, shall we say. Lacroix also talked
to a man called Léon Compère-Léandre, a twenty-eight-year-old
black cobbler who had an equally astonishing story, and one which
the circus agents and news reporters had forgotten in their rush to
embroider the Sylbaris myth. Léandre said the 'Lone Survivor' story
was nonsense. For he too had survived the terrible cataclysm, and
had the burns to prove it.

Léandre's story first appeared in a French daily paper called
Temps, and was later reprinted by the Astronomical Society of
France in August 1902. He described how, on the morning of
8 May, he was sitting on the doorstep of his house in the
southeastern part of Saint-Pierre, facing away from the great
mountain. He felt a strong wind blowing; the earth began to
shake, and the sky became dark. Léandre struggled back inside,
his arms and legs already burning:

> I hid under a table. At this moment, four others sought refuge in
> my room, crying and writhing with pain, although their garments
> showed no sign of having been touched with flame.
>
> At the end of ten minutes, one of these . . . (a young girl aged
> about ten) fell dead; the others left. I then got up and went into
> another room, where I found the father Delavaud, still clothed,
> and lying on the bed, dead. He was purple and inflated, but his
> clothing was intact.
>
> I went out, and found in the courtyard two corpses interlocked
> . . . Re-entering the house, I came upon two other bodies . . .
>
> Crazed and almost overcome, I threw myself upon a bed, inert
> and awaiting death. My senses returned to me in perhaps an hour,
> when I beheld the roof burning. With sufficient strength left, my

legs bleeding and covered with burns, I ran to Fond-Saint-Denis,
six kilometres from Saint-Pierre . . .

Léandre's story was barely reported by the newspapers. They
preferred to stick with Ludger Sylbaris, Lone Survivor of the
World's Worst Volcano: why spoil a good yarn with an awkward
new fact? Barnum and Bailey's Chief Press Agent, Tody Hamilton,
seemed to think the same way. Never short of an adjective or three,
Hamilton had already concocted a notice for the opening stand at
Madison Square Garden on 17 March 1903. Sylbaris would be *The
Sole and Only Survivor of the World's most Horrible Cataclysm*; *The
Modern Miracle*. And in case there are any doubters amongst you,
ladies and gentlemen: *His Identity and Absolute Genuineness indisputably attested, proved and established!*

NINE

SHOWTIME

T HERE IS only one individual photograph of Ludger Sylbaris in the Barnum and Bailey archive, and it is a most peculiar sight. The not-quite-so Lone Survivor of Saint-Pierre stands in front of a circus tent, staring dourly at the camera. He is wrapped in a white cloth, like a Roman senator, and carries a trowel in his right hand. His head is covered with an ugly, ill-fitting wig which appears to have escaped from one of the animal cages. Little wonder he has such a long face.

Either way, the picture is a mystery. The archivists at the Circus World Museum in Baraboo, Wisconsin, have no idea why young Ludger is dressed up like this; each of us holds the picture in turn and wonders aloud about its history. Perhaps this was how the poor man protected his wounds, says one. It must have been very hot that summer; look at his left hand, all scarred and shri-

velled! Maybe they were having a fancy dress party or something, says another. They would do that from time to time, when they got sick of all the travelling. As for me, I think he looks lonely and lost.

A handwritten note on the reverse doesn't take us much further. No dates or place names, just a simple inscription: 'Photo by Frank Crowe'. A riffle through the Route Book for 1903 reveals that Crowe played second violin and French horn in Barnum's Big Top band. Perhaps he and Ludger had become friends. Or maybe the violinist wanted to record one extraordinary fact. Sylbaris was the first black performer to appear in a Barnum and Bailey show, his remarkable story somehow excusing him from the company's informal colour bar. American blacks made up a large part of the circus road crew, but the sight of one of their brethren on a Barnum stage, before a largely white, East Coast audience was unprecedented. Given this sensitivity, it's worth noting how Barnum and Bailey presented their new recruit. Ludger Sylbaris was placed in the 'Museum': a loose, catch-all term for some of the more educative elements in that year's freak show. It was as if he could only be seen, in this white world, as a freak of nature: an object to be studied rather than understood.

An answer to the photographic riddle comes magically, accidentally. Among a pile of souvenirs from the 1903 tour, we find a neatly printed pamphlet called *Parade List*. Each day and in every town, the circus would proclaim its presence with a rowdy, raucous street parade. The *List* lays out everyone's duties, from the lowliest camel driver to the most delicate ballerina, describing what they should wear, and the order in which their floats should appear. Barnum's Parade was a fabulously costly affair: a dazzling pageant of twenty-nine coach-sized wagons, painted in various shades of gold and silver, scarlet and clover green. Each parade would start with the '40 Horse Hitch', a troupe of bay horses towing a gigantic replica of the world's two hemispheres. They were followed by a prowling, snarling line of lions and tigers, panthers and hyenas. Close behind came a pair of elephants with howdahs swaying from their uncomplaining backs. And after them, an array of lavish, beautifully tinted wagons upon which circus performers acted out all kinds of mythical and magical scenes. The *Fairy Tales* float included an obligatory Fairy Queen, complete with 'jewelled headdress, large wig and gold cloth sandals' and a Humpty-Dumpty Boy, dressed in what the *List* described as: 'Large white property head with peep holes where the eyes are'. Another wagon had the more prosaic title of *Our Country*: for which spectators got a wagon driven by Uncle Sam ('Hat, wig, chin whiskers, false vest') and a cast of former Presidents McKinley, Washington and Lincoln ('Hat, coat, watch-chain and beard').

What a spectacle it must have been. Clowns racing up and down driveways on unicycles, stealing hats and bursting balloons. What a noise they all must have made: marching down State and Main to the excited shriek of a calliope, its steam whistles fluting furiously. Every day the goal was the same: to 'crack the nut', to meet the circus's daily expenses and even make a little profit. Daily parades helped drum up interest for that night's show, and few children could resist following the cavalcade back to its overnight home: a rough patch of land near to a gleaming railroad track.★ The *Parade List* makes clear that every performer was expected to take part in these processions. Freaks, or at least able-bodied freaks, were no exception. The answer to our question lay here in the *Parade List*. Racing past *The Golden Age of Chivalry* (cast to include 'One Captive Maiden' from ballet) and *Funny Folks* ('One Jack-in-the-Box' played by Harry Friskey), I come across a tail-end wagon called *Africa* . . . and there he is. Playing a 'Nubian' of all things. The costume list prescribes 'wig, shirt, tights, shield, spear, shoes and rope', and everything falls into place. Even the trowel. Or is it a spear?

Ludger Sylbaris, sometime freak, sometime African tribesman, was in good company. Every member of his Africa float had been

★ Except in Germany, apparently. People were so impressed by the daily street parades on Barnum's European Tour, that they mistook them for actual circus performances. To restore ticket sales, the parades were cancelled.

recruited from the Side Show, with some casting decisions more inspired than others. Billy Wells, the Hard Headed Man, made an ideal Boer, at least metaphorically. The idea of Mohammed Soliman, Whirling Dervish and Fire Eater, as an Egyptian Infantryman was harder to imagine. I show the cast list to one of the Baraboo archivists, who is delighted we have found an answer to the photograph mystery. An unlikely bunch of Africans, I venture. 'Well, you know the old showbiz adage', she says drily. 'Work with what you've got.'

    And work they did. Life with Barnum and Bailey was much tougher than life in easygoing Saint-Pierre: everyone was on call from 9am until 10 or 11pm, six days a week. Each day began with a street parade, followed by an afternoon show at two and an evening show at eight. Side Show acts had to be in place an hour before that, to work the new audience. Nor did the day end there; once the evening gig had finished, performers were hustled off into railway sleepers, and dispatched like parcels to 'tomorrow's town'. One wonders what young Sylbaris made of it all: the unfamiliar trains hurtling from place to place; the old timers gassing on about lots, turns and tricks; the shitty stench of honey buckets rising up from underneath his toilet floor. Did Ludger make friends with any of his fellow freaks, or were the twin walls of language and culture too high to scale? Certainly, there was no time for his old roustabout antics. Barnum and Bailey ran a clean, Sunday school kind of show. Boozing, brawling, or any kind of activity which drew unwelcome 'heat' to the company would trigger an instant dismissal. Which was a shame if you thought circuses were *louche*, freewheeling affairs where you could make lots of money. As the trains chugged and chuffed over silver, moonlit tracks, the Lonely Survivor must have wondered whether it was all worth the effort. That Nubian wig didn't help either.

Barnum's new show won tremendous reviews. Every newspaper agreed that the Greatest Show on Earth's five-year absence in

Europe had only served to make it bigger and better than ever before. The reviewers could hardly contain their excitement. 'Circuses may come and circuses may go', declared the *New York Clipper*, 'but to New Yorkers none of them seem to be as enticing or marvellous as that with which the name of P.T. Barnum is associated.' 'The Greatest Show on Earth is still the greatest of them all', crowed the *Daily American*, while the *New York Tribune* judged 'each department stronger than ever before'. Critics were particularly taken with Cyclo the Kinetic Demon, who raced around a circular wooden cage on his bicycle, riding up the walls at right angles to the floor. Bolossy Kiralfy's opening pageant drew wave after wave of applause. As to the Freak Show, *Billboard* remarked that it held 'the most complete line of novelties that has ever been seen in one exhibition'. From its opening afternoon on Wednesday 18 March, until its closing night on Saturday 25 April, Barnum and Bailey managed to sell out Madison Square Garden twice a day for five weeks. 'Each time we see it, it seems better and grander than ever before', marvelled the *Clipper*, 'until one wonders when the limit will be reached.'

They would find out soon enough. As the Greatest Show on Earth wound its way through Pennsylvania and New Jersey, it ran into problems. Barnum and Bailey's new show – marvellous in its magnificence, stupendous in its size – was simply too big to move. Like a bloated, overweight monster, it lumbered across the East Coast leaving behind a trail of missed dates and cancelled shows. All of James A. Bailey's innovations seemed to backfire: the twelve-pole tent took an eternity to pitch and pull down; the French opera seats were heavy and awkward, and the electricity supply as skittish as a frightened horse. Then there was the hubristic scale of the show itself. The task of moving 1,200 people and 1,000 animals often brought the whole operation to a standstill. Morning parades had to be cancelled when wagons failed to arrive; afternoon performances were lost because the Big Top was not ready.

Rumours soon began to surface in the trade press. Barnum and Bailey's comeback show had ground to a halt, they said; overworked employees were threatening to strike over their sheer, backbreaking workload. On 30 May, *Billboard* reported:

BARNUM STUFF TOO HEAVY

Reports from the men who have left Barnum & Bailey Shows, indicate that the trouble is not so much a difference as to wages as on account of the heaviness of the stuff carried. Many men say it is a physical impossibility to move much of the material, and in consequence no help can be secured until the stuff is cut down. The show has lost several stands on account of the shortage of men, and it is evident that something must be done quickly or the show will be thrown into week stands exclusively . . .

All this compared unfavourably of course with the slick, professional operation being run by the Ringling Brothers, who had opened their season in Chicago on 9 April. Barnum and Bailey were trapped by their own imperial ambitions, by their determination to be the biggest and the best. By early July, press rumours had got so out of control that James Bailey's sidekick, Louis E. Cooke, was forced to issue a statement. Cooke admitted there had been difficulties. 'Our show is so cumbersome, so mighty', he wrote, 'that for a long time it was a perplexing proposition how we would ever be able to make the one day stands in time.' Cooke assured readers however that matters were now in hand, and the show was in 'apple-pie order'.

But this bluff public statement hid all kinds of troubles. Barnum and Bailey were failing to 'crack the nut' on a regular basis: the show was running at a huge loss, made worse by its massive outlay on new props and performers. According to historian Richard E. Conover, James A. Bailey spent $14,000 on French-made costumes for the American season. He also invested in thirteen new bandwagons. Given that the going rate for new parade chariots was anything between \$10–\$20,000 (the Two Hemispheres wagon was worth \$50,000), then one can assume an extra expense of well over \$100,000. 'The inevitable strain on overworked employees pyramided into labour trouble', Conover concludes, 'late arrivals and an unsuccessful season.' To aggravate matters, Barnum and Bailey were about to swing back into New York State, where they would run head to head with Ringlings for several days. Rival teams of billposters had already skirmished ahead of the two shows; the first clashes were set for Kingston on 3 June and Albany on 4 June.

A year was to pass before Martinicans felt safe enough to return to their homes. Yet eventually they did go back. Slowly, warily, they left government shanty towns around Fort-de-France and headed north to their family plots, as if responding to some inner conviction. Only there, beneath Pelée's cloud-wrapped summit, would they feel truly at home. One of the many thousands to make this journey was a young man called Gervais Marageot. According to a police report, Marageot left his makeshift home at Fond Lahaye in the middle of the night, along with his wife and six children. The *gendarme* stresses it was not an impulsive decision. M. Marageot was toiling in workshops for one and three quarter francs per day; his wife earned just one franc a day. The couple were miserable and homesick. Little by little, M. Marageot had absented himself from the civic workshop and slipped back to his land at Grand' Rivière. On that final night, 8 June 1903, he left for good. 'He preferred to return to Grand' Rivière', the policeman writes simply, 'to cultivate his own land.'

Relations between Paris and Fort-de-France also improved with the departure of Governor Lemaire in October 1903. His replacement, a genial, broad-minded Republican called M. Richard, took a very different tack, taking particular care to charm Senator Knight and his allies. Governor Richard's dispatches are more optimistic than those of the embittered Lemaire: partly, one suspects, because he inherited a more stable situation, but also because he felt more sympathy for his fellow islanders. 'The Martinican population is peaceful and listens willingly to appeals for reconciliation and good sense', he confided on 8 October. The new Governor also promised a 'new direction' for those without work. In November, he addressed an eager crowd: 'I reminded the refugees gathered around me, that they were part of a great nation where work is an honour and where professional begging is frowned upon. I was loudly applauded, and hands stretched out to grab hold of agricultural tools.' Some of the hurt inflicted by Maurice Bloch and Governor Lemaire was slowly being undone.

There remained the question of Saint-Pierre. No one knew what to do with their ruined town. Should it be abandoned altogether and left as a memorial to the dead – or was it better to start building once again, to inspire people with a spirit of renewal? Something had to be done. Thieves still preyed on the rubble, plucking rings and necklaces from skeletons and safes. They operated in gangs, and one senses a certain political touch to their work. In December 1902, twenty-three-year-old Raoul Milia was found guilty of breaking into a safe at the *Maison Lalung*, home to one of Saint-Pierre's oldest families. His brother Raphael, nineteen, was charged with the same offence at *Maison Dupuis*. Other members of the Milia family, including their sixty-year-old father Pierre, were also jailed. Pelée had given Martinique's criminals an unmissable chance to take revenge on their social betters; a macabre version of *Carnaval*'s upside-down world.

There was a more perplexing matter too.

Saint-Pierre was fast becoming a tourist attraction, with cruise ships darting into its blue bay to examine the ruins. The first visitors, on Sunday 3 January, came from an English yacht, the *Argonaut*. According to Governor Lemaire between 100 to 150 'sightseers' had come ashore, where they were escorted around the city by two bemused *gendarmes*. Two weeks later a German steamer, the *Moltke*, demanded a repeat performance for three hundred Americans. Lemaire raised two concerns with his Parisian bosses, neither of which had much to do with the propriety of such visits. First, he wanted to ensure proper evacuation procedures were in place in case Pelée erupted, a sensible enough precaution. Secondly, and not so sensibly, he demanded a major clear-up of the city streets in order not to offend American sensibilities. Saint-Pierre, scene of the world's most destructive volcano, was to be smartened up. 'In order not to make this spectacle too painful', he writes proudly, 'I have, over the past two weeks, taken care to bury the bones and cadavers left around each day by pillagers *sans scrupule*.'

Not everything went to plan. Mont Pelée itself was liable to misbehave without warning. On 25 January, a party of English, American and German sightseers from the steamer *Esk* had an uncomfortably close encounter with *La Montagne*. After an hour and a half of blithe meandering around Saint-Pierre's ruins, the three hundred or so visitors heard a distant rumbling sound. 'A dense fog rolled down the mountain', wrote Lemaire, 'directing itself at Saint-Pierre, and then continuing its descent via the Roxelane valley and the *Rivière des Pères*, before advancing several kilometres into the sea.' So alarmed were the visitors that about fifty passengers threw themselves overboard, and began swimming towards Carbet, two miles south of Saint-Pierre. It took a further two hours to recover the evacuees, all mightily upset by their experiences. Lemaire took the day's events in his stride. Martinique had seen much worse, and it did no harm to teach these mawkish tourists a little lesson. 'I seriously envisage the possibility of launching a new *genre* of sport', the Governor informed Paris, his tongue wedged firmly in his cheek.

1903 also saw the publication of John Flett and Tempest Anderson's exhaustive report *On the Eruptions of the Soufrière and on a Visit to*

Montagne Pelée. They shared Lacroix's view that a new form of volcanic eruption had occurred, 'of a type which hitherto has not been known to exist', and that in future such blasts should be known as 'Peléan Eruptions'. The most recent classification of volcanoes, by James Dwight Dana, had talked of Quiet, Explosive and Intermediate eruptions. Based on what they had seen in Saint-Pierre, the two Britons proposed a distinct new category of eruptive action. Although the Pelée and Soufrière blasts shared some features of Explosive eruptions, they also displayed several unique qualities of their own. Among them:

i) Discharges of 'incandescent sand' which raced down mountain slopes as a 'hot sand avalanche'.

ii) The presence of 'a great black cloud of gases charged with hot dust' which swept over the countryside at great speed, destroying every object in its path.

iii) The sharply defined zones of destruction. Beyond the zone of annihilation, men and animals were scorched by hot sand or mud. But 'beyond the limits covered by the great black cloud no effects are produced, other than those consequent on the rain of ashes which precedes or follows the avalanche'.

These features would be refined later by Lacroix, who offered more details on the 'glowing clouds' or *nuées ardentes*. But in essence, Flett and Anderson had laid the foundations for what they rightly recognised as 'this new branch of the science of volcanology'.

After establishing the basic physical features of Peléan eruptions, the two Britons went on to outline four distinct stages of such blasts. The early *premonitory* stage included minor earthquakes ('not so violent as to damage houses, but so frequent as to awaken apprehension') as well as increased emission of steam and ash from the summit. During the *preliminary* stages, these outbursts of steam, ash and rock increased in intensity. Fissures began to open on the volcano's flanks and, in the case of Mont Pelée, rivers became augmented with boiling mud. After reading the extensive newspaper reports leading up to 8 May, Flett and Anderson concluded that the preliminary stage in Martinique had lasted for over two weeks, starting around the time that Clara Prentiss heard 'three distinct shocks' on Wednesday 23 April. The 'mud lavas' which deluged the *Usine Guérin* on 5 May were part of this preliminary phase too.

The *climax* of a Peléan eruption came without any warning. After a slow build up of days or even weeks, a shattering blast would fill the air:

> The great black cloud wells out of the crater and rushes down the slopes, obliterating all trace of vegetation, annihilating every living thing in its path, and leaving behind it a desert of ashes. Its appearance is usually terribly sudden, a few minutes previously the volcano may have been emitting only a little steam and fine dust, perhaps more than usual, but not enough to awaken any general alarm . . .

It is not hard to detect the influence of Flett and Anderson's own experiences in these descriptions. Having seen Pelée's eruptive force at first hand, they were well aware of how suddenly, how craftily, the black cloud could descend. As a result, they were reluctant to criticise the French authorities as freely as the newsroom volcanologists of New York and Chicago. Their conclusions were more generous, more humane. Saint-Pierre had simply been overtaken by a disaster beyond anyone's comprehension. On 8 May, the city's residents were 'uneasy, but not madly excited', they write. 'Things looked no worse than they had done often during the previous five days . . . So sudden, so unexpected, was the great catastrophe, that death overtook most of its inhabitants before they knew what had happened.'

After these terrible events, the volcano would slowly slip back into repose. The *concluding* stages were, in many respects, similar to the pre-eruptive phases. Steam and ash continued to rise from the summit, but in smaller and smaller amounts. It was as if the whole appalling process had been set in reverse. Two days after seeing Pelée's glowing clouds in action, Anderson and Flett were astonished to find barely any trace of their adventure. As they sailed around Pelée's flanks, 'there might be nothing to indicate its deadly virulence except the hot water in the streams, and the thin coating of fine, pale grey ashes which had been scattered over its surface that very morning'. The Fire Mountain had vanished as quickly as it had appeared.

Flett and Anderson also devoted a great deal of space to the physical similarities between Mont Pelée and Saint Vincent's Soufrière. Both volcanoes had erupted at roughly the same time, and with similar spectacular effects. But beyond drawing attention to their obvious geological affinities – 'Each stands at the northern end of its respective island, an isolated volcanic cone, bearing a summit crater or craters' – the British geologists were unable to draw many firm conclusions. The evidence was contradictory. Pelée's area of devastation was sharply defined, and occupied only a quarter of the volcanic cone. In Saint Vincent, Soufrière's blast covered an area twice as large, while 'the total mass of material ejected by Pelée may be perhaps one tenth of that which the Soufrière has furnished'. Ash deposits on Saint Vincent were also five times deeper than those on Martinique, and stretched 700 miles out to sea.

Anderson and Flett explained these differences in terms of morphology. Pelée's ash cloud had surged through one narrow outlet on its southwest side: the infamous 'notch' which directed the fan-shaped blast down onto Saint-Pierre. Soufrière's eruption was much more diffuse, flying out in all directions. These physical differences may have helped to explain the lack of fumaroles or fissures in Saint Vincent and their conspicuous presence in Martinique, where Pelée's internal turbulence was directed at one specific point. But the two Britons were reluctant to speculate too much; the subterranean link between Soufrière and Mont Pelée would have to wait until a later time, when geologists had a finer understanding of the forces working beneath the earth's crust.

BARNUM AND BAILEY IN 1903
Contributed by Ralph A. Spencer, Assistant Press Agent

HARMONY was one of the crowning features of the season, and with no exceptions every one regretted the close of a most pleasant summer and fall with the Greatest Show on Earth . . .

Billboard, 3 December 1903

Barnum and Bailey limped into Albany, New York State, on Wednesday 3 June. The good news was that they were a day early. The bad news was that they had cancelled two shows in Kingston, N.Y. in order to make up lost time. Despite press statements to the contrary, the Greatest Show on Earth was still in a mess. Over the past week, they had missed a parade in Trenton, New Jersey, and now, 'owing to long run and numerous delays', had been forced to pull two entire performances. 30,000 paying customers had got away. At least Albany would give them all a chance to retrieve some lost ground. But it was here, on a scrubby lot about two miles out of town, that one man's circus trail came to an abrupt end.

The Lone Survivor of Saint-Pierre, the Most Marvellous Man on Earth, had got drunk, the Albany papers reported, and then stabbed one of Barnum's nightwatchmen in the groin. Barnum and Bailey's *Route Book* draws a self-censoring veil over the incident, ashamed that one of its favoured acts had proved such an embarrassment. In circus slang, Sylbaris had 'walked off the show', although the following week's *Billboard* suggested his performances were going to have a fairly limited audience in future:

CIRCUS GOSSIP

The French negro, the sole survivor of the Mont Pelée eruption who had been a feature of the Barnum and Bailey side show, is liable to spend the rest of the season in the workhouse at Albany, N.Y., where he is now detained on a charge of cutting with intent to maim.

Ernest Zebrowski, author of *The Last Days of St Pierre*, has uncovered two highly slanted accounts of Sylbaris's assault charge in the Albany press. Barnum's legal representative, Charles Andress, tells the *Albany Argus*: 'We brought [Sylbaris] to New York, and there spent money on him and saved him from dying. We clothed and took good care of the fellow, but he has always proved an ingrate and even officials of the show are afraid of him. We don't want to bother with him anymore.' The *Press Knickerbocker* helpfully adds: '[Sylbaris] likes North American fire water and drinks all he can get hold of. When under the influence of drink he is a fiend and is liable to attack anyone.'

In some ways, it was an appropriate end to Ludger Sylbaris's American adventure. The Lone Survivor of Saint-Pierre jail was back behind bars, guilty of the same, roustabout offence which had led him to prison in the first place. It seemed Barnum's had lost patience with Sylbaris. Maybe they also realised his half-true, half-false story was not quite what it seemed. At this point, Ludger disappears again, like the city which had once been his home. A year or so after Saint-Pierre vanished, Martinicans decided that its very name should also fade from view. As a gesture of respect and in recognition of the island's implacable grief, the words 'Saint-Pierre' were crossed off every map.

2001

TEN

LOOKING FOR LUDGER

THE ROAD is never straight. It twists and winds like a serpent, a tropical switchback ride. One moment we're driving past dark forest, the next we're racing up a bare cliff side, as if preparing for an emergency take off. Everyone on the bus seems remarkably calm about this. Except me, of course. The new boy, the wide-eyed visitor who's just been catapulted across the Atlantic in eight hours and isn't quite sure where he is. Clutching a rucksack against my chest, I can't help wondering what would happen if our *Espace* sailed through those low-slung crash barriers and nosed into the watery blue. There are worse ways to go, I reason, clinging childishly to a broken seat belt.

This being France the roads are perfect, as good as any in Provence or the Côte d'Azur. The street signs are also impeccably French, right down to those bright red slashes which indicate you have left the precincts of Schoelcher or Case-Pilote, Carbet or Bellefontaine. Unfurling to our left like a typewriter ribbon is a strip of charcoal-grey sand, which gets blacker and blacker as we head north. We pass the Paul Gauguin Museum, a bright red corrugated building with a tiny steeple – and all of a sudden we are there. *Saint-Pierre*, a navy-blue roadsign announces, *City of Art and History*. It is smaller than I had imagined: a snug little place, resting in the crook of a sparkling bay. From this distance, every house seems to be piled on top of another, as if the entire town has slid downhill. High above our heads *La Montagne* sulks behind its veil of mist.

A single carriageway leads into Rue Victor Hugo and for a moment one forgets what has happened here. At first glance, nothing seems to have changed since the elusive H.K. unpacked his tripod in 1901. To our left is the white clapboard Customs House with its ornamental clock; to the right stands Saint-Pierre cathedral, complete with twin bell towers. All is as it should be. The truth reveals itself unexpectedly. Just off Saint-Pierre's main street there is a two-storey house of quite unusual colour. Its ground-floor brickwork is black and uneven while the upper floor is caramel yellow: the two floors are as distinctively different as rock strata. With a shock, you realise an act of civic cannibalism has taken place. The foundations of new Saint-Pierre, *Ville Renaissante*, have been built directly upon the remains of the old.

As your eyes adjust, you begin to see more ruins: a merchant's town house reduced to a stone shell; a pile of charred pillars and church statuary; a ragged row of seafront warehouses. Saint-Pierre is still a city of the dead, a *nécropole*, where thousands of bodies are preserved beneath our feet. The city's current inhabitants – all 5,000 of them, barely a quarter of the 1902 population – have tried to tame these spirits by turning their home into a tourist attraction. The traces of Saint-Pierre's theatre and its lunatic asylum have been restored with money from the European Union: a political invention which no Pierrotin could have imagined. The old quarrel with *la Métropole* has moved on a little: Martinique is now a *département* of France, one of the so-called 'Dom-Toms' (*Départements et Territoires d'Outre Mer*) which have opted for autonomy within Republican France rather than outright independence.★

Even Ludger Sylbaris has joined the tourist game. Saint-Pierre's most famous resident has lent his name to the *Cyparis Express*, a motorised train which putters around town offering guided tours of various ruins. The curious can step into young Ludger's solitary cell, preserved exactly as it was on the morning of 8 May 1902: the city

★ Although tensions between Caribbean countries and their old European masters can still flare from time to time. Witness the remarks of Britain's Overseas Aid Secretary Clare Short, responding to Montserrat's demands for help after a devastating volcano in 1997. 'They say £10,000, double, treble and then think of another number', she said. 'It will be be golden elephants next.'

jailbird has achieved some kind of posthumous fame. And yet, there remains something odd about the Sylbaris story, something which does not quite fit. The guide books shrug their shoulders: 'Whether he was an inspired thief or a Miracle of Pelée', writes one, 'he died carrying his secret.' But having come this far, it seems a pity not to pursue things a little further.

To start with, there is the endless confusion over that name. After Sylbaris became famous, his adventures were reported by newsmen and scientists under a variety of exotic and improbable aliases:

LOUIS-AUGUSTE CYPARIS
'SAMSON'
RAOUL SARTERET
EUCHER CYPARIS
PIERRE BACHÈRE

I seek advice from Mademoiselle Maioitte Dauphite, curator of Saint-Pierre's Historical Museum. She shows me a photocopy of Ludger Sylbaris's birth certificate and the matter is settled. Or so it seems. A few months after leaving Martinique, I have a phone conversation with an archivist called Jeanne Cazassus. When I raise the matter of Ludger Sylbaris and his many splendid names, she laughs. 'Maybe they are all correct', she says. 'No one wrote anything down in those days, so people could have several different names. They might all be true, all at the same time.'

I run into similar problems when trying to establish what Sylbaris did after leaving Barnum's Circus. Local legend says he won a pardon and went to work on the Panama Canal. He died in 1929, still a celebrated figure in Martinique. But again, the trail runs cold. There are no Cyparises or Sylbarises in Saint-Pierre; I ask Mademoiselle Maioitte if she knows of any surviving relatives. 'None', she says, smiling. 'He has left no trace.' A pattern is emerging: the more I try to find out about Ludger Sylbaris, the more he vanishes like a *quimboiseur* into thin air.

Ville Renaissante

There is one other source of information. Martinique's phone book lists two people with a similar-sounding name – Cyparisse – living at Trinité on the east coast. After drawing a blank with my first call, I expect much the same from the second. But Marcelle Cyparisse proves me wrong. She talks slowly and carefully, rather bemused by this inquiry. 'The prisoner in Saint-Pierre?' she asks. 'Yes . . . He was my Great Uncle, I think. My late father's Uncle, you see.' There are six surviving relatives, she explains. Five sisters and one brother. Do any of them know anything about Ludger, I wonder. 'No. Not at all, I'm afraid', she sighs. 'We never knew anything about him. If you find anything out, do let us know!'

Perhaps it is appropriate, given these fugitive facts, that Saint-Pierre's memory is best preserved in fiction and poetry. The words of Martinique's most celebrated writer, Aimé Césaire, are infused with volcanic imagery, a sense of imminent disaster. In the *Notebook of a Return to the Native Land*, Césaire summons 'fumaroles of anguish' and 'mountains uprooted at the hour when no one expects it'. His memory is tormented by 'lava and brush fires, and blazes of flesh and blazes of cities . . .' For Césaire, Pelée is a constant, claustrophobic presence on his island, and a reminder of how callously France has treated its Antillean outpost over the centuries. 'So much blood in my memory', he whispers.

One of Césaire's most energetic heirs, Patrick Chamoiseau, takes a more mischievous approach. In his novel *Texaco* (1992), Chamoiseau presents the disaster from the perspective of two young lovers, Esternome and Ninon, who are separated by Pelée. Their tale, Chamoiseau cackles, is one of 'Barbecued Love'. Like Césaire, he deftly combines the languages of official France and unofficial Creole, weaving them together into new patterns. This unique blend of spoken and written language is vividly displayed in Chamoiseau's account of the 8 May eruption. Esternome is woken up by Pelée's blast, and goes off in search of Ninon, his missing lover:

> One morning a huge bang blogodooom shook him into con-
> sciousness . . . Manic fleeing shook the Quarter. A fragrance of
> sulfur, of scorched-red wood, singed life, thickened the air. Each
> and every one around was screaming, Soufrière has exploded!
> Soufrière has exploded! . . . On the horizon, a night that defied
> the sun was rolling down.

Although Chamoiseau protests that too much has already been written about 'that horror', he also feels the need to bear witness, to remember. In his description of that day, one senses a little of Pelée's terrible enchantment: its ability to transfix all who saw it:

> [Esternome] floated in smoke. He trembled in an airless smell that
> had spread everywhere. He flapped his wings in silver ash. He saw
> black stones as light as soap bubbles fly toward him . . . He
> walked on . . . not seeing anything any more, so much had he

seen. A tide of ash. A deposit of still heat. The stone's red glow. Intact beings stuck to wall corners, going up in strings of smoke. Some were shrivelled up like dried grass dolls. Children savagely interrupted. Bodies undone, bones too clean, and oh how many eyes without looks . . .

Esternome never finds Ninon. Like hundreds of real people, he searches the ruins of Saint-Pierre wailing *Ouéti Ninon?* without success. By preserving such lives on paper – lives which were never celebrated in the *Bulletin Officiel* or the pages of *Les Colonies* – Chamoiseau performs his own act of remembrance.

The destruction of Saint-Pierre also inspired two British writers. Jean Rhys, a native of Dominica, captures something of the town's *louche* charm in a short prose piece called 'Heat'. Rhys was eight years old when Pelée erupted. She recalls watching a vast volcanic cloud massing over Saint-Pierre that night, a memory which she was unable to shake for the rest of her life:

> There was a huge black cloud over Martinique. I couldn't ever describe that cloud, so huge and black it was, but I have never forgotten it. There was no moon, no stars, but the edges of the cloud were flame-coloured and in the middle what looked like lightning flickered, never stopping. My mother said: 'You will never see anything like this in your life again.'

Rhys's father takes a less sentimental approach. As soon as boats are sailing again between Dominica and Martinique, he visits Saint-Pierre and returns with a pair of brass candlesticks, stolen from a derelict church. 'The heat had twisted them into an extraordinary shape', writes Rhys. 'I stared at them all through meals, trying to make sense of the shape.' As time passes, she also tries to make sense of Saint-Pierre: a town with a wicked reputation, or so the British believe. Myth has overtaken reality. 'I read all this,' concludes Rhys, 'then I thought but it wasn't like that, it wasn't like that at all.'

But the most evocative book about Saint-Pierre remains Patrick Leigh-Fermor's 1953 romance, *The Violins of Saint-Jacques*. Leigh-Fermor lightly fictionalises the events of 8 May 1902 by setting them on an invented island called Saint-Jacques des Alisés. It is carnival time in the city of Fort de Plessis, and the white planters are dancing so furiously that no one pays any attention to the volcano's first appearance, 'a deep and ominous rumble . . . above the notes of the orchestra'. Leigh-Fermor cleverly adapts many of the real events which struck Saint-Pierre in its final days. When ash begins to fall upon Fort de Plessis, his characters mistake it for snowfall; a schooner coated with flakes seems to be 'made of icing sugar and rigged with a web of rock-crystal'.

Death comes quickly. A young Frenchwoman called Berthe de Rennes is the only survivor. As she watches Fort de Plessis disappear beneath a curtain of black cloud, Berthe reflects on the vanity of human wishes, in much the same way as those sailors who watched the last, haunting moments of Saint-Pierre:

> The only fact I was able to assimilate for a time was the immense, the blind and brutal and annihilating event of the island's destruction; a thing so irresistible and indifferent to ordinary life that the death of the Jacobeans and my own survival seemed a matter of trivial, almost frivolous lack of consequence.
>
> Eruptions and cataclysms and plagues and the colliding of planets were the only real, the only inevitable events, and the human activities that happened to lie in their path, and which are destroyed with such blind ease and ignorance were of as little real importance as the doings of insects . . .

The architect of all this destruction still sits calmly above Saint-Pierre, as oblivious as ever to its human neighbours. These days, visits to the summit of Mont Pelée are arranged by Saint-Pierre's Tourist Board. Our guide on this damp Sunday morning is a *Métropolitaine* called Madame Villerin. Brisk and energetic, she takes us up into the hills in her four-wheel drive. Madame Villerin has lived in Martinique for over ten years, seduced by the island's climate and people. 'It is the most beautiful place in the world', she says, and at that moment I am inclined to agree with her. Fields of swaying green cane flash past our windows, and the sea is a dreamy blue. It is a perfect day for Pelée. Yet the higher we climb, the more overcast the sky becomes; we are heading into a wall of grey cloud. By the time our jeep reaches Morne Rouge, one-time home of Father Mary and his patient Ludger Sylbaris, we are enveloped in a drizzly mist. The streets are empty, and Madame Villerin's windscreen wipers are working at full tilt. We pull into a layby and look upwards. Pelée has vanished behind a white curtain; *La Montagne* has eluded us, as it eluded Louis Garaud and Angelo Heilprin in their time. Madame Villerin shrugs her shoulders. 'Madame La Montagne is not happy today', she says. 'You will have to come back another day.' Sadly, there is no second chance.

Despite the exhaustive work of Lacroix and Heilprin, Hovey, Anderson and Flett, Mont Pelée's internal mechanisms remain a mystery. The lack of surviving witnesses means there is no definitive account of what happened at eight o'clock on Thursday 8 May 1902. Yet Pelée's awakening did force scientists to rewrite their classification of volcanoes, adding a fourth category to their list. Peléan eruptions propel hundreds of tons of superheated gas and debris down a mountainside: a phenomenon broken down today into *pyroclastic flows* and *pyroclastic surges*. Pyroclastic flows are denser and faster moving than pyroclastic surges; they contain heavier, more mobile debris. Although these terms of reference are some-what elastic, volcanologists today prefer to class 8 May 1902 as a pyroclastic *surge*; a similar kind of blast wave rode down the slopes of Mount St Helens in 1980. Pelée has roused itself one more time since the events of 1902. In September 1929, a series of *nuées ardentes* rolled into Saint-Pierre, but early evacuation meant no lives were lost. To keep an eye on Pelée, an American volcanologist called

Frank Perret built an observatory high above the city; it remains in use today, watching Pelée's every move.

Over the years Saint-Pierre has slowly rebuilt itself – with less swagger than in the past perhaps, but with a certain style. The first settlers came in 1912: Saint-Pierre's natural harbour made it hard to resist. By 1927, some three thousand people had returned to the town. (After Pelée roared back to life in 1929, this fell to thirty in a few hours.) And yet the people remember. No longer do they regard Pelée as *un volcan débonnaire*. Everyone knows the odds are in favour of another eruption from Fire Mountain – and soon. 'There was an interval of twenty-seven years between the last eruptions (1902–1929)', writes volcanologist Fred Bullard, 'but the 1792–1851 interval was fifty-nine years, and the 1851–1902 interval was fifty-one years. Obviously this does not establish a pattern, but two of the three intervals between historic eruptions were fifty to sixty years.'

Before leaving Saint-Pierre – *Paris of the Caribbean, Pearl of the Antilles* – I visit the *Église du Fort* and the cathedral. One is never far from the old town, the dead town. A set of architectural drawings by one Emile T'Fla Chabba show how the *Église du Fort* must have looked in its prime: a stout Norman church with three-foot-thick walls overlooking the sea, and a trim Italian bell tower. All that remains today is a scatter of rocks, pillars and razed arches. Each of the pieces has been laid sideways with a yellow number printed neatly on its base, as if someone was trying to stick the blocks back together with the help of a DIY manual.

My only feeling – there can only be one feeling – is one of awe. Nature usually needs two or three thousand years to do this kind of damage. To imagine such destruction being wrought in less than five minutes is beyond comprehension. One of the guide books claims Mont Pelée erupted with a force 'forty times stronger than that of the Atomic Bomb in Hiroshima', a fact which only heightens my sense of unreality. A natural disaster as powerful as Hiroshima was bad enough. But I cannot imagine one which has a destructive power forty times greater. When it came to the destruction game, nature could still beat man hands down: crushing his dreams with brutal ease. Like the Parisian journalist Remy Saint-Maurice, I feel as if I have chanced upon a civilisation many thousands of years old, the weathered relics of a time and place impossibly distant from our own. Usually, one walks around cities with a comforting sense of the threads which tie past to present. The past reassures us with its stoic presence, its statuesque stolidity. Here, there is no such connection. Only a reminder of how transient, how fragile our gestures will prove to be.

The cathedral graveyard offers little consolation. Its blackened boundary wall still bears the marks of that fire storm on 8 May. The graveyard itself has been turned into a permanent memorial, its charred and wilted railings seemingly untouched for almost a hundred years. Beneath the south wall, there is a simple stone memorial to the Hurard family. Near the entrance, a small marble urn commemorates those teachers at Saint-Pierre *Lycée* – among whom is counted Gaston Landes – who died on that day.

Although the graveyard is deserted, one senses another spirit in the air: someone or something with a message to impart. Perhaps it is one of the island's *revenants*, a returning spirit like Lafcadio Hearn, that eternal traveller. Sitting here over one hundred years ago, beneath the shadow of Mont Pelée, he had a premonition. A premonition which returns this hot January morning with uncanny force. Beware the island paradise, our *revenant* whispers, for '*where Nature is most puissant to charm, there also she is mightiest to destroy . . .*'

NOTES

SELECTED REFERENCES

Prologue: The Most Marvellous Man on Earth

Ludger Sylbaris's amazing story is related in the *Barnum and Bailey Official Program and Book of Wonders* for 1903. More details appear in *The Realm – A Magazine of Marvels* (1903), Charles Andress's scrapbook cum Route Book: *Day By Day with Barnum and Bailey* (1903 and 1904) and a supplementary programme, *The Arenic World* (1903).

For circus life at that time, see: W.L. Alden, *Among the Freaks* (London, 1896), W.C. Thompson, *On The Road with a Circus* (1903), pp 67–85, and H.W. Root, *The Ways of the Circus – Being the Memories and Adventures of George Conklin, Tamer of Lions* (Harper, New York, 1921), pp 174–175. See also John Lentz, 'The Revolt of the Freaks – A Classic in Circus Publicity', *Bandwagon*, Vol. 21, No. 5 and Joe McKennon's splendidly foul *Circus Lingo* (Carnival Publishers, Sarasota, 1980). On Barnum's financial troubles, see Richard E. Conover, 'The Affairs of James A. Bailey' (McCaddon Papers, Princeton, 1957).

Barnum's 1903 Side Show is beautifully captured in the photographs of Charles Andress and the Florenz Family. Both collections are kept at the Circus World Museum in Baraboo, Wisconsin.

Chapter One: Petit Paris

H.K.'s postcards – and dozens of similar photographs – are held by the Hayot Collection, Fort-de-France. They are also reproduced in Solange Contour's anthology, *Saint-Pierre: La Ville et le Volcan avant 1902* (Paris, 1988).

For Saint-Pierre, see Louis Garaud, *Trois Ans à la Martinique* (Paris, 1895); Salavina, *Trente Ans de Saint-Pierre* (Fort-de-France, 1910. Repr. Éditions Caribéennes, 1986); Rene Bonnéville, *Le Triomphe d'Églantine* (Repr. Horizons Caraïbes, 1976). The most evocative account remains Lafcadio Hearn's *Two Years in the French West Indies* (Harper & Bros, New York, 1890).

For basic facts and figures: Gaston Landes, *Notice Sur la Martinique* (1900) and the *Annuaire* or State Almanac for 1901. The Governor's activities for that year are outlined in Martinique's *Bulletin Officiel*.

On Creole, see J.J. Audain, *Recueil de Proverbes Créoles* (Port-au-Prince, 1877); Louis Jahan Désrivaux, *Les Fables de La Fontaine* (1869) and Lafcadio Hearn, *Ghombo Zhebes: Petit Dictionnaire des Proverbes Créoles* (Repr. 1998).

On *Carnaval*, three talks to Saint-Pierre's Rotary Club provided a great deal of information: Liliane Chauleau's 'Distractions et Vie Culturelle à Saint-Pierre' (1973) and 'La Vie Saint-Pierre d'Antan' (1975); Marie Chomereau-Lamotte's 'Saint-Pierre en ce temps là' (1981). An exhibition at Saint-Pierre's Chamber of Commerce in 2001 also provided a lot of evocative detail.

Chapter Two: Death to the Whites!

Extracts from Aimé Césaire's *Notebook of a Return to the Native Land* are reproduced with permission from Clayton Eshleman and Annette Smith (eds), *Aimé Césaire: The Collected Poetry* (University of California Press, 1983).

The best guide to Martinique's early history is Armand Nicolas's three-part *Histoire de la Martinique* (Harmattan, 1996), particularly Volume 1: *Des Arawaks à 1848*. See also Solange Contour, *Guadeloupe – Martinique dans les Revues Illustrées du XIXème Siècle* (Paris, 1996), and M. Terrée, 'L'Élargissement de la vie politique' in Jacques Sabatier (ed.), *Historial Antillais*, Vol. IV, pp. 329–349.

Biographical details on Amédée Knight and Marius Hurard are taken from editions of *Les Colonies* and *L'Opinion* for 1900 and 1901, held at the Bibliothèque Schoelcher, Fort-de-France. Further information from Jack Corzani (ed.), *Dictionnaire Encyclopédique des Antilles et de la Guyane* and Camille Darsières, *Joseph Lagrosillière: Socialiste Colonial* (Éditions Désormeaux, 1996), p. 275. The row between Amédée Knight and *La Dépêche Coloniale* is reported in the editions of 15 Nov. and 22 Nov. 1901.

On events at François, see 'Le Massacre du François' in *Historial Antillais*, Vol. IV, pp 381–383.

Chapter Three: La Montagne

On Pelée's past activity: Césaire Philémon, *La Montagne Pelée et L'Effroyable Destruction de Saint-Pierre* (Paris, 1930); Alfred Lacroix, *La Montagne Pelée et Ses Éruptions* (Paris, 1904); Alexandre Moreau de Jonnès, *Histoire Physique des Antilles Françaises* (Paris, 1822), pp. 45–58. Lafcadio Hearn, *op. cit.*, also has a chapter on Mont Pelée, pp. 254–293.

Early attitudes to volcanoes are comprehensively explored in Haruldur Sigurdsson, *Melting the Earth – The History of Ideas on Volcanic Eruptions* (OUP, 1999) and Fred Bullard, *Volcanoes of the Earth* (University of Texas, 1976).

For Gauguin's letters from Martinique, see Roger Cucci, *Gauguin à la Martinique* (Calivran Anstalt, 1979). The Paul Gauguin Museum at Carbet also holds many interesting mementoes.

Tempest Anderson's amateur spirit is embodied in the Preface to *Volcanic Studies in Many Lands* (London, 1903). A second volume, published in 1917, includes a posthumous tribute by T.G. Bonney.

Gaston Landes is remembered in *La Revue des Cultures Coloniales*, Vol. 10, No. 101, pp. 314–315. See also, Françoise Thésée, *Le Jardin Botanique de Saint-Pierre, Martinique, 1803–1902* (Éditions Caribéennes, 1990).

On the antics of Saint-Pierre theatre: Maurice Nicolas, 'Le Théâtre de Saint-Pierre au XVIIIème siècle – Les Années Difficiles', *Annales des Antilles*, 1, pp. 53–64 and 'Le Théâtre de Saint-Pierre pendant les premières années du XIXème siècle – Les Années Essentielles', *Annales des Antilles*, 4, pp. 109–128.

Chapter Four: On the Brink of Hell

Most of the events leading up to 8 May are covered, in some detail, by Lacroix, *op. cit.* They are also described by Angelo Heilprin, *Mont Pelée and the Tragedy of Martinique* (Philadelphia, 1903) and George Kennan, *The Tragedy of Pelée* (New York, 1902) – and less reliably by Frederick Royce, *The Burning of Saint-Pierre and the Eruption of Mont Pelée* (Chicago, 1902). Each book also contains an account of Ludger Sylbaris's picaresque adventures – as does Solange Contour's second anthology, *Saint-Pierre: La Catastrophe et ses suites* (Paris, 1989).

Louis Mouttet's diplomatic career is outlined in Corzani, *op. cit.* For a more jaundiced account of his life – and some rather tendentious arguments – see Gordon Thomas and Max Morgan-Witts, *The Day Their World Ended* (Souvenir Press, 1969). A more accurate version of events (along with a bitter critique of Thomas and Witts's book) is laid out by Martinican historian Jacques Petitjean Roget, 'À Propos du Livre, *Le Volcan Arrive*' published in *Annales des Antilles*, 17, pp 3–89.

Chapter Five: Not One Alive

The account of events at Fort-de-France telephone exchange on 8 May is taken from Ministerial File C25/D216 at the Centre des Archives d'Outre

Mer (CAOM), Aix-en-Provence. A report on Prosecutor Lubin's trip to Saint-Pierre that day can be found in the same file.

Vicar-General Parel's experiences are reprinted in Heilprin, *op. cit.*, pp. 85–108; the various accounts of sailors in Saint-Pierre harbour are reproduced in Kennan and Royce. See also Jean Hess, *La Catastrophe de la Martinique – Notes d'un Reporter* (Paris, 1902).

On the death of Gaston Landes, see Lacroix, *op. cit.*, pp. 283–286.

Chapter Six: A Miracle

Amédée Knight's first visit to Saint-Pierre on 9 May is quoted in Solange Contour's *Saint-Pierre: La Catastrophe et ses suites*, p. 141. For more first-hand accounts see George Kennan, *op. cit.*, pp. 88–92. His meeting with Ludger Sylbaris is described on pp. 74–80. On calculation of casualties, see Lacroix, *op. cit.*, p. 303.

Father Mary's first-hand account of Ludger Sylbaris's rescue is at CAOM, File C25/D 216. See also Contour, *La Catastrophe et ses suites*, pp. 84–87.

Vice-Consul Devaux's correspondence is held at the Public Record Office, London: Consuls General, FO 27/3596–1902. James Japp's time as British Consul in Saint-Pierre is recorded in FO 27/3506, 3512 and 3547.

Remy Saint-Maurice's report on 'Les Désastres de la Martinique' is from *L'Illustration* 3095, 21 June 1902, pp. 449–451 and 3096, 28 June 1902, pp. 466–469.

Chapter Seven: The Great Secret

On the natural phenomena generated by 8 May, see Heilprin, *op. cit.*, pp. 271–318. For the American missions to Martinique: E.O. Hovey, 'Martinique and Saint Vincent – Preliminary Report', *Bulletin of American Museum of Natural History*, 16, 1902 pp. 333–373; T.A. Jaggar, 'Field Notes of a Geologist in Martinique and Saint Vincent', *Popular Science Monthly*, 61, pp. 352–368. See also *National Geographic Magazine*, 13, 1902.

France's relief effort in Martinique is well covered by files at CAOM. For Bloch's mission, see C25/D 212; Lhuerre's difficulties are covered in C25/D215, C58/D483 and C58/D477. The latter also includes Jules Cambon's correspondence from Washington.

For Heilprin's ascent, see the chapter 'To the Storm Cloud of Pelée's Crater' in *Mont Pelée and the Tragedy of Martinique*, pp. 151–165.

Chapter Eight: Glowing Clouds

On Barnum's return, see *Billboard*, 28 March 1903, and *New York Clipper* of same date. Details of that year's Spectacle are related in *The Book of Wonders*, *op. cit.*, and in the permanent exhibition at Circus World Museum, Baraboo.

For the events of 9 July: Tempest Anderson and John S. Flett, 'Report on the Eruptions of the Soufrière in St Vincent in 1902 and on a visit to Montagne Pelée in Martinique', *Transactions of the Royal Society of London*, Vol. 200, 1903. Heilprin's return to Martinique is covered in *Mont Pelée . . .*, pp. 216–243.

Lemaire's difficulties after 30 August are to be found at CAOM, C25/D217 and C58/D483. For Perney's sketches and study of Pelée's Dome, see Lacroix, *op. cit.*, pp. 108–161.

Chapter Nine: Showtime

On Barnum's Parades, see Greg Parkinson, 'James A. Bailey's Last Parades: 1903 and 1904', *Bandwagon*, Vol. 26, No. 3, 1982. On Circus publicity, Philip B. Kunhardt, *America's Greatest Showman* (Knopf, 1995) and Tody Hamilton's article 'The Press Agent' in Charles Andress (ed.), *Day By Day with Barnum and Bailey* (1903 and 1904). The Circus World Museum, Baraboo, also holds moving pictures of a Barnum parade in 1904.

For the return of refugees, see CAOM, C25/D218, C58/D477 and C25/D219. The question of tourists in Saint-Pierre is raised by Lemaire in C25/D221.

Chapter 10: Looking for Ludger

Extracts from Aimé Césaire's *Notebook of a Return to the Native Land* are reproduced with permission from Clayton Eshleman and Annette Smith (eds), *Aimé Césaire: The Collected Poetry* (University of California Press, 1983).

Extracts from Patrick Chamoiseau's *Texaco*, translated by Rose-Myriam Réjouis and Val Vinkurov reproduced with kind permission of Granta books. See also Chamoiseau's other translated works: *Solibo Magnificent* (Granta, 1998), *Strange Words* (1998) and *Childhood* (1999).

Jean Rhys's story 'Heat' is taken from *Tales of the Wide Caribbean* (Heinemann, 1985). Extracts from Patrick Leigh-Fermor's novel *The Violins of Saint-Jacques* published with kind permission of John Murray Publishers.

Every reasonable effort has been made to trace copyright holders of material reproduced in this book, but if any have inadvertently been overlooked the publishers would be glad to hear from them.

ACKNOWLEDGEMENTS

Lots of people helped me to research this book. I'd particularly like to thank the following individuals and institutions.

In Martinique: Mme. Paule Delaunay-Belleville and Mme. Jeanne Cazassus of the Service de Patrimoine, Saint-Pierre; Mlle. Maiotte Dauphite and Mme. Roselyne Gomess at the Musée Historique; M. Eddy Ebroin at Prêcheur Town Hall and Mme. Ophéline Villerin; the Gauguin Museum, Carbet; M. Louis-Joseph Trudemp at the Bibliothèque Schoelcher, Fort-de-France; Mme. Lyne-Rose Beuze and Mme. Caroline Porticop at the Musée Régional; M. Loïs Hayot and Mme. Marcelle Cyparisse.

In France: staff in the Newspaper and Periodicals department of the Bibliothèque Nationale, Paris and the Archives Nationales; the Centre des Archives d'Outre Mer (CAOM), Aix-en-Provence. In the United States: Meg Allen and Erin Foley at the Circus World Museum, Baraboo, Wisconsin.

In Britain: staff in the Rare Books and Maps departments of the British Library; the Public Record Office, Kew; the Royal Society Library; Rhodes House, Oxford; The London Library.

Professor Steve Sparks of Bristol University took time out from a very busy schedule to cast a volcanologist's eye over the final text – for which I am very grateful. Colin Harding of the Museum of Photography, Film and Television in Bradford offered advice on early twentieth-century photographic techniques.

I'd also like to thank the following friends and colleagues:

At Bloomsbury, my editor Rosemary Davidson was always ready

with imaginative advice and encouragement; Bill Swainson and Chiki Sarkar helped ease the way; Edward Faulkner copy-edited with patient precision. At A.P. Watt, my agent Natasha Fairweather was wonderfully wise and supportive – as were Sarah Castleton and Rob Kraitt. At ITN, I'd like to thank Jim Gray, the editor of Channel Four News, for allowing me to work part-time.

Finally, there's friends and family. Dietlind Lerner and Chris Thomas made the Parisian research even more enjoyable, as did Susanna Brighi and Anthony Rendall; Monika Vielberth let me lease her fine flat; Emily Kennedy – for brain food; Thalia Eley – for inspirational mountaineering metaphors; and Rachel Ward – for believing in the whole project, even when less devoted individuals (i.e. me) were having doubts.

Peter del Tufo helped to explain the history of postcards; Imogen Cornwall-Jones found Jean Rhys's account of the disaster. Gaby and Desa Rado, Zoe Silver and Alison Hindell, Alex Carolan, Parissa Nahani and last but not least, my partner Marina Zenovich – *sa mnogo ljubavi.*

My parents, Alwena and Gwynne Morgan, volunteered to be the long-suffering research team. My brother Robert offered lots of valuable comments on the manuscript. This book is for them, with thanks.

LIST OF ILLUSTRATIONS

78 Advertisement from *La Revue des Cultures Coloniales*, reproduced with permission of Bibliotheque Nationale, Paris.

80 Postcard of Saint-Pierre Theatre, reproduced from Contour, *op. cit.*

85 Postcard of Saint-Pierre harbour. Reproduced with permission of Musée Regional d'Histoire, Fort-de-France.

89 Picture of Louis Mouttet, reproduced with permission of Musée Historique, Saint-Pierre.

92 Photograph of Ludger Sylbaris, courtesy of Hayot Collection, Fort-de-France.

102–103 Family Group, Collection Salles. Reproduced with permission of Musée Regional d'Histoire, Fort-de-France.

109 Photograph of Ludger Sylbaris's cell taken by author, January 2001.

123 Photograph of the *Roraima* from Frederick Royce, *The Burning of Saint-Pierre and the Eruption of Mont Pelée* (Chicago, 1902).

129 Diagram taken from George Kennan, *The Tragedy of Pelée* (New York, 1902).

141 Photograph of Rue Victor Hugo after the eruption taken from Heilprin, *op. cit.*

142 Photograph of Place Bertin after the eruption taken from Heilprin, *op. cit.*

150 View from Morne d' Orange, reproduced courtesy of Underwood and Underwood, New York.

166 Photograph of ruined sugar refinery taken from Solange Contour, *Saint-Pierre: La Catastrophe et ses suites* (Paris 1989).

176 Photograph of Pelée in eruption taken from Heilprin, *op. cit.*

184 Billboard advertisement for Barnum and Bailey, courtesy of Feld Entertainment Inc. and Circus World Museum, Baraboo, Wisconsin, and with kind permission from Ringling Brothers and Barnum and Bailey.

186 Advertisement taken from *Day by Day with Barnum and Bailey* (1903), Circus World Museum, Baraboo, Wisconsin, and with kind permission from Ringling Brothers and Barnum and Bailey.

197 Photograph of Notre Dame de la Delivrande, Morne Rouge from Solange Contour, *Saint-Pierre: La Catastrophe et ses suites* (Paris, 1989).

201 Postcard of The Tower of Pelée taken from Solange Contour, *Saint-Pierre: La Catastrophe et ses suites* (Paris, 1988).

202 Photograph of M. and Mme Lacroix from Alfred Lacroix, *op. cit.*

209 Photograph of Ludger Sylbaris reproduced courtesy of Circus World Museum, Baraboo, Wisconsin.

223 Photograph of Saint-Pierre today taken by author, January 2001.

228 Photograph of Saint-Pierre today, reproduced courtesy of Martinique Tourist Board.

Endpaper maps designed by Richard Horne.

A NOTE ON THE AUTHOR

Peter Morgan is a reporter for ITN's Channel Four News. He has written several plays for radio and theatre. His first radio play won the Society of Authors new writing award.

A NOTE ON THE TYPE

The text of this book is set in Bembo. This type
was first used in 1495 by the Venetian printer
Aldus Manutius for Cardinal Bembo's *De Aetna*,
and was cut for Manutius by Francesco Griffo.
It was one of the types used by Claude
Garamond (1480–1561) as a model for his
Romain de L'Université, and so it was the
forerunner of what became standard European
type for the following two centuries. Its modern
form follows the original types and was
designed for Monotype in 1929.

Macouba

Grand´-Rivière

Basse-Pointe

Montagne Pelée

Le Prêcheur ▲

Morne Rouge

Saint-Pierre

Le Carbet

Trinité

Bellefontaine

Case-Pilote

FORT-DE-FRANCE

Le François

Trois-Îlets

MARTINIQUE